Watching Television Audiences

Cultural theories and methods

JOHN TULLOCH

Professor of Media Communication, Cardiff University

A member of the Hodder Headline Group
LONDON
Co-published in the United States of America by
Oxford University Press Inc., New York

First published in Great Britain in 2000 by
Arnold, a member of the Hodder Headline Group,
338 Euston Road, London NW1 3BH

http://www.arnoldpublishers.com

Co-published in the United States of America by
Oxford University Press Inc.,
198 Madison Avenue, New York 10016

British Library Cataloguing in Publication Data
A catalogue record for this book is available from the British Library

Library of Congress Cataloging-in-Publication Data
A catalog record for this book is available from the Library of Congress

ISBN 0 340 74141 4 (hb)
ISBN 0 340 74142 2 (pb)

1 2 3 4 5 6 7 8 9 10

Production Editor: Rada Radojicic
Production Controller: Bryan Eccleshall

Typeset in 10/12pt Sabon by Phoenix Photosetting, Chatham, Kent
Printed and bound in Great Britain by MPG Books Ltd, Bodmin, Cornwall

What do you think about this book? Or any other Arnold title?
Please send your comments to feedback.arnold@hodder.co.uk

Contents

Acknowledgements

The author and publishers would like to thank the following for permission to include copyright material:

David Buckingham for extracts from Buckingham, D., *Public secrets: 'EastEnders' and its audience* (1987) and Buckingham, D. (ed), *Reading audiences: young people and the media* (1993); Polity Press for extracts from Hodge, R. and Tripp, D., *Children and television: a semiotic approach* (1986); Routledge Ltd for extracts from Ang, I., *Living room wars: rethinking media audiences for a postmodern world* (1996); Westview Press for extracts from *Enlightened racism: the Cosby show, audiences, and the myth of the American dream* by Sut Jhally and Justin Lewis. Copyright © 1992 by Westview Press, a division of Perseus Books L.L.C. Reprinted by permission of Westview Press, a member of Perseus Books, L.L.C.; and University of Pennsylvania Press for extracts from *Beverley Hills, 90210: television, gender and identity* by E. Graham McKinley. Copyright © 1997 E. Graham McKinley. Reprinted by permission of the publisher.

Every effort has been made to trace copyright holders of material reproduced in this book. Any rights not acknowledged here will be acknowledged in subsequent printings if notice is given to the publisher.

1

Introduction

Looking back over nearly thirty years of research and teaching in media studies, I am struck by how little of that time I spent on 'methodology'. The reasons are easy to spot. In particular, there has been a considerable and (in my view) justified suspicion of 'objective' empiricist methodologies which have been so profoundly critiqued by the armory of theories sweeping the fields of film and television studies since the late 1960s. Thus it is that I have prestigious colleagues in the UK who still say they are 'critics not researchers', and who nominate the social sciences as 'the enemy'. Thus, too, a recent colleague in Australia, with whom I was designing an 'Audience and Reception' postgraduate module, questioned the need to teach methodology at all.

This was a question that the School of Communication staff teaching the other (quantitative) half of this 'Media Audience' postgraduate subject would never have dreamed of asking. Yet, from my cultural studies colleague's perspective, as a post-Barthesian specialist in literary theories of 'reading', it was an entirely appropriate question, as we shall see in this chapter.

My colleague said that 'methodology' was not part of his competence. His particular 'binary' was that of 'theory' and 'criticism', rather than 'theory' and 'method'. So how, he asked, did one actually do focus group work or long interviews? What were they *for*? Could I convince him that he (and the audience studies students) would be any better off if they knew about 'methodology'? What did this additional repertoire of 'methodology' add to the 'theory' that students debated already? Most importantly, how could I answer some pretty foundational critiques that poststructuralist theories were mounting against approaching the everyday experiences of people as some kind of 'truth', whether by focus group, long interview, survey, or any other methodology?

This chapter begins to answer these questions. Why, in other words, is there a need for a book on television audiences that emphasises theory and method together? I will start to answer these questions from a personally reflexive position, and then build up to a more general 'meta'-theoretical response. I am taking this 'bookend' (personal/global) approach to this introductory chapter (as well as the concluding one) for theoretical reasons that will become apparent as we proceed.

But there are also strategic reasons. Since returning to Britain I have found my Australian colleague's view widespread here also; and not just in the critical literary theory end of cultural studies. I have heard colleagues convince younger scholars that important sources of research funding like the ESRC (Economic and Social Research Council) are probably not for them ('the enemy' again). I do not share this view. I never did; and least of all at a time when there is a clear move within media and cultural studies to re-synthesise more global theories of communication with localised ethnographies of production and audience (Alasuutari 1999). Consequently, I see the readers of this book as both the kinds of media/cultural studies academics who think of social science funding bodies as 'against them' and their students (who have perhaps done a year or two of university work already and are now shaping up to do a more specialised 'audience' course).

So where, then, do we start in the 'current debate' – given the wideranging poststructuralist critique of methodology as an objectivist mystique of modernity?

A personal audience story

When I first thought about writing a book about *Doctor Who* in the early 1980s, it was as something of a fan. The twentieth anniversary of *Doctor Who* was fast approaching, and I had watched virtually every episode since its beginnings in November 1963. I had also taught about it in media studies courses in the late 1970s at the University of New South Wales; and I had found that students there got some of the same pleasures I did from the gently parodic and reflexive signature of the show at that time. Only later was I to recognise this as the 'Douglas Adams' (author of *A Hitchhiker's Guide to the Galaxy*, and script editor on *Doctor Who* in 1977–8) period. This ignorance made me only 'something of a fan', because in fact fans worldwide were busy at that time (and thereafter) excoriating Douglas Adams's notorious '17th season' of *Doctor Who* as containing several of the 'worst episodes of all time'.

The fact that neither I nor any of my UNSW (University of New South Wales) students 'read' this period of *Doctor Who* in terms of a 'Douglas Adams' signature indicated that we were not 'real fans'. If we had been, we would have attended fan conventions and read fanzines, where we would very quickly have realised that the period of *Doctor Who* that we were enjoying so much was a very *particular* one in both local and international fan communities. Globally, this very localised moment in the *longue durée* of *Doctor Who* as a series was establishing mythical status. But this was not myth in Barthes's sense as the historical seen as 'natural' and unchangeable. The fans knew as well as any professor of media studies at that time that texts were produced in very finite, local conditions of production, and that the texts (if not the means of production) could be changed.

I was soon to find out about this as I began researching my book, interviewing fans in Britain and Australia, attending their conferences, reading their articles and letters in fanzines, and so on. But even prior to this stage I knew that *Doctor Who*, over the twenty years that I had watched it, was not an unchanging and unitary programme. After all, I reasoned, as an audience member *I* had changed a lot. When I had started watching it in 1963 I was a young Cambridge University undergraduate, whereas now, by 1983, I was a father watching *Doctor Who* regularly with two young sons of my own. But as well as these personal developments in my daily life, I had also changed quite profoundly politically and epistemologically over that time. In 1963 I had been an empiricist historian (whose methodological and political conservatism was further exacerbated by being brought up on family 'eyewitness' narratives which privileged a particular version of British imperial history in India – in which my family had actively participated for two hundred years). Whereas by 1988 I was a 'post-1968' radicalised graduate in Marxist and 'conflict' sociology.

I had started my Master's degree at Sussex University in 1968, without actually knowing it *was* '1968', as it later came to be mythologised. It was there (at Sussex University) and then (in 1968) that my overlapping family/Cambridge history narratives of 'communist world orders', of Vietnam as 'domino effect', and so on had to meet the incisive (but on reflection, personally gentle) critique from other Master's degree students, of the calibre of Tony Bennett, Paul Q. Hirst, Janet Woollacott, and many others to whom I owed the chance to live intellectually in new and exciting ways.

My own intellectual story is, I am sure, a familiar one; and it is repeated in each generation; as, for example, neo-Marxist theorists have encountered critique from poststructuralists and postmodernists in their turn. But (as far as I know) only I, among this body of Master's degree students at Sussex University, was 'something of a fan' of *Doctor Who*. Only I had been watching it for five years already, and would still be watching it fifteen, even twenty years later. If *I* had changed so much during that time-frame, yet still enjoyed it, what did that tell me about the narratives of *Doctor Who*? About how the programme constructed its audiences? And how did my own variously developing identities relate to it now, in the late 1970s/early 1980s as I talked with my students about it, and as I prepared to write a book about it?

For example, what had led me to choose a particular *Doctor Who* episode, the 1974 'Monster of Peladon' to open up discussion in sociology of mass communication classes at the University of New South Wales? This was certainly not an episode that a 'real' fan would have chosen, since it ranked neither among the 'best' nor the 'worst' episodes 'of all time' in their various fanzine histories. Indeed, fanzine writer Gary Hopkins opened his story review of the episode by suggesting that 'The Monster of Peladon' was 'taboo' (and therefore not very 'becoming' as) *Doctor Who*.

> Next to sex and religion, party-politics has normally been something of a taboo subject in *Doctor Who*; and yet 'The Monster of Peladon' dares to touch a political nerve with its depiction of a miners' revolt and a class system not unlike those that existed in the UK in 1974. It is interesting to speculate that writer Brian Hayles may have been avenging 'The Curse of Peladon' (Serial 'MMM') which, as a result of another miners' strike, had become a casualty of power cuts and blank TV screens two years earlier. However, such radical posturing does not become *Doctor Who* and a decade later 'The Monster of Peladon' might well have been censored for blatant anti-Conservatism.
>
> (1985, p. 5)

This is a familiar fan reading: evident both in its specific comment (the archivalist emphasis on 'Serial "MMM"'; the reading of Brian Hayles' miner's strike *intra*textually, in terms of an earlier *Doctor Who* episode) and in terms of its similarity with other juxtaposed narratives under the same covers of this fan-written Cybermark series account of 'The Monster of Peladon'. In this set of reviews, there were (as in other volumes in the series):

- extracts from shooting scripts;
- technical notes;
- production office notes (focusing on the departure of not only Jon Pertwee as the Doctor, but the series producer and script editor as well, leading to the perennial worry among fans that could this be 'the end for *Doctor Who*').
- pointed discussions of the Doctor reacting callously in this episode 'to the . . . death of others' (Hopkins, 1985, p. 5). This was a major emphasis of *Doctor Who* fan discourse in the mid-1980s when this review of 'The Monster of Peladon' was written (Tulloch and Jenkins 1995, p. 160), but not in 1974 when the episode was made.

These were the British fan preoccupations with 'The Monster of Peladon'. But what were mine? Why did I choose this 'unbecoming' episode to discuss *Doctor Who* with my students. And, even worse from the fans' point of view, why did I choose to follow it up with discussion of a Douglas Adams episode?

Obviously part of it was to do with the institutional formation in which this 'audience' discussion was taking place. This was a 'sociology of mass communication' course I was teaching, and so issues of class and feminism which the episode foregrounded had their own 'expert' intertexts among other reading the students were doing. So it seemed natural to choose it in relation to this kind of content.

But, when I later looked back on this choice of 'The Monster of Peladon' as I began seriously to get into my *Doctor Who* audience research, it seemed to me that I had also chosen it because of my own biographical and historical negotiations: between, for example, my 'University of Sussex' self and my biographical self. My father (a 'British Raj' conservative), was especially virulent as we watched television news footage of the British miners' strike in 1974; and our emotions would become so intense during television coverage of the miners' strike ten years later, in 1984, that we found we could not speak to each other about it at all. Maybe here, in my late 1970s university class, I was negotiating different narratives, histories and identities that I could not easily speak about in front of the TV at home? Certainly, it was my father's comments about the 1974 miners' strike that I reiterated to the producer and script editor of this episode as I interviewed them later (Tulloch and Alvarado 1983, pp. 53–4). I was not fully aware of this when I first chose that episode for class discussion. But I certainly needed to recognise it as I engaged with the preferences of a new body of experts, the fans, and as I began to write the book.

So audience response, and audience research, can be private-sphere 'deep stuff', embedded in the micro-narratives of our most personal histories, identities, emotions and understandings, as well as within the broader public sphere institutions of school, university, the media, the unions, government, and so on (Tulloch and Jenkins 1995, ch. 7). How we go about gaining access to – and then at least partially understanding – those mixed and muddled negotiations of our own (and other people's) narrativised identities does actually matter. And without my one-to-one interviews with *Doctor Who* fans my own personal/professional/political negotiations of this text might not have appeared to me quite so clearly.

This is just the beginning of my answer to my colleague about why methodology matters. As Barbara Adam and Stuart Allan have said, we need to begin our theorising about cultural life from 'the position of "nowhere": inescapably local, partial and fragmentary, and yet contextual, interconnected and globalizing' (1995, p. xvi). These questions of methodology and theory have implications at the most personal, local level. But how, then, do we find methods of access that are fine-grained and local enough, and yet relate theoretically to the 'interconnected' and 'globalizing' too?

From personal to academic accounts

What is the point theoretically and methodologically of my reflexive personal story? How does it tell us any more about focus groups, long interviews, and other qualitative methods of accessing audiences? In researching my *Doctor Who* books, why did I decide on a range of qualitative audience studies, including participant observation at fan conventions, accompanied by an 'ethnography of production' (spending six months around BBC studios, locations, offices and canteens during 1983)? Why was I so directly 'approaching the audience' (and the production of *Doctor Who*) in this way?

Part of the reason had to do with academic, rather than personal, histories. Reception analysis was itself, just at that time, beginning to 'watch the audience'. Earlier, at the beginning of the 1970s, the 'linguistic turn' of dominant versions of structuralism had gone strongly down the 'screen theory' path of the 'inscribed reader' of television 'texts'. Althusserian Marxian/structuralist notions of 'Ideological State Apparatuses' and the media's 'interpellation' of viewers as subjects, and Lacanian psychoanalytic rejection of the agentive, unified self, had been blended in various ways with Metzian semiotics and feminism to produce powerful critiques of 'humanism', 'the real', and everyday 'common sense'. (For useful critical accounts among audience theorists of this period see, for instance: Morley, 1980; Lewis, 1991; McGuigan, 1992; Moores, 1993; though the reader should also turn to some of the profoundly important work of this 'screen theory' period itself, as collected in the series of *Screen Readers*.)

What I have been charting so far was my personal/academic negotiation of 'expert knowledgability' as I approached my early audience research of *Doctor Who*. Central here was the fact that I was influenced by, but also dissatisfied – both as historian and sociologist – with, 'screen theory'. My own dominant grounding at Sussex University in 'genetic structuralism' left me, in the end, equally dissatisfied with the linguistic turn by the early 1970s, and open to the more sociological semiotics of writing and research at the Birmingham Centre for Contemporary Cultural Studies (particularly evident in Stuart Hall's 'encoding/decoding' model of TV news reception). This emphasised the 'determinate moments' of both television production and reception, and the materiality of cultural power that lay between these two 'moments'. Thus Hall and others at the CCCS opened out the agenda for an empirical audience research programme which focused on the different social and discursive positioning of various subcultures as interpretive communities. Hall's emphasis on 'professional' discourses in encoding, and on 'negotiated' and 'oppositional' discourses in decoding media texts, not only helped me think about my, my father's and the fans' response to 'The Monster of Peladon', but also helped underpin the choice of an 'ethnography of production'/audience interview binary for my *Doctor Who* research project.

Out of the Birmingham CCCS work came the *Nationwide* project on the encoding and decoding of television current affairs discourse (see chapter 10); and subsequently the internationally path-breaking books by David Morley and Charlotte Brunsdon, *Nationwide* (1978) and Morley's *The 'Nationwide' Audience* (1980). These books helped articulate for me a text/audience analysis in parallel to the one I had in process with my *Doctor Who* research. It also seemed to justify *post hoc* my initial choice of 'The Monster of Peladon', since Morley, too, emphasised 'political' readings of

TV texts. Morley, it was, who began to 'watch the audience' of actual social subjects in his 1980 book, helping to inaugurate a decade or so of 'actual audience' research. This included other important empirical work on specific genres by Dorothy Hobson, Charlotte Brunsdon and Ien Ang (soap opera), Henry Jenkins (science fiction), Janice Radway (the romance novel), Marie Gillespie (on Indian families' viewing of Hindi films on video), Ann Gray (on VCR technology use and film genre preferences), among many others. Meanwhile, a different brand of academic researchers was conducting ethnographies of production in relation to TV genres. This included Ed Buscombe and Manuel Alvarado's book on the private eye series *Hazell*, which was an important stimulus to our own *Doctor Who: The Unfolding Text* (Tulloch and Alvarado, 1983). Coming at the same time as I was conducting my own first audience focus groups in the late 1970s/early 1980s, this 'ethnographic turn' in media studies (together with epistemological criticism of 'screen theory' approaches to representation by Terry Lovell in *Pictures of Reality*, 1980) was important in helping clarify for me what I described earlier as dissatisfaction with dominant screen and reception theory.

Several commentators were later to criticise the so-called 'ethnographic turn' – particularly in audience research during the 1980s – for being too superficial and limited *as* ethnography (Radway, 1988; Nightingale, 1989). Anthropology was generally taken to be an originary source of reference in these criticisms. Thus Radway said:

> In anthropology, of course, an ethnography is a written account of a lengthy social interaction between a scholar and a distant culture. Although its focus is often narrowed in the process of writing so as to highlight kinship practices, social institutions or cultural rituals, that written account is rooted in an effort to observe and to comprehend the entire tapestry of social life.
>
> (Radway, 1988, p. 367)

By this account, the ethnographies of television production that were beginning to appear in the early 1980s were much closer to being 'true' ethnographies than the 'active audience' analyses of the same period. Researchers of the former did spend considerable lengths of time within the various cultures of the TV industry, whereas audience researchers (particularly in Britain) tended to rely on qualitative interviews and brief observation (my own work in the mid-1980s on the Australian soap opera *A Country Practice* was symptomatic of this, in that, while I spent several months with the production team, I relied for my audience analysis on nine focus group interviews). Moreover, the authors of the production studies contextualised their 'narrowed' accounts in terms of the 'entire tapestry' of television life and work. For instance, Alvarado and Buscombe were able to trace a particular use of set design and colour in *Hazell* to the political economy of British television, and to the subcultural values of its lighting professionals.

Similarly, Tulloch and Alvarado related the alternating 'history'/'science fiction' generic formats of the early *Doctor Who* to the loss by the BBC of
monopoly over television audiences, and the ensuing 'quality/commercial'
dichotomies within its various professional cultures. So in these and a variety of other ways the professional discourses and idiolects of television production were seen as embedded in the economies and broadcasting histories
of their time. In contrast, David Morley's account of television and gender
in one housing estate near London (in his book *Family Television*) was
increasingly cautious about its overall generalisability.

Following on these criticisms of 'audience ethnography' research, a much
more radical critique of the tradition was already emerging. This was a
rejection of the 'metaphysics of presence' itself; that is the notion that there
is a 'real world out there' at all, independent of a narrator, and accessible via
the daily life experience of an 'authentic' respondent. Earlier, under the
influence of various forms of structuralism (of Levi-Strauss, Althusser, Saussurian
semiotics and Lacanian psychoanalysis) human experience was increasingly
seen as an 'effect' (of unconscious rules and myth-logics in the human mind,
of 'ideological state apparatuses', of language, of the 'mirror stage' in infancy).
From this perspective, human subjects were simply the 'bearers' of history
and ideology, were 'spoken' or 'interpellated' by structures; and authorship,
in Barthes's lingering phrase, was dead. 'Structuralism views experience not
as the ground of culture but its effect, the product of the ways in which
individuals are transformed into thinking, feeling and perceiving subjects of
different kinds in the context of differently structured relations of symbolic
exchange' (Bennett *et al.*, 1981, p. 12).

The 'lived experience' which Raymond Williams and others of a more
'culturalist' persuasion were seeking in order to open out our 'expert' analysis to different voices outside our own local and historical horizons was now
seen to be no source of 'authentic' knowledge at all. As Bennett *et al.* put it,
within the structuralist perspective, 'the diverse forms of human agency –
the forms in which men and women think, feel and act out their lives – are
the product of cultural determinations, not the other way around' (Bennett
et al., 1981, p. 12).

If that is so, why then do we need to draw on methodologies that give us
access to people's 'lived experience', by way of ethnographic field work,
long interviews, focus groups and other qualitative methods? In the 1980s,
why did we not simply continue to analyse the 'text' and the 'structures' that
'determine' the text, as the screen theorists had been doing for a decade?
And if our only access to the 'real' is via either our own or other people's
structurally determined 'narratives', how can we legislate between these?
What is the point of even going beyond the personal narratives with which
I began this chapter? Why do we not, as John Fiske suggested in the early
1980s at a conference on new television audience theory, simply conduct
our audience analysis as individuals seated in front of the television screen?
The attempt to embed ourselves, as Radway suggests, in another culture in

order 'to comprehend the entire tapestry of social life' will become an infinitely regressive task as we disclose more and more subcultures (and multiple subjectivities within those subcultures), each with their own 'determined' validity as accounts of what they see, and each also 'determined' by their interaction with the analyst's own language.

A quick response to that worry is: 'Well yes, that is exactly what sociologists and anthropologists do. That *is* reality, as it is constructed, sedimented in various formations of power, negotiated, dissolved or reformed in time and space.' To move on from my own (biographically/institutionally located) use of 'The Monster of Peladon' to *British, American, or Australian* fan readings of it, or to become aware of a different producer's take on 'politics' in *Doctor Who* via an ethnography of production, is not necessarily privileging one account as more 'real' than another. Rather it is trying, as Adam and Allan ask us to do, to find the 'now here' – the local, partial and fragmentary micro-narrative – and yet to contextualise it also, to interconnect it, to globalise it.

But quite how we think about doing that brings us to a longer response *vis-à-vis* how we come to theorise qualitative research methodology itself. How do we understand the relationship between methodologies that give access to other people's 'lived experience' and theories about what that 'data' actually means? These methodological, theoretical and epistemological debates around television audience theory were themselves part of broader academic ferment over 'meta'-theory and 'grand narratives' to which I will turn next, as I still hunt the answer to my colleagues' questions about why methodological debates in audience studies (and media studies more generally) matter. I am working, then, in this first chapter, progressively from a personal (briefly reflexive) narrative, via the field of professional academic decoding/audience theory, to wider issues of debate about modernity/postmodernity, poststructuralism and the 'risk society'.

How might I move from the more personalized account of myself as 'ethnographer' in the previous sections, to a broader one that positions all of us (academics and students) as qualitative or ethnographic researchers? Are there wider patterns in which we can find our own personal/academic histories embedded?

Five moments of qualitative research

In a useful 1990s overview, Norman Denzin and Yvonna Lincoln speak of 'the five moments of qualitative research' this century. Other researchers may choose to articulate this history differently. But Denzin and Lincoln's narrative is useful to my task because it draws attention to the way in which qualitative methods have themselves been embedded in a relationship between researchers as particular kinds of narrator and their theoretical (paradigm) assumptions.

For these two authors, the 'traditional period' of qualitative research (from the early 1900s to World War II) focused on the study of 'other' (alien, foreign and strange) cultures via the '"objective", colonizing accounts of field experiences' (1998, p. 13) by positivist researchers. This was the period of the heroic Lone Ethnographer, 'the story of the man-scientist who went off in search of his native in a distant land' (Denzin and Lincoln, 1998, p. 14). Its ethnographic texts were organised according to four beliefs: 'a commitment to objectivism, a complicity with imperialism, a belief in monumentalism (the ethnographer would create a museum-like picture of the culture studied), and a belief in timelessness (what was studied never changed)' (1998, p. 14). As Denzin and Lincoln argue, this model of the ethnographic researcher continues in many quarters to the present day, though not without critique from current postmodernisms; and they quote a retired Harvard anthropology professor complaining at a 1980 conference of her discipline shifting from a 'distinguished art museum' into a 'garage sale' (1998, p. 15). A key moment in this early tradition of ethnography was the Chicago school's interpretive 'slice of life' sociology. Here Depression-era outcasts were accessed by academic sociologists, who used the language of ordinary people under the mantle of 'a social science version of literary naturalism' (1998, p. 15). Yet these ethnographies were, Denzin and Lincoln say, very particular kinds of narrative. They were morality tales; usually working through the three stages of 'existence in a state of grace, seduction by evil and the fall, and finally redemption through suffering' (1998, p. 15). In this they were not so different from the Hollywood gangster narratives of the same Depression period.

The second moment Denzin and Lincoln call the 'modernist phase'. This, building on the earlier social realism stage, extended through the 1950s and 1960s, attempting to formalise rigorous qualitative methods. A new generation of young researchers were drawn to ethnomethodology, phenomenology, critical theory and feminism, and wanted thereby to access the voices of the underclass. A canonical text of this period was Howard Becker *et al.*'s *Boys in White*, where causal narratives were central. Here the researchers used a multi-method approach. This combined open-ended and quasi-structured interviews in attempting to make qualitative research talk about probabilities. In this they took their 'cue from statistical colleagues. . . . Thus did work in the modernist period clothe itself in the language and rhetoric of positivist and postpositivist discourse' (1998, p. 17). The ethnographer now was also a cultural leftist romantic. 'Imbued with Promethean human powers, they valorized villains and outsiders as heroes to mainstream society . . . and held to emancipatory ideals' (1998, p. 17). Generally, though, theirs was an ironic/tragic tale, whose end came during the Vietnam War with its ferment of new dominant ideas, including a mix of labelling theory, conflict theory and dramaturgical analysis.

Denzin and Lincoln's third moment – of 'blurred genres' (from about 1970 to 1986) – saw ethnographers and qualitative researchers gaining in

stature with the 'ethnographic turn'. But by now they had a vast comple-
ment of paradigms, methods and strategies to mix and (maybe) match.
Theories ranged through symbolic interactionism, constructionism, natural-
istic ethnography, postpositivism, phenomenology, ethnomethodology, critical (Marxist) theory, semiotics, structuralism, feminism and various ethnic
paradigms. Methodologies included grounded approaches, case studies, historical, biographical, ethnographic action and clinical research; and these
variously drew on qualitative (open-ended and semi-structured) interviewing, observation, visual and documentary methods, and personal experience. Clifford Geertz's 'thick description' of detailed events, rituals and
customs (such as his Balinese cockfight analysis) became the paradigm
account, as anthropologists admitted that all their writings were interpretations of interpretations. The 'local situation' became the subject of expert
and lay narratives. On the one hand 'genre dispersion was occurring: documentaries that read like fiction (Mailer), parables posing as ethnographies
(Castaneda), theoretical treatises that look like travelogues (Levi-Strauss)'
(1998, p. 18). On the other hand, poststructuralism (Barthes), micro–
macro descriptivism (Geertz), liminality theories of drama, performance
and culture (Turner) and deconstruction (Derrida) were challenging the
familiar 'expert' genres and narratives at their epistemological foundations.
'The golden age of the social sciences was over, and a new age of blurred,
interpretive genres was upon us. The essay as an art form was replacing the
scientific article' (1998, p. 19).

'What we call the fourth moment, or the crisis of representation, appeared
with *Anthropology as Cultural Critique* (Marcus and Fisher, 1986), *The
Anthropology of Experience* (Turner and Bruner, 1986), *Writing Culture*
(Clifford and Marcus, 1986), *Works and Lives* (Geertz, 1988)' (1998, p. 19).
In Denzin and Lincoln's account, the 'profound rupture' of the mid-1980s
problematised all over again the issues of validity, reliability and objectivity
which qualitative researchers thought they had settled in earlier phases.
Reflexivity became central, embedded in critical and feminist epistemologies,
and epistemologies of colour. The fact that, on the one hand, informants
routinely lie to their anthropologists, and that, on the other hand, naturalist
literary conventions encouraged authors routinely to edit themselves out of
their texts, led to the conventional ethnographic narrative (of, sequentially,
'doing fieldwork', 'collecting data' and then 'writing up') being thrown into
disarray. A different type of text emerged, a memoir in which the anthro-
pologist her/himself became a central character in the story that was told.
Writing rather than fieldwork became the focus of attention, as a method of
inquiry that developed through successive stages of self-reflection. This was
an attempt at a 'new politics of textuality that would refuse the identity of
empirical science' (Clough, 1992, p. 16; cited in Denzin and Lincoln, 1998,
p. 21). Intertextuality was also a focus, since 'the field worker's texts flow
from the field experience, through intermediate works, to later work, and
finally to the research text that is the public presentation of the ethnographic

and narrative experience. Thus do writing and fieldwork blur into one another. There is, in the final analysis, no difference between writing and field-work' (Denzin and Lincoln, 1998, p. 21). My own earlier biographical comments on the way in which Hall's and Morley's texts 'flowed' through my own empirical audience research on *Doctor Who* are given their broader theoretical frame here.

The fifth (and current) moment in Denzin and Lincoln's account is one where the 'ethnographer's authority remains under assault today. A double crisis of representation and legitimation confronts qualitative researchers in the social sciences' (1998, p. 21). The structuralist/linguistic turn has thrown into doubt the possibility that qualitative researchers can ever directly capture lived experience, since such experience is created in the social text that the researcher her/himself writes. So 'representation' of lived experience is highly problematic methodologically. Notions of validity, generalisability and reliability become even more problematic. Thus, in the midst of this crisis of representation and legitimation, theory asks 'How are qualitative studies to be evaluated in the poststructural moment?' (1998, p. 22). As Denzin and Lincoln argue, this fifth moment of 'double crisis' (of representation and legitimation) means that theories 'are now read in narrative terms, as "tales of the field" (van Maanen, 1988). . . . The concept of the aloof researcher has been abandoned. More action- activist-oriented research is on the horizon, as are more social criticism and social critique. The search for grand narratives will be replaced by more local, small-scale theories fitted to specific problems and specific situations' (Denzin and Lincoln, 1998, p. 22). Small – and local – is now beautiful.

Denzin and Lincoln willingly admit that their temporal map of 'five moments' is 'like all histories, somewhat arbitrary' (1998, p. 22), that earlier historical phases are co-present with the current one; and indeed that it is precisely this co-presence, multiplication and fragmentation of qualitative research which currently leads to the availability of choice and academic agency according to multiple methodological canons, to competing criteria of evaluation, and to a ferment of debate. I have chosen to privilege their particular 'history' of five stages here because it focuses centrally on questions of theory and methodology, and also because it is clear about the way in which different dominant academic paradigms help determine this work. Their focus is

- on specific *research narratives*, as tales are told within these theoretical paradigms ('morality tale', 'tragic tale', 'genre dispersion', 'memoir', 'tales of the field');
- on the kinds of *agency* (e.g. as heroic Lone Ethnographer, cultural leftist romantic, or reflexive memoir writer) inscribed and generated by these paradigms;
- on the *canonical theoretical/empirical* texts/authors that are markers of the dominant paradigms (Chicago School, Becker *et al.*, Geertz, Marcus etc.); and

- on the *mediated relationship* imposed on the accessing of 'everyday experience' by these canons, authorships, narratives and methods.

We have shifted, then, from my personalised narrative (how I came to use this or that qualitative method or text in researching *Doctor Who* audiences) to a history of personalised narratives. Yet each is contained within the rule-laden logics, categories and classifications that determine what counts as 'truth' or as 'authentic' experience in these various paradigms. So to that extent, 'the forms in which men and women think, feel and act out their lives' are (as Bennett says) the product of 'structured' academic determinations. But how, then – if the notion of the validity of our research in relation to the world 'out there' is lost in a crisis of representation – can we avoid academic solipsism? In discussing 'audience' worlds, how can we do more than 'theorise' about them, like *Doctor Who*'s timelords – intellectuals whose pleasure resides in contemplating, without action, the infinite plurality and difference of the universe?

The following chapters will explore these, and my colleague's, questions by way of a number of audience case studies of various television genres where academics like myself have watched (and analysed) audiences watching the screen. The particular audience studies I discuss here – of crime series, soap opera, 'television violence', news, current affairs and documentary, cartoons, take-home videos, sitcom, science fiction and cult television – are my own choice of studies which I have found of enormous value in my teaching and my thinking about audience research. I do not claim to be representative, either in the TV genres studied (nothing here, for example, on audiences for TV sport or high cultural 'classic' series) or in my coverage of the academic studies discussed (and many important studies are, inevitably, not discussed here). To be representative or archivalist in this book is not my aim; which is to focus on the relationship of theory and method in television audience analysis via a variety of valuable, even path-breaking approaches within the broader field of cultural studies. My main point is to draw attention to their place among the changing theoretical paradigms which have brought qualitative methods so much to the foreground in social and cultural research over the last few decades. In addition, I want to say something about the different 'moral frames' that researchers have themselves brought to the audiences they have studied – frames, for example, of 'pleasure' and of 'risk' which are then situated within broader, macro-social critical assumptions. Here we have the pleasurable play of difference within postmodernism, or the cataclysmic democracy of 'risk modernity'. Although my main focus will be on the methodological detail and particular theoretical assumptions of specific audience studies, these other frames will never be far away.

One final point about the frames circumscribing this book. My brief is to talk about *television* audiences and *academic* analysis (valuable discussion of the moral frames surrounding public pressure groups and television has taken place elsewhere: see Barker (1984), Sparks (1992), Barker (1997), Hill (1999)). Clearly, no sophisticated understanding of theories and methods of audience analysis can stop with television. That there is a significant need to go beyond this to examine the 'audiences' of new technologies, few readers of this book will doubt (and Matthew Hills, whose work I look at in the final chapter, has begun to do this in very innovative ways).

But, perhaps less obvious to media and cultural studies scholars – despite their current focus on the 'everyday' – is the need also to visit audiences of live cultural performances. This should include theatre in its widest sense (from Shakespeare to street carnivals), music (high and popular), painting, sculpture as well as a host of new arts. So I see the television genre examples of this book as no more than a starting point in a much broader project which will, I hope, continue to be reflexive about the theories and methods we bring to the audiences, texts and performances that we study.

2

Beyond celebration: from local ecstasy to global risk

In their 'critique after postmodernism', Barbara Adam and Stuart Allan challenge recent theory's tendency towards an 'ivory tower' self-referentiality. Adam and Allan accept poststructuralism's

- critique of 'meta-narratives'
- pluralisation of 'reality'
- contextualization of 'truth' and 'validity'
- reflexivity
- emphasis on the tentative fluidity of 'local' stories and accounts.

But they also challenge poststructuralism's outcomes.

> This is to say that, despite its theoretical potential for active engage-
> ment, commitment and 'life politics' (Giddens 1991), this type of theory
> recurrently prioritizes cultural plurality and invention for their own
> sake. The rich diversity of cultural forms, practices and identities is
> being celebrated at the expense of a critical analysis of their implica-
> tion in the daily renewal of the pernicious logics of class, sexism,
> racism, homophobia, ageism and nationalism, amongst others, that
> are all too indicative of 'postmodern' societies.
>
> (Adam and Allan, 1995, p. xv)

'Celebration' and 'critical analysis' are the key terms in opposition here; and it is the latter that recognises the 'pernicious logics' of human risk as matters of daily renewal and routine. Contrary to celebratory notions of diversity, for the authors these logics constitute both local and global *orders of risk* of the following: poverty and structural unemployment; domestic violence and women's public exposure to harassment, fear and exploitation; racial disad-vantage and racist politics at the heart of our corporate-consumer 'multi-culturalisms'; gay bashings; older people's impoverished invisibility; nationalist wars and 'ethnic cleansing'; biotechnological exploitation of 'underdeveloped' societies. These orders of risk only have to be listed, the authors suggest, to point to the obscenity of an academic discourse that is solipsistically locked into self-referentiality. Hence it is time already to beware the reflexive position of my first chapter. It is because of these 'pernicious logics' that this book on audience theory and methodology deliberately takes its narratives into the field of risk, anxiety and pain, as well as the more recently fashionable pleasure, ecstasy and celebration.

Reflexivity – important as it is to our theory and to our method – needs to be more widely based. And to make this claim is not, I believe, to be 'spoken' or 'interpellated' by the 'structures' (for example, of this or that 'Left' narrative). It is simply to agree with the rhetorics of many governments and peoples in the world today (for example, those recently involved in the wars in Kosovo and East Timor), on behalf of democratic participation, and a fairer, safer and more equitable citizenship.

Moreover, as Ien Ang tells us, we already are (as academics and students) part of the universe of power relations. So the honest thing is to admit to it, and to our particular stake in it. Thus Ang argues for *both* an 'ethnography of storytelling' *and* a careful reflexive account of our relationship as researchers to these relations of power and participation.

> This contemporary cultural condition – postcolonial, postindustrial, postmodern, postcommunist – forms the historical backdrop for the urgency of rethinking the significance of ethnography, away from its status as realist knowledge in the direction of its quality as a form of storytelling, as narrative. This does not mean that descriptions cease to be more or less true; criteria such as accurate data gathering and careful inference making remain applicable. . . . It does mean that our deeply partial position as storytellers . . . should be . . . seriously confronted. . . . The point is not to see this as a regrettable shortcoming to be eradicated as much as possible, but as an inevitable state of affairs which circumscribes the . . . responsibility of the researcher/writer as a producer of descriptions which, as soon as they enter the uneven, power-laden field of social discourse, play their political roles as particular ways of seeing and organising an ever-elusive reality.
>
> (Ang, 1996, pp. 75–6)

Ang, we notice, emphasises that 'more or less true' descriptions, 'accurate data gathering' and 'careful inference making' are still important. She is, in other words, concerned with a demonstrably valid methodology. But at the same time, she insists on the importance of being (theoretically and politically) reflexive so that we are as aware as we can be about the kind of 'arbitrary closure' (Stuart Hall) which, as academic theorists, we are placing on other people's 'everyday' participation in reality. There *is* a reality, but it is embedded in the negotiation of different discursive practices.

> Once again, this does not mean that people's involvements with media as audience members in everyday situations are not real or non-existent; it

only means that our representations of those involvements and their inter-relationships in terms of 'uses', 'gratifications', 'decodings', 'readings', 'effects', 'negotiations', interpretive communities' or 'symbolic resistance' (to name but some of the most current concepts that have guided audience research) should be seen as ever so many discursive devices to confer a kind of order and coherence onto an otherwise chaotic outlook of the empirical landscape of dispersed and heterogeneous audience practices and experiences. The question, then, is what kind of representational order we should establish in our stories about media consumption.

(Ang, 1996, p. 77)

Like Denzin and Lincoln, and like Adam and Allan, Ang's 'what kind of representational order?' does not embrace objectivism ('a wish to build an ever more "comprehensive theory of the audience", which would by definition be an unfinishable task' (Ang, 1996, p. 78)). Rather Ang calls for a radical contextualism, and a cultural politics that is concerned with the ways in which 'unequal power relationships across the board' work through 'the intricate intersections of the diverse and the homogenous, the complicated interlockings of autonomy and dependence' (1996, p. 143).

Ang does not (and neither do I) accept the position of researcher-as-fan, which finds in the postmodern condition an ecstatically pleasurable diversity of audience readings. She takes to task in this regard John Fiske's approach to audience 'ethnography', and his discovery of a 'semiotic democracy' of television separate from a political economy of its institutions; where a 'popular' reading of television genres is, by definition, also a progressive one. As Ang says,

'if the ethnography of reception wants to elaborate its critical function, it cannot avoid confronting more fully what sociologists have dubbed the micro/macro problematic: the fact that there are structural limits to the possibilities of cultural democracy *à la Fiske*, that its expression takes place within specific parameters and concrete conditions of existence. In short, we need to return to the problematic of hegemony.

(Ang, 1996, p. 140)

So, on the one hand, as an audience theorist, Ang insists on ethnographic reflexivity: 'I must know on whose behalf and to what end I write. . . . That is, our stories cannot just tell "partial truths", they are also, consciously or not, "positioned truths" ' (Ang, 1996, p. 78). This is the inevitable responsibility of 'expert' discourse. But on the other hand, she speaks of 'concrete conditions of existence', in which 'the hegemonic specified' includes – centrally – the transnational media system. Ang argues that the overarching media communication empires of Rupert Murdoch *et al.*, are very specific, and are historically developing 'structural and global configurations of hegemony, within which contemporary practices of media reception and consumption evolve' (1996, p. 143). It would be ludicrous to suppose that the structural intervention which globalised corporations make into all forms of popular entertainment do not delimit the 'infinite diversity of viewer meanings' which some postmodernist media theorists celebrate; and to this extent Ang agrees with structuralist notions of cultural determination.

But equally ludicrous, says Ang, is the opposite, pessimistic tendency, that there is

> a definitive and unambiguous, general theoretical answer to this question – as the theory of cultural imperialism has attempted to do (Tomlinson 1991) – precisely because there is no way to know in advance which strategies and tactics different peoples in the world will invent to negotiate with the intrusions of global forces in their lives. For the moment, then, we can only hope for provisional answers – answers informed by ethnographic sensitivity to how structural changes become integrated in specific cultural forms and practices, under specific historical circumstances.
>
> (1996, p. 143)

Drawing on Denzin and Lincoln's 'fourth moment' theorists Marcus and Fisher, Ang argues that '"since there are always multiple sides and multiple expressions of possibilities active in any situation, some accommodating, others resistant to dominant cultural trends or interpretations, ethnography as cultural criticism locates alternatives by unearthing those multiple possibilities as they exist in reality"' (Marcus and Fischer, 1986, p. 116; cited in Ang, 1996, p. 149).

It is crucial to discover these alternative voices – often partial, fragmentary and highly localised – in people's various everyday realities. But it is equally important to remember that it is 'in this very living out of their everyday lives that people are inscribed into large-scale and historical relations of force which are not of their own making' (Ang, 1996, p. 137). Hence, the 'critical potential of an ethnography of audiences . . . evinces global and historical consciousness as well as attention to local detail' (Ang, 1996, pp. 148–9). Ang is therefore bringing together Denzin and Lincoln's fourth and fifth moments of methodology/theory: an emphasis on authorial reflexivity fused with a focus on local problems and specific situations – and yet without forgetting the 'global' concerns of their third moment (the leftist romantic's emancipatory ideals).

The 'answer', then, to my colleague's question – what is the point of talking about methodology, or of the different uses in different local contexts of focus groups, long interviews, and structured surveys? – is that these are ways of giving us research access to other people's 'multiple possibilities as they exist in reality'. But this is never an innocent procedure. On the one hand, the question – and how we ask it – will provoke an answer that is a 'yes' or a 'no' on behalf of an emancipatory and democratic politics. On the other hand, 'theory' is crucial here too; otherwise we are faced, as Meaghan Morris has said, with the cultural studies 'banality' of *just* local contexts; of an endlessly proliferating collection of 'ethnographic' audience studies as one or other audience group makes its particular meanings in relation to one or other television genre. This banality, as Morris argues, lies in the fact that where we lack a macro-cultural critique, we are doing no more than endlessly repeating the 'Truth' that audiences 'in modern mediatised societies are complex and contradictory, mass cultural texts are complex and contradictory, therefore people using them produce complex and contradictory culture' (Morris, 1988, p. 22; cited in Ang, 1996, p. 137).

Some macro/local contexts

How then might we establish a 'global and historical consciousness', while at the same time giving due attention to the local and the reflexive? In the remainder of this chapter, I look at two recent (and academically 'hegemonic', to use Ang's term) meta-theoretical approaches which focus on this interplay *beyond* the era of modernity's 'grand narratives'. We return to Ang's emphasis on a reflexive analysis of the everyday within the 'global and the historical' by looking at two recent approaches to the 'global' everyday.

Postmodernism's 'era of simulation'

How shall we (as 'audiences') best gain access to the nature of the 'contemporary' and the 'global'? As we saw in the case of Ien Ang, media theorists often look at the media itself, and the media's corporate globalisation, as a conceptual mode of access to understanding what the 'everyday' feels like in the contemporary world. Douglas Kellner takes this approach, in arguing that:

> the analysis of media culture within its matrix of production and reception helps illuminate its artefacts and their possible effects and uses, as well as the contours and trends within the broader socio-political context. Since the forms of culture produced by giant media and entertainment conglomerates are an immediate and pervasive aspect of contemporary life, and since media culture is both constituted by and constitutive of larger social and political dynamics, it is an excellent optic to illuminate the nature of contemporary society, politics, and everyday life.
>
> (1995, p. 5)

Focusing on the globalising nature of the media and its particular 'contemporary' modes of representation has itself had spectacular visibility within the academic field of media studies (as well as within the media and advertising industries themselves) – from Marshall McLuhan's 'global village' to Baudrillard's postmodern world of the 'simulacra' and 'hyperreal'. Baudrillard's discourse of the postmodern has been not only very significant in media and cultural studies, but also one of the most extreme in postulating a complete rupture with the world of modernity.

In his *Ecstasy of Communication* – a title which is highly indicative of the kind of moral thrust of Baudrillard's discourse – he argues that we have entered a new stage in the history of the subject, where identity is so splintered and kaleidoscopic as to have become akin to that of the schizophrenic.

> In spite of himself the schizophrenic is open to everything and lives in the most extreme confusion. . . . Stripped of a stage and crossed over without the least obstacle, the schizophrenic cannot produce the limits of his very being, he can no longer produce himself as a mirror. He becomes a pure screen, a pure absorption and resorption surface of the influent networks.
>
> (1988, p. 27)

There are a number of telling features in this comment. One is Baudrillard's universalising and essentialising of his 'subject' by calling it 'he'. Second, this inactivity is re-emphasised by the reference to a failure of agency and performativity. Baudrillard's receiving subject has been 'stripped of a stage' for projecting and constructing 'himself' ('He becomes a pure screen'). Third, there are the strong emphases on words to do with representation – mirror, screen – which technologically determine the subject in a relationship of 'pure absorption'.

Like many other postmodern theorists, Baudrillard emphasises the fragmentation of the subject. Jameson, too, argued that the discontinuous and fragmented mode of experience is a central feature of postmodern culture and its audiences. But Baudrillard's theory of the 'implosion' of subjects into fragmented masses has gone perhaps furthest in arguing for a new information society where the subject is no more than a 'term in the terminal' (1988).

For Baudrillard 'TV is the world' – a 'hyperreal' world where simulation dissolves social action in an endless flicker of images. Reality and signification fuse. The nuclear meltdown at Five Mile Island has no 'core' reality beyond television's images of it, the television event having 'supremacy . . . over the nuclear event which itself remains . . . in some sense imaginary' (1984, p. 18). As regard the Nazi extermination of Jews, 'Properly speaking it is *Holocaust* the television film which constitutes the definitive holocaust event' (1984, p. 24). And – in a famously outrageous prediction – Baudrillard argued that there could be no 'real' Gulf War, since it had already been played out in simulation.

In 'the era of simulation' everything becomes interchangeable, says Baudrillard: the left and the right in politics, the beautiful and the ugly in fashion, the useful and the useless in any exchange of objects, the true and the false in media messages about reality. 'All the great humanist criteria of value, all the values of a civilization of moral, civic and practical judgments, vanish in our system of images and signs. Everything becomes undecidable' (1988, p. 128).

This is a contemporary world marked by consumption of the most expansively passive kind. Indeed, it is a world marked *only* by consumption; and here Baudrillard's postmodernism links hands with that of Lyotard who challenged any epistemological 'grand narrative' – including Marx's meta-theory about human identities derived from human production. Whereas Marx argued that the alienation of human labour at the workplace was the site and focus of change within capitalist relations of production, Lyotard rejected such 'narratives of emancipation'.

> In contemporary society and culture – postindustrial society, post-modern culture – the question of the legitimation of knowledge is for-mulated in different terms. The grand narrative has lost its credibility, regardless of what mode of unification it uses, regardless of whether it is a speculative narrative or a narrative of emancipation.
>
> (Lyotard, 1984, p. 37)

Since, in this formulation, theory itself – even emancipatory theory – had become the source of oppression of the subject within this or that iron cage of 'expert' narrative, the release of the subject from unity, control, narrative process and humanist agency was indeed (to use Baudrillard's term), 'ecstasy'. Image diversity was choice itself in an endlessly moving prolifera-tion of tastes.

Modernity had based its wager on two affirmatives: that humanity would control and fix the meaning of nature through knowledge; and that the agent of this progress would be the free, equal and knowing subject. Consequently, the expert's rationality and knowledge was at the heart of this system. In contrast, the postmodernist claim is to replace meaning (as in knowledge = control) by affect. As Munson argues, 'Without origins or sta-ble meanings, there is no real source of "impassioned commitment". Postmodern media culture creates the conditions of fandom, of affective investment in appropriated objects wherein investment further empties them of meaning' (Munson, 1993, p. 14). The fashion stream has replaced 'commitment' (whether to scientific evolution, class revolution or any other 'impassioned' grand narrative); and Munson goes on to argue that particu-lar parts of the television medium are at the forefront of this postmodern shift.

> The talkshow has become the ideal vehicle for showcasing and even *becoming* the fashion stream. Its audience participation makes the stream uniquely accessible. Gender, race, ethnicity, lifestyle, handicap, personal problem, unique experience – such differences are no longer

repressed in this 'third stage'. They become the talkshow's emphasis. Confronting boredom and channel clutter with constant, intensified novelty and 'reality', talkshows offer a variety of Others to the fluid spectatorial self. The talkshow mingles the 'professional' or 'expert' with the 'amateur', the guest or participant who appears by virtue of particular personal experience or simple audience membership.

(Munson, 1993, p. 15)

Circularity and undecidability are characteristic of the talk show, as they are of the postmodern condition itself; and in this condition of 'affective invest-ment', the performance of diverse and fragmented daily experiences (as in the talk show genre) in 'hyperlocal' media space constitutes a new public sphere. But whereas Habermas' notion of classical public space was based on the free and equal formation of public opinion through rational dis-course (where we all aspire to knowledge and expertise), this 'alternative' public sphere is one of affect, contextualised experience, diversity and frag-mentation.

Many other commentators, however, have noted that this vision of 'choice' (as an endlessly moving stream of fashions and tastes) is remarkably close to that of the capitalist advertising industry, which itself quickly took up postmodernism's celebration of fragmentation and pastiche. As Kellner says,

Perhaps the very lack of a cultural dominant and the mixing of a vari-ety of aesthetic styles and strategies, such as one sees in advertising is postmodern. Yet contemporary Marlboro advertising campaigns sug-gest that the highly paid and often sharp interpreters of the contempo-rary scene in the employment of corporate capital see the continuing existence of traditional identities, where masculinity is still important, combined with a modern concern for power and enjoyment as a con-tinuing social force. . . . [C]ontemporary culture is highly fragmented into different taste cultures which respond by producing quite differ-ent images and values. A megacorporation like Marlboro goes after all these audiences, thus one sees a certain heterogeneity in its image pro-ductions with different appeals sent out to different audiences accord-ing to market segmentation. . . . Thus, it is capital itself which is the demiurge of allegedly postmodern fragmentation, dispersal of identity, change and mobility. Rather than postmodernity constituting a break with capital and political economy as Baudrillard (1976) and others would have it, wherever one observes phenomena of postmodern cul-ture one can detect the logic of capital behind them.

(1995, pp. 256–7)

So, like Adam and Allan, Kellner continues to find exploitative logics. And, although focusing on a very different form of advertising – the 'Meeting Point' columns of local newspapers ('FEMALE 18, blond and fun loving, seeks hunky black guy, 18–25, must be exciting & enjoy music and clubs. Cardiff') – Glenn Jordan and Chris Weedon come to a similar conclusion, and a similar critique of postmodernism (but with a different spin to Munson's point that race and ethnicity are no longer repressed within postmodernism).

> Within the endless stream of commodities on offer in the international capitalist market of the 'Post-Modern Age' are symbols and fantasies of racial Otherness. It is sometimes assumed that People of Colour – Black and Brown bodies, minds, character and culture – are despised in the dominant representations of race in Western culture, i.e. that racism works *only* by suppression, domination and exclusion. We wish to suggest . . . that the reality is otherwise: Blackness, for example, is often *celebrated* in the dominant – that is to say, racist – culture, especially by those in the dominant group who regard themselves as liberal, avant-garde and/or cosmopolitan.
>
> (Kellner, 1995, p. 150)

Like Kellner, Jordan and Weedon point to a mix of the discourses of modernity and postmodernity within the hegemonic power relations of racist and capitalist societies.

> In hegemonic and popular discourses, in modern and postmodern systems of representation, the Black is strong, powerful and, on the dance floor, football field and basketball court, a smooth mover. . . . This is the continuation of a long tradition – but with a difference: whereas from the sixteenth to the nineteenth century 'it was this black body that was most "desired" for its labor in slavery', today 'this body . . . is most represented in contemporary popular culture as the body to be watched, imitated, desired, possessed'.
>
> (hooks, 1992, p. 34; cited in Jordan and Weedon, 1995, pp. 156, 158)

Thus, Jordan and Weedon argue, it may be the case that postmodernist theory 'offers a framework from within which to question long-established Truth, narratives of History and the exclusion of marginalized and oppressed groups' (1995, p. 162). But this will only be the case if we remember that

> core aspects of the cultural politics of racism are reproduced in the 'cosmopolitan' capitalist market place of our Post-Modern world. . . . Surely the crucial point is that it is not adequate to theorize difference merely as plurality, the play of the signifier or as an effect of cultural diversity. Difference, like 'free choice', in racist and sexist societies is an effect of power.
>
> (Jordan and Weedon, 1995, p. 162)

So, whether the audience of these advertisements is the young white (or black, or yellow) female smokers of Marlboro cigarettes worldwide, or the 'blonde and fun loving' young white female in Cardiff, Baudrillard's 'ecstasy of communication' is still embodied in very traditional relations of commoditisation and power. Ecstasy there may have been for the 'blond and fun loving' young woman in Cardiff, but this was never separate from the situating of bodies in material relations and representations of power.

Perhaps the point is that while modernism is still inscribed within postmodernism (as Kellner argues), important aspects of the postmodern were also integral to the devlopment of modernism. Munson remarks that the

> notion of audience participation in commercialised entertaiment goes back at least to the nineteenth century lyceum, the women's service magazine, and – in an integration of spectator into performance space – the turn-of-the-century amusement park, dance hall, and cabaret. . . . The working women and prosperous urbanites who practised such forms of leisure approached them as *trans*gressive, *pro*gressive, and *ex*pressive gestures, mixing people of different backgrounds in a nocturnal pursuit of self-actualizing risk.
>
> (Munson, 1993, p. 11)

The point, then, is that the society of risk, diversity and fragmentation was increasingly the doppelgänger of the society of scientific meaning (for the development of this in science fiction, see Tulloch and Alvarado, 1983, ch. 3). The risk society, featuring the slippage from the social/rational subject to the disordered self, lay deep in the very engine house of modernity.

The 'risk society'

On first observation, Ulrich Beck's current notion of the 'risk society' is a very different 'global' view of our everyday world from that of Baudrillard. Risk theory is currently very prominent (in academia, among user groups and in government circles) as the twentieth becomes the twenty-first century (Lupton, 1999); and offers itself as an alternative in its analysis of 'late' or 'risk' modernity from that of 'post'-modernity. Here we move from Baudrillard's pleasure and ecstasy to Beck's anxiety and risk.

Nevertheless, there is substantial common ground between postmodernist and 'risk modernity' theory; most notably in their critique of the 'grand narratives' of the Enlightenment tradition (such as science and Marxism). Like Baudrillard *et al.*, Beck argues for a global society in which we are increasingly free from controlling and normative expectations, whether of class or modern institutions. Baudrillard speaks of everything becoming 'undecidable', while Beck emphasises the 'incalculability' (between prediction and action) obsessing all sectors of society. Like Baudrillard, there is a distinct pessimism in Beck's theory.

But there are also significant differences. Whereas for Baudrillard pessimism is embedded in the cynicism of the 'bad masses' – 'The mass knows that it knows nothing, and it does not want to know. The mass knows that it can do nothing, and it does not want to achieve anything' (1988, p. 216) – in Beck's case, the pessimism is about 'bad science'. The scientific engine of the earlier society of 'goods' – the belief in an improving and evolving enlightenment of the mind and control of natural forces via technology – has in fact been widely *seen* to contain its own doppelgänger. Science and technology, far from being producers of the enlightenment, have helped produce the gas chambers of Auschwitz, the nuclear disaster of Chernobyl, the chemical death at Bhopal, the greenhouse effect, pollution, global warming, genetic engineering.

Even more centrally, for Beck risk is potentially not only catastrophic but also 'democratic'. In his view people who suffer the other risks of late modernity (such as unemployment because of new technologies, or the choices of job mobility versus family stability) are highly aware of them as everyday experiences, choices and tensions. Moreover, these economic risks clearly still have socio-economic variabilities. In contrast, environmental risks that 'induce systematic, and often *irreversible* harm, generally remain *invisible*' (Beck, 1992, p. 23); and can affect entire populations. While (as with technologically induced environmental risks) 'risky underemployment' is 'a development whose far-reaching consequences and risks are not calculable for political consciousness and action either' (Beck, 1992, p. 144), its victims have a reflexive relationship with its daily consequences. In contrast the inability of scientists in risk modernity to be sure of risk calculation and avoidance can lead to catastrophes which, while invisible, 'are based on *causal interpretation*, and thus initially only exist in terms of the (scientific or anti-scientific) *knowledge* about terms' (Beck, 1992, p. 22–3).

Beck sees the familiar dangers of everyday life as 'drenched with experience' (1997, p. 123). But it is the invisibility of environmental hazards that lifts this aspect of the risk society out of the everyday domain; which is why the media becomes so important in his theory. 'What eludes sensory perception becomes socially available to "experience" in media pictures and reports. Pictures of tree-skeletons, worm-infested fish, dead seals (whose living images have been engraved on human hearts) condense and concretize what is otherwise ungraspable in everyday life' (Beck, 1995, p. 100). It is this existence of a natural and social reality 'beneath and behind' these images that the media can draw attention to in Beck's view, in what is foundationally a critical realist reading of the media and its audiences. The human effects of environmental catastrophes begin to show at the surface. 'What scientists call . . . "unproven connections" are [for parents] their "coughing children" who turn blue . . . and gasp for air with a rattle in their throat. . . . The immediacy of personally and socially experienced misery contrasts today with the intangibility of threats from civilization, which only come to consciousness in scientized thought' (Beck, 1992, p. 61, p. 52). In this experiential way, victims of risk 'themselves become small, private alternative experts in risks of modernization. . . . The parents begin to collect data and arguments' (Beck, 1992, p. 61). How important then – both for these 'parents' and even more for those whose children do not 'gasp for air'- might the media be!

Yet for Beck the media – as knowledge-processing systems – are themselves part of risk society.

> As the risk society develops, so does the antagonism between those *afflicted* by risks and those who *profit* from them. The social and economic importance of *knowledge* grows similarly, and with it the power over the media to structure knowledge (power and research) and disseminate it (mass media). The risk society in this sense is also the *science, media and information* society.
>
> (Beck, 1992, p. 46)

When Beck points to the differentiation of communication forms within the public sphere 'from the global television network to the school newspaper' (1992, p. 196) he is not, as Cottle (1998) suggests, involved in an epistemological 'slippage' but realistically pointing to both the potential 'cognitive' role of the media and the power discriminations of their varied forms. Beck no more forgets the power of 'market forces' over the mass (as compared with school) media than he does in his analysis of the family within risk society. But it is especially *because* of the potentially catastrophic, invisible nature of environmental risks that the 'risk society = media/knowledge/information society' equation becomes so important for Beck in relation to *those risks*.

Given his general view (together with other risk theorists like Lash) that class and other systemic differences within modernity would give way (as a result, for Beck, of 'risky underemployment') to differences of knowledge within the information order, the 'invisibility' of environmental risks becomes a paradigm case for his theory. Beck's particular use of terms for the potential role of the media – that they can help imagistically to 'condense and concretize what is otherwise ungraspable in everyday life' – is identical with that of critical realist media practitioners themselves (Tulloch, 1990, ch. 5); and needs to be remembered at the same time as his more pessimistic conclusion that 'market forces' (e.g. the media's penchant for short-term risk 'fashions') working together with the public relations spin-doctors employed by risk industries will continue to control a 'media-dependent, manipulable' (Beck, 1997, p. 123) public. Again, Beck is close to both critical realist practitioners and theorists (like the Frankfurt School) in arguing that 'Television isolates *and* standardizes' in removing people from 'bounded contexts of conversation, experience and life' (Beck, 1992, p. 132); but also in offering, as a wager, the potential of a different kind of media. '[T]he democratisation of criticism that becomes possible in risk society implies that the necessary attentiveness and clarity of criticism in the interplay of government and opposition will falter if at the same time criticism, even radical criticism, does not prove its principles and expand its footing in the public mass media' (Beck, 1997, p. 147).

However, unlike 'modernist' critical realists who pin their wager on contradictions between classes, Beck finds his potential for a liberating conflict in a different struggle; namely the dialogue over the uncertainties of science and 'expert' knowledge – in other words, in 'reflexivity' as a contest between experts and counter-experts. 'We are dealing with "scientific battles" waged over the heads of the workers, and fought instead by intellectual strategies in intellectual milieux' (Beck, 1992, p. 113). Environmental hazards, says Beck 'are produced by business operations, to be sure, but they are defined and evaluated socially – in the mass media, in the experts' debate, in the jungle of interpretations and jurisdictions, in courts or with strategic–intellectual dodges, in a milieu and in contexts, that is to say, to which the majority of workers are totally alien' (Beck, 1992, p. 112). And *yet*, the media may – via its possibilities for imagistic condensing and concretising – perform as 'cultural eyes through which the "blind *citoyens*" can perhaps win back the autonomy of their own judgement' (Beck, 1992, p. 20).

So risk is not simply something imposed upon us by science and technology. It is also something chosen and calculated upon. Although the property and power relationships within this period of 'reflexive' (or 'risk') modernity remain constant, and while the society still makes decisions on the pattern of the old industrial society, new 'debates and conflicts which originate in the dynamic of risk society are already being superimposed on interest organisations, the legal system and politics' (Beck, 1996, p. 28). Whereas for postmodernist theorists the risk (and ecstasy) of the contemporary world lies in the dethronement of experts by (pluralised) lay knowledge, Beck's risk society is, in fact, a world of experts-in-contradiction. Certainly, as a global concept, risk society 'describes a stage of modernity in which the hazards produced in the growth of industrial society become predominant.' (1996, p. 29). But the point is that these risks are not calculable as certain knowledge.

> Industrial society, which has involuntarily mutated into risk society through its own systematically produced hazards, balances *beyond the insurance limit*. The rationality on which this judgment is based derives from the core rationality of this society: *economic* rationality. It is the private insurance companies which operate or mark the frontier barrier of risk society. With the logic of economic behaviour they contradict the protestations of safety made by the technicians and in the danger industries, because they say that in the case of 'low probability but high consequence' risks the technical risk may tend towards zero, while at the same time the economic risk is potentially infinite. . . . Insurance experts contradict safety engineers. . . . Experts are relativised or dethroned by counterexperts. . . . Ultimately industries responsible for damage (for example, the chemical industry for marine pollution) must even expect resistance from other industries

affected as a result (in this case fishing and the business dependent on coastal tourism).

(Beck, 1996, pp. 31, 32–3)

For Beck, risk society sees a systemic transformation of industrial society in three areas. First, there is the increasingly dark relationship of modern industrial society to the natural and cultural resources whose reserves are being used up (Beck includes here, as well as environmental resources, cultural resources like the nuclear family and housewives' labour which made men's paid labour possible). Second, there is the intellectual and discursive relationship of society to the hazards which it is producing and which are exceeding its own conceptions of security (so that all sectors of society – business, the law, academia, and especially politics – are now talking 'risk' discourse). Third,

> the exhaustion, dissolution and disenchantment of collective and group-specific sources of meaning (such as belief in progress, class consciousness) of the culture of industrial society . . . leads to all the work of definition henceforth being expected of or imposed upon individuals themselves. This is what the concept of 'individualising process' means. . . . They are . . . expected to live with the most diverse, contradictory global and personal risks.
>
> (Beck, 1996, p. 29)

Whereas Baudrillard's 'masses' become simply the context-local bearers of multiple, shifting and fragmented identities composed of a proliferation of media signs, Beck's 'individualised individuals', deprived of even the us/them commonalities of the Cold War, live in a 'networked media world, which compels not love-thy-neighbour, but love of whoever is far away.' In this condition, individuals in the risk society 'must repeatedly discover and justify even their own personal foreign policy in personally changing constellations' (1996, p. 30).

This is one of Beck's relatively rare references to media audiences; and he is interested in the media here not as a defining phenomenon of postmodernity (as in Baudrillard, even though there are distinct similarities in their focus on dethroning expertise), but as just some of the many circuits of communication within reflexive modernisation. For Beck this is to emphasise the automatic transition from industrial to risk society as *all* its institutions become aware that what once appeared 'functional' and 'rational' (i.e. the products of science and technology) now appear as a threat to life in incalculable ways. The media, then – along with the law, the medical profession, the economic and insurance professions, and so on – predominantly speak risk discourse.

This, of course, has a profound implication for any theory of audience response. This is especially so, given that, despite Beck's talk about individualisation in a world of 'diverse, contradictory global and personal risks', there is a parallel devaluation of everyday agency in Beck as there is in Baudrillard. In Baudrillard's case, the mediated 'mass' is the effect of an endless play of images and 'simulacra'. In Beck's analysis, despite the talk about both reflexivity and reflection, the everyday 'risk individual' seems almost as helpless, since he/she is subject in even the most intimate decisions to little more than a choice between experts (see Wynne, 1996, p. 76).

Somewhat contrary to Beck (and closer to some postmodernist theorists of television audiences, like Livingstone and Lunt, 1994), Brian Wynne has emphasised that 'the fundamental sense of risk in the "risk society" is risk to identity engendered by dependence on expert systems which typically operate with such unreflexive blindness to their own culturally problematic and inadequate models of the human'. Wynne's focus is thus on the way in which 'scientific expert knowledge . . . denigrates specialist lay knowledges' and 'defines lay resistance as based on ignorance or irrationality rather than on substantive if unarticulated objections to those inadequate constructions of lay social identity which the expert discourses unwittingly assume and impose' (1996, p. 68). In Wynne's 'risk' analysis, we move beyond Beck's notion of an automated, societal reflexivity, back to the kind of political reflexivity emphasised by Ien Ang. We also return directly to the relationship between 'global' and 'local', to questions of how we theorise this relationship, and – beyond that – to questions of methodology: how, as theorists, we gain access to the 'everyday'?

For Wynne, 'specialist lay knowledge' – as in his well-known case study of Cumbrian sheep farmers' response to the Chernobyl disaster – is crucial. Like Ang also, Wynne's political reflexivity is on behalf of a more emancipatory and democratic theory and method. It is, he argues, the reintegration of 'lay' with 'expert' knowledge, and with it the 'reintegration of the deleted issues of human agency, responsibility and value which may lead to the democratisation, legitimation and epistemic pluralisation of science' (Wynne, 1996, p. 70). Still, Wynne's emphasis on 'specialist lay knowledges' does not immediately help us in considering the role of the media in this process (we will look at Livingstone and Lunt's highly specific emphasis on lay knowledge in television talk shows in the final chapter).

It is a feature, in fact, of Baudrillard's, Beck's and Wynne's theories of (respectively) 'post' and 'risk' modernity that they say very little about the actual products of media culture. Despite the emphasis on media in their globalising theories, they say so little about the everyday world of media producers and audiences. What Cottle (1998) says of Beck is true of Baudrillard also. Both theorists lack an empirically based middle-level theory of the media, concerned with the everyday narratives of production and reception.

In this context, Pertti Alasuutari's recent description of the 'third generation' of media reception studies points us in useful directions beyond the 'experts' of Baudrillard, Beck and Wynne.

> The third generation resumes an interest in the programmes and pro-
> gramming, but not as texts studied in isolation from their usage as an
> element in everyday life. Furthermore, it adds a neglected layer of
> reflexivity to the research on the 'reception' of media messages by
> addressing the audiences' notions of themselves as the 'audience'.
>
> (1999, p. 7)

Alasuutari sees as an important starting point for 'third generation' analysis the emphasis of Allor (1988), Grossberg (1988) and Radway (1988) that 'there isn't really such a thing as the "audience" out there; one must bear in mind that audience is, most of all, a discursive construct produced by a particular analytic gaze' (1999, p. 6). In particular, Alasuutari is interested here 'in the place of expert knowledge produced by media researchers in enhancing or quieting down the public concerns, and in reproducing or transforming the frames within which the media and "audiencing" are perceived' (1999, p. 7). We need also to be interested in the expert 'analytical gaze' of media producers who perceive their audience in virtually every aspect of their everyday professional practice.

'Audiencing' then becomes the centre of many 'expert' circuits of communication: of government and other moralists, media professionals, academic researchers, and the 'specialist lay knowledge' of audiences (as fans) themselves. Like Ang, Alasuutari is arguing on the one hand for an analytical focus on the representational orders which academics (and many other 'experts') place on 'the audience', but on the other hand he is emphasising the need for a renewed concentration on the 'big question' of the 'cultural place of the media in the contemporary world' (1999, p. 7). By considering this in terms of the 'moral frames' through which the public 'conceive of the media and its contents . . . as representations – or distortions – of reality', and by examining the role of 'experts' (media researchers, producers, moralists and others) in 'enhancing or quieting down' these public concerns – he is arguing for an analysis which is both 'global' in its public context and reflexive in relation to academic (and other) analytic paradigms.

Like Denzin and Lincoln, Alasuutari addresses critical anthropology's concern with the 'voice' of the ethnographer. But here he argues for the additional advantage we have as researchers of television of being able to draw on our 'specialist local knowledge'. '[I]t is ridiculous to think of a media ethnography in terms of so-and-so many months of participant observation: "fieldwork" has actually started years before we knew anything about a particular site we are going to study' (Alasuutari, 1999, p. 8) – as in my case with *Doctor Who*.

Thus we have, as television researchers, both 'expert' and 'local' knowledge. Alasuutari is concerned with how this local 'specialist lay knowledge' becomes 'expert knowledge' by way of our theoretical and methodological commitments. He speaks of 'audiencing' rather than 'audiences', because of the discursive nature of our methodological constructions. Producers, audiences, moralists and researchers of media are all part of the audiencing process. How the interviewees in a group discussion speak about particular television programmes tells us, most of all, about 'what are the embedded problems and concerns that evoke it as a topic? What are the viewpoints and subject positions taken in the discourse' (Alasuutari, 1999, p. 16)? For example, *Doctor Who* fans speak reflexively about their own compared with the 'average viewer's' watching of the programme. Fans in interviews see themselves as audiences that 'look back' at an episode: via video-recordings, convention discussions and fanzines. In contrast, the 'average viewer' (whose continued watching is crucial to the survival of the show) does not 'look back'; and so fans worry about unresolved narratives that leave this other audience 'up in the air' – in case they switch off. Consequently, as well as the intra-textual references that fans enjoy (for example the fourth Doctor's fight to the death with the Master on a radio-telescope, which drew fans' memories back to their very first confrontation many years before), fans also highlight 'as data' in their interviews other properties of the text (such as a clear and resolved narrative) which they think is necessary to keep the 'average viewer' hooked and the programme alive (Tulloch and Jenkins, 1995, p. 156).

Thus, as Alasuutari argues, viewers are (no less than producers or researchers or moralists) constantly active in 'audiencing'. That is, they reflexively construct themselves and others as 'audiences', watching themselves watch the television text; and the particular properties of the text that they reference as 'data' depend on the frames within which these 'me/other' audiences are constructed. 'Third generation' audience research, for Alasuutari, requires a sociological focus on the moral frames within which viewers, moralists, producers and researchers 'talk': as audiences justify their media preferences, producers persuade about the demographics of their new television idea, researchers explain the particular audience focus of their research (explaining the shift, for example, from a 'deficit citizenship' focus on current affairs to women's pleasures in soap opera), or moralists explain the latest mass killing via renewed 'risk to young viewers' discourse.

It will be these daily 'audiencing' discourses of 'ecstasy' and 'risk', rather than the meta-theories of Baudrillard or Beck, which will provide my focus of selection in the chapters that follow. My brief from the publishers was to focus on the audiences for different genres of television. But in order to avoid Meaghan Morris's 'banality of just local contexts' charge against cultural studies, I have wanted to situate these different genres of audience within a developing local/global account. My own slant on this has been to take a number of academic 'audiencing' texts which I have found personally valuable over the years in helping me watch audiences watch particular television genres. As with my approach to *Doctor Who* as a subject for research, the choices here will be personally and professionally embedded. There is neither any intention nor possibility of being 'representative'. Rather my task is to re-read these (for me) key texts that have watched and talked about audiences watching television; to unpack their methodology, their theory, and their discursive focus; and then to consider how each does (and does not) help me understand 'audiencing' better.

|3|

Some histories of the television cop series

The full title of this book, *Watching television audiences: Cultural theories and methods*, specifies its particular brief. That is to say, among the many foci on 'audiencing' as a macro/local phenomenon it might take, this book emphasises particularly the **academic researcher/TV audience** relationship within cultural studies. Audiences watch the screen, and we also – as researchers and writers – watch them watching, as active members of Alasuutari's 'moral frames'. But how do we understand that multiple 'watching'?

In recent years there has been a ferment of current theoretical debate about:

- ontology (what is the nature of being human, of reality?);
- epistemology (what is the relationship between the researcher and the audience, between those who inquire and those who are 'known'?); and
- methodology (how do we access the world, and gain knowledge of the 'other'?).

Denzin and Lincoln have noted that researchers face 'an embarrassment of choices [that] now characterize the field of qualitative research. There have never been so many paradigms, strategies of inquiry, or methods of analysis to draw upon and utilize' (Denzin and Lincoln, 1998, p. 22). They argue that the paradigms of qualitative and ethnographic research have become so multiple and fractured during the historical 'stages' that they describe, it is now possible for 'any given researcher to attach a project to a canonical text from any of the above-described historical moments' (1998, p. 22).

In this book's first substantive chapter on a particular television genre and its audiences, I want to begin to illustrate some of the general arguments of the first two chapters by choosing as 'canonical', or at least symptomatic, research texts on television police series between the 1970s and 1990s. These will mark the shifts and flows within academic interpretive communities during that period, and illustrate the ways in which globalising and middle-level theories of media generated their own symptomatic methods of accessing 'the audience'. If we compare these shifts with those described by Denzin and Lincoln (chapter 1), we will then see how important it is to examine the *specific* reading formations in different academic communities in different places at different times within the broader academic history they are describing.

Interpretive communities: encoding ideological effect

During the 1970s the significant work on cop series that influenced my media teaching was British. The dominant debate here included a mix of Althusserian notions of police as ideological state apparatus, Barthesian concepts of the textual conversion of history into myth, and Gramscian notions of hegemony, as well as feminist critiques of police and patriarchy within critical criminology. This was a period, as Denzin and Lincoln say, of 'blurred' genres within academic paradigms. But in the field of television studies this diffusion was significantly contained within the framework of critical (Marxist) theory, semiotics, structuralism, feminism and psychoanalysis. It was around these that the debates within and between the two British 'international leaders', the Birmingham Centre for Contemporary Cultural Studies (CCCS) and the journal *Screen*, mainly occurred.

There were, of course, differences of view also within these two organisations, which sometimes get lost from view in retrospective histories of the 'origins' of cultural studies in Britain. *Screen*'s constituency of film and media secondary teachers, for example, often tended to cluster around its 'teacher education' journal *Screen Education*, and there were strong debates and editorial resignations over issues of 'plain speaking' as against 'jargon' between these two journals in relation to their respective audiences. Some of the key pieces on police series during the 1970s were printed in *Screen Education* and tended towards a 'conflict' sociology rather than post-'linguistic turn' set of theoretical agendas, and also more towards a 'Birmingham Centre' emphasis on encoding, preferred readings, ideology and hegemony than to the textualist mix of psychoanalysis and structuralism at *Screen*.

Typical of this period was Geoff Hurd's analysis in *Screen Education* of *The Sweeney*, the British police series staring John Thaw and Dennis Waterman as a pair of Flying Squad cops who occasionally bent the rules in their quest for justice. Hurd argues that the series emerged out of a particular moment in British police history when public knowledge of police corruption in relation to organised crime was increasing, when (as also recently in New South Wales) a new police commissioner was appointed on an anticorruption ticket, and when cop series like *The Sweeney* worked to resolve these 'points of tension' within British society in an acceptable way. The lead character, Regan, is given a mandate by the series narrative to be 'entrepreneurial' in his rule-breaking, because 'If the law is inviolable . . . the rules are not and the viewer is presented . . . with a context in which the police are absolved from normal rule-governed behaviour' (Hurd, 1976, p. 50). By constructing its narrative flow across a series of oppositions – police vs. crime, law vs. rule, professional vs. organisation, authority vs. bureaucracy, intuition vs. technology, masses vs. intellectual, comradeship vs. rank – *The Sweeney* could construct its 'good' (intuitive, entrepreneurial, comradely, plebeian) police by emphasising this cluster as 'everyday professional' in contrast to top-down, controlling hierarchies (whether in crime or police organisations).

To break the rules was 'good' as long as it was 'professional'; and meanwhile other 'half-formed' public worries (about, for instance, the increasing use of science and technology for public surveillance) could be defused. In one episode the topic of science training in the police force was introduced via a narrative that opposed Regan to a young university-trained policeman whose scientific expertise was justified only because, in the narrative finale, he was shown to have the same 'professional' qualities as Regan (for a semiotic interpretation of this episode see Drummond (1976)).

In Hurd's critical-realist analysis, science was a problem, not as the 'grand narrative' soon to be challenged by poststructuralists, but because of its significant potential to extend the surveillant power of one of Althusser's ideological state apparatuses. Moreover, from a critical Marxist point of view, the police series created myth (in Barthes's sense) out of the real history of class relations. *The Sweeney*, Hurd argued, articulated compulsively the apparently timeless myth of the 'professional' as the good policeman, 'simulating the division of a world along lines not derived from class and thereby divorcing the issues surrounding crime from any class analysis' (1976, p. 39). Yet, by appealing to the 'plebeian' qualities of its heroes (this was the part which made Dennis Waterman famous for his 'wide boy', Cockney-style individualism, which he was later to develop further in *Minder*), *The Sweeney* could pull in a working-class audience and make this a top-rating, peak viewing series. For Hurd, the cop series was therefore hegemonic, in Gramsci's sense, in so far as it encouraged people to assent to their own exploitation.

For Hurd and others the myths of TV cop series papered over the contradictions within capitalism at a key moment of public debate in one of its key apparatuses, the police force. Both 'centred biographies' like *The Sweeney* (focusing on the anomic, isolated cop in an alienated world) and 'de-centred' police series like *Z-Cars* (depicting a world of extended, collective police work) were subgeneric variations that resolved the same contradiction: the separation of most people from agency within the social division of labour. In both subgenres of police series, Hurd argued, major conflicts faced by police (with organised labour and with racial groups) which reflected antagonisms fundamental to the relations of production of contemporary capitalism were displaced on to non-'structural' oppositions (professional vs. organisation, intuition vs. technology, etc.).

A number of things will be apparent from Hurd's analysis (which was a familiar approach in this period: see also Dennington and Tulloch (1976) and Clarke (1986)). First, the TV police genres were seen as historically situated, *working textually* to displace very specific ideological (time/place) 'contradictions'. Correlatively, the method of analysis was also textual. Similarly, Bennett and Woollacott argued in their 1980s analysis of the James Bond phenomenon, that different genres operate (and become popular with audiences) at different historical moments, each at the 'fault lines' of society. Whereas the police genre related to the dominant 'law and order' debate of the 1970s, so the Bond films operated in the early 1960s 'both to shift and stabilise identities at a time when existing ideological constructions had been placed in doubt and jeopardy, when . . . the articulating principles of hegemony were in disarray and alternatives had not been successfully established' (Bennett and Woollacott, 1987, p. 280).

Second, the theoretical model overlaying the analysis was of the kind formulated by Stuart Hall in the early 1970s, within a Marxist sociological framework of television as a *structure with ideological effect*. Hall argued that a central rhetorical encoding device within the media was a three part move of displacing, individualising and re-binding, a process which masked and mythologised the contradictions within capitalism. Thus, in Hurd's formulation, *The Sweeney*:

- masked and displaced (the labour contradictions within capitalism);
- fragmented and individualised (focusing, for example, on Regan's world of existential angst where heroes sacrificed families, leisure and safety for their job); and
- re-bound within a new 'imaginary' coherence (reconfiguring the different individuals within the 'good police professional').

Third, the *audiences* for these police series were not analysed empirically, but deduced from text analysis and from the ratings popularity of the programmes. The emphasis was on the ideological encoding of these texts, following Hall's critique of American 'effects' studies of audiences. Here Hall argued that audience analysis that focused on individual changes in attitude and behaviour (as in the TV violence debate) was misplaced. Rather, textual ideology-critique revealed how television worked to reproduce, rather than change, the hegemonic order. From this point of 'encoding' analysis, it then seemed a natural development to follow up with empirical 'decoding' (audience) analysis of these ideological messages, as David Morley did at the beginning of the 1980s with his 'Nationwide' analysis (*see* chapter 10). The evolving generic focus of this encoding/decoding trajectory was on the socio-political contents of, first, police series, next, the current affairs genre.

However, little or no empirical audience work of this 'decoding' kind was ever done in relation to cop series. Rather Denzin and Lincoln's 'blurred genres' period took the analysis in different directions. The 'ethnographic turn' focused analysis of police series on *production studies* like Alvarado and Buscombe's *Hazell* (1978, a private eye series based on a former cop) and Albert Moran's *Bellamy* (1982, an Australian police series). Here, a background emphasising the political economy of television served to underpin the 'thick' description of professional production idiolects and values-in-practice. For example, Alvarado and Buscombe showed in *Hazell* how ITV's search for a peak-viewing replacement for *The Sweeney* led to the notion of something 'similar-but-different' in its 9 p.m. slot. To replace the guns-and-car-chase scenario of *The Sweeney* with something different, a more laconic, voice-over, film noir style was conceived by a producer deliberately selected for herself being 'different' (i.e. entirely inexperienced in making cop series). Alvarado and Buscombe then showed how this concept was worked through the tribulations of professional practice. The technical supervisor, for example, opposed the producer's and designers' film noir chiaroscuro contrasts because they conceived of the television audience as one that sat in fully lighted sitting rooms rather than in the darkened cinema that served film noir. In the end not much was left of the film noir concept visually, other than the filmed credit sequence, the voice-over, and a painting of the sets as a poor simulation of the 'uneasy' *mise-en-scène* of film noir. As a teacher, one could therefore simply begin a lecture with a shot of one of these interior sets of *Hazell* and trace televisual stylistic devices back through an ethnography of production to the 'real' basis in the political economy (ratings) of commercial television. Clearly, this kind of analysis augmented, with little contradiction, the Marxist sociology of Hurd's and others' more textualist accounts of the police series.

Meanwhile, more textualist approaches, like Gillian Skirrow's analysis of *Widows*, were drawing on the notion of textual 'excess' (developed during the 1970s in screen theory analysis of Hollywood melodrama) to point to tensions between *mise-en-scène* and performance on the one hand, and the narrative of violence and action on the other. For Skirrow, *Widows'* foregrounding of film noir *mise-en-scène* (where women are active and ambitious) and its performative emphasis on women learning to act like male gangsters (as a 'de-naturalisation of the signifier of male sexuality', Skirrow (1985, p. 177)) opened out a different kind of pleasure for women viewers. On the one hand, Skirrow's work was part of a developing debate within feminism on film narrative and female pleasure. On the other hand, it was also part of a new and larger debate (as in Ien Ang) that refused to instrumentalise pleasure, as ideology-critique tended to do. So that by the mid-1980s at least, the police series and closely related genres were beginning to be seen as purveyors of pleasurable fantasy as well as of hegemonic ideology. Series like *The Sweeney* and *Miami Vice*, James Donald argued, refracted rather than reflected their time, and were an active constituent in their historical moment, 'working its ideological tensions, anxieties and fantasies into fictional forms' (Donald, 1985, p. 123).

A third development during the 'blurred genres' 1980s was around theories of the cop series *as genre*. Analyses such as Skirrow's were restoring human agency to the analysis of drama as myth by positioning specific (textually defined) audiences as potentially performative elements in the *process* of genre. Whereas Skirrow focused on the potential audience aspect of this, other theorists like John Fiske were pointing to the ambiguating effect of the production process. Steve Neale had forcibly argued that television genres are never simple 'ideological' narratives (i.e. stories that led from the initial 'lack' of the crime to the final 'plenitude' of the capture), as, for example, in Propp's classic analysis of the folk tale narrative, which had been a canonical text in early structuralist textual analysis in the 1970s. Rather, Neale argued, the narrative process within any particular genre simultaneously inscribes the text across a number of discourses which are in constant relations of equilibrium/disequilibrium. These are continuing and parallel narrative relations of coherence and contradiction, which enabled, Fiske argued, new 'angles of interest' to remake the police series according to their particular time/space co-ordinates. In the 1980s, police series like *Cagney and Lacey, Charlie's Angels* and *Juliet Bravo* placed women in roles which were both 'caring' and active. Thus contemporary American TV male-action series, like *The A-Team*, were 'challenged by the admission of feminine values . . . strongly in *Remington Steele* and very threateningly indeed in *Cagney and Lacey*' (1987, p. 222). Similarly, Alan Clarke argued that the conflict between core 'human' values in the police series and contradictory current discourses (about police corruption, feminist critiques of patriarchal culture, the threats of science and technology, etc.) was what kept the genre fresh and socially responsive.

Clearly this argument (which was to be raised in relation to the multiple narratives within soap opera also) altered the balance of analysis from television drama as an 'ideological effect' of capitalism to one where new fissures opened up, and new possibilities for agency and resistance appeared at both the production and audience levels. By now, in the mid-1980s, we were well into the decades of the cultural studies 'resistance' tradition that Alasuutari describes as one of the main instrumentalist directions in 'expert' academic discourse. This kind of analysis also offered potential overtures to the ethnographic studies of production (which had by and large eschewed both text/ideology and audience analysis), in so far as it suggested ways in which various 'expert' paradigms circulating in the broader social context (such as feminism or environmentalism) could become part of 'lay' readings via the production process of popular TV series. What Stuart Hall had called the 'professional' encoding position within popular television could be relied upon to access these new 'expert knowledges' continuously from other circuits of communication, as television producers tried to keep their product fresh and (as Alvarado and Buscombe argued in the case of *Hazell*'s ratings relationship to *The Sweeney*) 'similar but different'.

Postmodern series

The similar disappeared within difference as postmodernist and post-structuralist theories began to impact on analyses of cop series. As we have seen, Baudrillard foregrounded the schizophrenic identity, while Deleuze and Guattari celebrated the nomadic and the schizoid aspects of subjectivity. Kellner notes that one sees

> in Baudrillard and other postmodern theorists that the autonomous, self-constituting subject that was the achievement of modern individuals, of a culture of individualism, is fragmenting and disappearing, due to social processes which produce the levelling of individuality in a rationalized, bureaucratized and consumerized mass society and media culture. Post-structuralists in turn have launched an attack on the very notions of the subject and identity, claiming that subjective identity is itself a myth, a construct of language and society, an overdetermined illusion that one is really a substantial subject, that one really has a fixed identity.
>
> (1995, p. 233)

Kellner points to the way in which the crime series *Miami Vice*, together with MTV, became a key television text in the explication of the postmodern condition. Thus Gitlin pointed to *Miami Vice*'s postmodern blankness, and Grossberg spoke of the series as nothing but a 'surface' composed of 'a collection of quotations from our own collective historical debris, a mobile game of Trivia' (1987, p. 28). In this it was more akin to the billboards that successively flash past us than to any 'text' which we might want to analyse and interrogate. It is, some theorists argued, this 'indifference' (to meanings, ideology, etc.) of *Miami Vice* that makes it a representative postmodern text, a 'flat' text in Jameson's sense, when he argues that the most marked feature of postmodernism is 'the emergence of a new kind of flatness or depthlessness, a new kind of superficiality in the most literal sense' (1984, p. 60). This representation of society's surface of appearances as *all there is*, concealing no 'deep structures' or 'causal mechanisms' (Lovell, 1981a; Allen, 1985; Tulloch, 1990), was pointedly at the expense of materialist (critical realist) accounts of cop series in the 1970s which emphasised (as in Hurd) the textual displacement of 'underlying' class contradictions.

As Kellner says, the 'cutting edge of image and sound production' (1995, p. 238) in *Miami Vice* displays for the viewer a succession of 'artificial images, emphasizing South Florida colours of flamingo pink, lime green, Caribbean blue, subdued pastels, and flashing neon' (1995, p. 238) backed by four-track stereo rock music and 'replicating the music video form of MTV'. This celebration of image and sound (with sometimes entire songs in the background of action) tended to drag the attention away from the storyline. 'Image frequently takes precedence over narrative and the look and feel

become primary, often relegating . . . narrative meanings to the background' (Kellner, 1995, pp. 238–9). In addition to this 'waning of affect'
(Jameson) where postmodern texts become flat successions and intensities
of the moment only, the character of the two undercover officers, Crockett
and Tubbs, and of their boss Castillo, are 'fragmented and unstable', as
their 'schizoid dichotomy' (Kellner, 1995, p. 243), their 'multiple identities
and multiple pasts . . . intersect in unstable ways with the present' (1995,
p. 241).

In fact, Kellner himself adopts a postmodernist theoretical stance, arguing against 'the Althusserian position, taken at one time by *Screen*, which
claims that ideological texts interpelate individuals into subject positions
that are homogenous, unified and untroubled'. In contrast, Kellner argues,
'the "subject positions" of media culture are highly specific, contradictory,
fragile, and subject to rapid reconstruction and transformation' (1995, pp.
239–40). But Kellner does not adopt a postmodernism separate from a critical analysis of political economy. He locates the fashion and identity discourses of *Miami Vice* within the 1980s Reaganist emphasis on wealth,
affluence, fashion, style and image. This emphasis was both influenced by
this US/1980s materialist consumer society and performatively transcoded
it. For example, 'Crockett's unconstructed Italian jackets, his tennis shoes
without socks, his T-shirts and loose pants, his frequently stubbled beard,
his changing hairstyle and so on produced a model for a new male look, a
new hip alternative to straight fashion' (Kellner, 1995, p. 240).

Further, Kellner argues for specific subcultural *audience* readings of
Miami Vice within its broader 'problematics of identity in contemporary
techno-capitalist societies' (1995, p. 240). So, 'Crockett and Tubbs and
their colleagues are arguably role models for macho white males, blacks,
Hispanics, women, and teenagers. . . . Thus, quite specific gender and role
models and subject positions are projected, as are quite different images of
sex, race and class than are usual in the typical mediascapes of [the] television world' (1995, p. 240). We note Kellner's use of 'arguably' and 'projected' since (as in the earlier 'ideological effects' period) no empirical
audience research was conducted.

Kellner's emphasis is on the *performativity* and *reflexivity* of postmodern
identity, as the focus of modernity's subjectivity (in one's occupation and
one's family) is replaced by identity as a function, of leisure, pleasure, play,
'cross-dressing' and gamesmanship. Thus the macho 'modern' single-iden-
tity cops of *Dragnet* (with its moralistic, authoritarian personality in Sgt.
Friday) and *The Untouchables* (Elliot Ness's incorruptibility) are replaced
by *Miami Vice*'s Crockett and Tubbs who 'assume different hairstyles,
looks, roles, and behaviour, from show to show, season to season' (1995, p.
244). In contrast Friday and Ness now seem extraordinarily repressed in
their mono-logical professional masculinity. Consequently, in so far as
'there are emancipatory possibilities in the perpetual possibility of being
able to change one's self and identity' (1995, p. 247), Kellner reads this as a

Loan Receipt
Liverpool John Moores University
Learning and Information Services

Borrower: Kenneth Longden
Borrower ID: 185589
Loan Date: 26/07/2007   Loan Time: 14:52

Watching television audiences
Tulloch, John
Barcode: 31111009067067   Loan Type: 1 Day Loan
Due Date: 27/07/2007   Due Time: 23:59

Science fiction audiences
Tulloch, John
Barcode: 31111011602495   Loan Type: 3 Day Loan (I
Due Date: 30/07/2007   Due Time: 23:59

Risk and everyday life
Tulloch, John
Barcode: 31111010758793   Loan Type: 21 Day Loan
Due Date   21/09/2007   Due Time: 23:59

Fines will be charged on late returns.
Please retain receipt in case of dispute.

26/07/2007 loan-receipt-00

progressive tendency in *Miami Vice*. Ecstasy and pleasure, rather than risk, was the focus of this postmodern textualist analysis, in spite of the genre's substantive focus on violence and crimes against the person.

On the other hand, however 'unstable, fluid, fragmentary, disconnected, multiple, open and subject to dramatic transformation' the characters of *Miami Vice*'s cops are, the series 'nonetheless privileges certain male subject positions' (1995, p. 244), together with a generally negative view of black, Hispanic and Third-World people of colour. Moreover, *Miami Vice* both criticises the excesses of capitalism and glamorises its high-powered economic crime – 'an ambiguity that runs through the series and which constitutes postmodern identity as ambivalent and beyond traditional "good" and "bad" role models' (1995, p. 245). So, against Grossberg's analysis of the 'flat' and 'indifferent' *Miami Vice*, Kellner argues that it is 'highly polysemic and is saturated with ideologies, messages and quite specific meanings and values. Behind the high-tech glitz are multiple sites of meaning, multiple subject positions, and highly contradictory ideological problematics' (1995, p. 239). What these different sites of meaning and subject position are, in Kellner's analysis, is still, however, read from the text.

Cop series, cultivation, risk and the fear of crime

If pleasure and human agency were the evaluative focus of these 1980s postmodern trends, another strand of media sociology was continuing to focus on underprivilege and risk. During the early 1970s developments in new criminology theory allied closely with media studies to produce a range of important works about 'deviance' and 'moral panics' (as for example in S. Cohen and J. Young's edited compilation, *The Manufacture of News: Social Problems, Deviance and the Mass Media* (1973)). A symptom of this was the title of one of my own media courses at that time, called 'Cinema "Deviance" and Social Control'. As regards TV cop series, this era of work is best summarised and extended by Richard Sparks' book, *Television and the Drama of Crime* (1992). An important feature here was that Sparks gave himself two agendas, which together widened out debate about police series and at the same time brought them into contact with empirical audience research.

First, was the agenda of 1970s/1980s textual analyses that I have been describing. Here Sparks pointed in particular to the relationship between new strategies of policing, changing representations of police on television and changing public perceptions of the dimensions of the crime problem. In particular, the 'withdrawal of the police-officer into the panda car necessarily lessened the extent of public interaction with the police, and presented a less reassuring image of the police-officer's role and powers. The common law tradition of the constable as little more than a citizen in uniform could no longer be sustained' (1992, p. 15). These 'very changes in the relationship between police and public, themselves the source of some anxiety, also made the public more dependent on mass media for knowledge or reassurance' (1992, p. 26).

There are two crucial issues that Sparks addresses here: the influence that this greater distance between the public and everyday policing had on television representation; and the effect of this on public anxiety about risk generally. This 'criminology' dimension is Sparks' central interest.

As regards representation, 'the increasing distance of the sphere of dramatic action from public experience affords greater dramatic license, more schematic narratives, more action and less contamination by the equivocations of the real' (1992, p. 27). *The Sweeney*'s Flying Squad was, Sparks argues, thus merely the precursor of a series of British and particularly American 'new wave' cop shows (*The Professionals, Kojak, Columbo, Rockford Files, Starsky and Hutch*) which, in line with the 'dissolution of the settled moral and aesthetic dimensions of the classic Western' (1992, p. 27) in the films of Leone, Penn and Peckinpah, implied a 'demand for a more restless and mannered representation, often known . . . as hyper-realism' (1992, p. 27).

By the early 1970s the cop show had entirely supplanted the Western as the dominant genre of narrative fiction on US television, largely on the basis of its superior demographics. The cop show drew an audience which was not necessarily larger but which had a younger, more affluent, urban profile. The urban audience seemed to prefer the *contemporary* mythology of the enforcement of the law in a recognisable city over the traditional Western myths of the foundation of the law in American frontier history (1992, pp. 27–8).

Thus Sparks embeds what Denzin and Lincoln call the 'double crisis of representation and legitimation' (1998, p. 21) within the wider field of social and media representation. But, elaborating his second agenda, Sparks asks why it was that the urban audience liked this kind of cop series? Here Sparks, like Ang, spoke against the 'danger of taking too instrumental a view of the relations between social and political development and the sphere of representation' (1992, p. 28). An audience's *pleasures as well as their anxieties about risk* are as important in understanding the selection of television shows that they regularly watch as any instrumental issue of television's 'ideological effect'. Crucially, narrative pleasure was preceded by a deep sense of risk.

> Fear and anxiety must emerge again here as they are always key terms in the analysis of crime fiction, especially in relation to television. The argument . . . that for at least a fraction of its audience the medium itself is a focus of anxiety, is thus only part of the story. For the implications of the narratives of crime and law enforcement are always in varying degrees unnerving or reassuring, and the extent to which they are experienced as pleasurable lies largely in the dialectic between

these terms. Thus, the debate about whether or not television 'causes' fear of crime . . . suffers from a failure to recognize that the narrative is directed towards precisely the area of tension between anxiety and resolution.

(Sparks, 1992, p. 25)

'Fear of crime', risk and emotional *affect* thus become become a key focus of Sparks's shift of cop series interpretation towards audience analysis; and this 'fear' in his analysis is contained within a contemporary crisis of legitimation. The 'analysis of law and order as a public issue must include not only debates about specific policies or measures but also a consideration of its value as a talisman, as a potent index of the integrity of society as a moral order' (1992, p. 29). As the fictional representation of crime and law enforcement on television responded to changes in policing and its social context, so the myth of crime and punishment would vary in its inflections around an underlying 'set of preoccupations: order, community, integrity, masculinity, danger and the need for retribution' (1992, p. 30).

This second agenda that Sparks opened up, about audience anxiety and public legitimation, drew into his book quite another set of academic 'key texts' from those conventionally addressed in textualist accounts of police series. On the one hand, Sparks was working within and beyond the 'new criminology' of the 1970s (itself strongly influenced by critical Marxist theory). Like these 'left realists', Sparks criticised the top-down nature of the 'new administrative criminology' (also emerging in the 1970s/1980s) because it suggested 'that fear is extraneous, excessive, generated by something other than its ostensible objects, and to this extent irrational' (1992, p. 8).

Strongly embedded in quantitative surveys, this new administrative criminology, Sparks argued, was a symptomatic example of top-down 'expert' research which reduced 'lay knowledge' to the level of 'irrationality'. But colluding with it, in the view of left realist media criminologists like Jock Young, was the 'left idealism' of the radical media theorists and criminologists of the 1970s, who looked at the way in which the media constructed 'deviance', and instituted 'moral panics' and 'deviancy amplification spirals' in relation to 'others' such as Hells Angels, vicars as pederasts, 'free-loving, drug dealing' rock music festival crowds, and so on (Cohen and Young, 1973). Young argued against 'those idealist theories which portray moral panics as media instigated events without any rational basis and against those writers who talk glibly of irrational fears of crime without specifying what a rational fear would look like' (1987, p. 333, cited in Sparks, 1992, p. 8). So Sparks strongly supports Young and other left realist criminologists who brought the focus of fear of crime analysis back to the daily experience of actual women, black youths and other oppressed groups: of risk, harassment and exploitation in the home, at the workplace, from the police, and so on.

But Sparks also criticises the left realists for an *over-rationalist* account of human anxiety. He argues that

- despite so much emphasis among left realists on the concept of rationality, the term itself is left largely undefined – fear is rational in their discourse only if it is wholly accounted for by an *antecedent level of objective risk*. This, Sparks argues, 'simplifies the way in which people respond to their social and physical surroundings, and constitutes the kind of *derogation of lay experience* which the realists are concerned to avoid' (1992, p. 10);
- there is an equation among left realists between the 'reality' of a risk and the rationality (or appropriateness) of an emotional or dispositional state called fear (or worry, or anxiety, or concern). All of this work (by administrative criminologists and left realists alike) has unduly simplified notions of what fear actually is as a mode of experience and perception;
- what from the point of view of an outside observer looks like an actuarially calculable risk is, from the point of view of a potential victim more like a case of *uncertainty*. Perhaps fear of crime is as much a product of subjective uncertainty as of risk (in Mary Douglas's sense of a situation 'governed by known probabilities' (1986, p. 43; cited in Sparks, 1992, p. 11). Thus different senses of the term 'fear' may be operative for different circumstances and groups of people (e.g. women compared with men, and older people compared with the young), not just in 'quantity' but in kind. 'In most cases what we mean by fear of crime is not so much a calculation of probabilities as a set of "intuitions" grounded in experience' (1992, p. 11). While left realists are right to argue that fears are well-founded (and *grounded)*, it is harder to separate it out from other experiences, troubles and hazards than they suggest. It is deeply implicated in our sense of well-being, and takes place among the 'anxieties which press in on everyone' in modern societies (Giddens, 1990, p. 49; cited in Sparks, 1992, p. 12).

On the other hand to this engagement with key texts in the new administrative criminology and in left realism, Sparks's other reference is to work in fear of crime and audiences. This area of television audience research had been dominated by primarily quantitative accounts, the most influential of which were as follows

- George Gerbner's 'cultivation thesis', which tried to establish a relationship between heavy television viewing and people's fear of a 'mean world'. By comparing heavy with light viewers' perceptions of risk, Gerbner and his colleagues at the Annenberg School for Communication argued that a heavy diet of television makes American citizens prisoners of fear, hiding in protected high-rise apartments or suburbs, and calling for authoritarian solutions to the inner-city problems of poverty and underprivilege.

- Barry Gunter's more individually and psychologically based research, which argued that the relationship between fear of crime and television viewing may be the opposite to Gerbner's hypothesis. Rather than heavy television viewing leading to a 'mean world' perception of the occurrence of crime and violence in society, selective perception and selective viewing by anxious personalities might *account* for the heavy viewing of certain kinds of television programme. Overall, Gunter favoured a notion of 'circularity' in his fear of crime and television analysis. 'Greater fear of potential danger in the social environment may encourage people to stay indoors, where they watch more television, and are exposed to programmes which tell them things which in turn reinforce their anxieties' (Gunter, 1987, p. 88).

Sparks took a very different approach from either Gerbner or Gunter. He argued that

- a limitation of both criminological ('administrative') and cultivation theory's worries over the mass media and fear of crime is the calibration of levels of fear against indices of exposure to risk of the feared outcomes. This is a legitimate but not exhaustive concern, because fear is not simply a quantity to be measured. It is, rather, a mode of perception which is perhaps constitutive of personal identity. To this extent it is not accurate to speak of fear as simply being 'caused', even by a specific precipitating event;
- thus one should always see fear of crime as not 'irrational' but as intelligibly summarising a *range* of more diffuse anxieties about one's position and identity in the world.

Sparks therefore found Gerbner wanting in his failure to analyse:

- the pleasure people get from being made uncomfortable;
- how viewing is constituted as a situated activity;
- how differently it may be engaged with by viewers in diverse social locations;
- the spurious isolation of TV viewing as a causal factor behind statistical correlations.

Despite his similarities here with Gunter's criticisms of Gerbner, Sparks also argued *against* Gunter's selective exposure hypothesis. 'The inference that crime drama is "beneficial" because reassuring is an over-simple inversion of Gerbner's position. It still takes insufficient account of the lived experience of fear-of-crime problems and is based on a similarly reductive interpretation of texts' (1992, p. 97).

There are two parts to Sparks's comment here: (a) the critique of reductive interpretations of media texts, and (b) the insufficient account of lived experience. Sparks's book focuses primarily on the first of these: establishing a better account of television crime drama 'texts' than Gerbner's 'ideological effect' approach.

How can we, Sparks asks, get past the standard 'expert' criminological accounts of fear of crime which rely (at least implicitly) on a notional rational agent, and thus give very little insight into the nature of fear of crime *as a dimension of experience*? If 'what we mean by fear of crime is not so much a [rationalistic] calculation of probabilities as a set of "intuitions" ' (Sparks, 1992, p. 11) about 'experiences and hazards and troubles' (Sparks, 1992, p. 12), then what methodological procedures for understanding this global/local relationship might we adopt?

Television, Sparks argued, is one of the most important as well as routine purveyors of the 'paleo-symbolic dynamic of fear'. The paleo-symbolic (following Gouldner) is the 'emotional underpinning' (Sparks, 1992, p. 41) on which any successfully 'rational' transmission of knowledge depends.

Kellner, another media theorist who recognises the 'underneath symbolism' of the paleo-symbolic, elaborates on this 'emotional underpinning' role of key scenic images.

> Paleosymbols are tied to particular scenes that are charged with drama and emotion. For example, Freud found that certain scenic images, such as a child being beaten for masturbation, or discovering his parents having sex, have a profound impact on subsequent behaviour. The images of these scenes remain as paleosymbols which control behaviour, for instance, producing guilt accompanying masturbation, or infusing sex with great fascination and attraction or fear and repulsion. Paleosymbols are not subject to conscious scrutiny or control; they are often repressed, closed off from reflection, and can produce compulsive behaviour. Thus Freud believed that scenic understanding was necessary to master scenic images.
>
> (Kellner, 1995, p. 107)

Kellner therefore argues that resonant images – of non-conformist rebels like James Dean, of nude swimming and easy sex at Woodstock, of body-building, arms training and violent action from *Rambo*, of vampire-like, predatory women from *Fatal Attraction* and *Basic Instinct* – may detach themselves from specific narratives and stay in the viewer's mind, thus deeply influencing one's perceptions of other races, classes and genders. 'Media culture provides powerful images and scenes for identification that may directly influence behaviour, providing models of action, fashion and style' (Kellner, 1995, p. 108).

For Sparks, the paleo-symbolic level of television crime shows relates to a crisis of legitimacy. He believes that as the police series replaced the Western as the most popular action television genre, so its particular '*command iconography*' (relating especially to fears of the modern city) underpinned its narratives. Like Hurd *et al.*, Sparks argues that the routine, daily scheduling of popular police series narratives where 'good guys' beat the 'bad guys' reproduces a certain kind of ideological order. But it is important in Sparks's argument that this routine 'ideological effect' frame is based on non-rational, deep emotional responses to television as an iconic, participatory and profoundly familiar form (as in its repeated imagery of the city). Emotionally charged images connoting 'deep' (but not necessarily fear-specific) anxiety then interact, Sparks suggests, with routinised ('good guy defeats bad guy') police narratives in a relationship which ensures a dramatic 'resolution' (rather than a rational, 'intellectual clarification').

It is in this popular genre, he argues, that people are offered – for their pleasure – troubling and risky issues which, in other media genres are likely to cause fear and concern. In particular, the city offers the public's main 'landscapes of fear'. And since the city, as Stuart Hall has argued, is 'above all the concrete embodiment of the achievement of industrial civilization' (Hall *et al.*, 1978, p. 145), the media's emphasis on the breakdown and dislocation of social order in the city helps engender a crisis of authority and legitimation about modernity itself. At some intuitive and local level, this becomes a crisis in the belief of our 'master narratives' of civilisation altogether.

Sparks thus elaborates on the *ambivalent but central* television representations of the city in the police genre. Public violence now inheres in the actions of law enforcers who themselves often find social organisation too extensive to control or even comprehend. Meanwhile, their violent actions are played out in the kinds of public city spaces that are often all too recognisable to viewers, both as places of everyday work and leisure, and as ritualised 'landscapes of fear'. Thus, Sparks argues, ambivalence and tension beset both the crime series' agents of law *and the viewers who watch them*; and the risk/pleasure tension for viewers is played out *between the narrative and the iconic levels* of television. One simple way in which this can happen is for the local, 'known' and ambiguous images of the city to be embedded in a police series narrative which begins in a familiar locale (a police station, office, or home), moves outward into the dangerously ambivalent scenes of the city to encompass its crime, risk and police pursuit, and then finally returns to a place of safety (the police station again). 'Most crimes take place either outdoors or in public and non-domestic buildings. . . . "Indoors", on the other hand is usually a space of reflection, planning, discussion but also banter and intimacy' (Sparks, 1992, p. 127). It is for that (paleo-symbolic) reason that images of armed 'home invasion' are so shocking as 'especially personal affronts' (1992, p. 127).

This is Sparks's approach to a more sophisticated textual analysis. He also argues, however, that the interpretation of television viewing should be more about how individual people *talk* than in the formal study of texts. 'I am centrally interested in reaching an understanding of television narratives . . . conceived in terms of their likely "realisations" by viewers viewing in determinate settings' (Sparks, 1992, p. 49).

But despite saying this, Sparks does not actually do this kind of situated and local audience analysis himself. So his book does not address empirically the local specificities of audience negotiation with paleo-symbolic images and the anxieties and pleasures associated with narrative, scheduling, place and genre which he analyses.

Tales from the field: fear of crime and the media

A large consultancy study conducted by the Centre for Cultural Risk Research at Charles Sturt University (CCRR) in Australia extended Sparks's valuable divergence from both the dominant paradigms in 'fear of crime' studies of the media: cultivation analysis and left realism. This continued Sparks' emphasis on the **pleasures and anxieties** (in addition to the rationalities) involved in watching crime 'city street' drama via narrative resolution (1992, p. 39), and the scheduled pleasures of 'doxic' routine (1992, pp. 50–1). If television itself has the underlying power of the **emotional** and paleo-symbolic, cop series as a television genre may augment this with the power of the **ideological**: that is, following Eco, via a 'doxic' ritual of reiteration which reaffirms rather than informs. The analytical task, then, for Sparks becomes the examination of these paleo-symbolic and ideological relations of television crime in the context of people's other daily practices and discourses. Television brings the public world of power, threat, and ideological resolution into the private world of emotions and fear. But there it becomes part of our 'mutuality of interaction' (1992, p. 47): it is part of our talk, gossip, and so on.

A case study

We interviewed many people during the Fear of Crime study; this is the story of just one of them.

 Angela is a single parent, having left her husband some years ago because of physical and emotional cruelty. She lives in the New South Wales tourist belt of the Blue Mountains, which has historically been an area where single women parents have looked for work in the hotel industry. Angela, though, is a part-time teacher, having been 'downsized'. Angela had been a union representative in her last full-time teaching position, and it is arguable that she lost this job indirectly as a result of her work in this role. Now out of full-time employment, and a single parent with a late teenaged, unemployed son, Angela is poor. She tells us that she watches television more now that she is older because she cannot afford to go out. She watches on one channel only, in black and white, because she cannot afford an antenna. The channel is the Australian Broadcasting Company, which, as she says, makes her selection of cop series limited. In the old days of employment and a husband, however, Angela did have colour and a number of channels, and her choice of programme then was much the same.

NARRATIVE PLEASURES

Just prior to her interview, Angela had been to a trade union show, where she had enjoyed the gender-bending of the Polish Solidarity choir. With this in mind, and given her union background, her response to our first question was perhaps surprising.

Q: If you watch cop shows, do they make you feel better or more ill at ease about the world, or don't they make any difference?

A: Better about the world. I like the idea of there being *law and order*.

Judging from her 'law and order' opening, we might have expected a conventionally conservative moral frame to Angela's sense of 'audiencing', with attendant fears of crime: drugs, sex, Asian immigrants, etc. Yet our knowledge of Angela already suggests a contradiction here. We did not expect the television pleasures of this woman with quite strong feminist and anti-racist sentiments to be driven by a 'law and order' moral frame.

Her response to the *narrative* question, however, began to reveal how her structural (and situated) social position resolves this apparent contradiction.

Q: Do you prefer the shows where the good guys regularly win?

A: That doesn't really make much difference. I don't care. The good guy doesn't have to win. The story is more important and the characters. If it's a cop show I do enjoy mystery, finding a solution at the end. . . . And I enjoy the characters being realistic, well-rounded, other things happening in their lives apart from the story . . . outside of the text and the action. I like that in cop shows.

In terms of Roland Barthes's narrative codes, Angela is emphasising her pleasure in two of them: the hermeneutic code of puzzles and mysteries; and the cultural code – here a preference for the epistemologically 'real', with 'well-rounded characters', a density of detail from the world beyond the action-narrative, and so on. We followed this response with the Gerbner 'mean world' question to Angela as a heavy viewer.

Q: In your experience, have crime images in the media become more mean and cynical in recent years, or not?

A: Yes. There's [the appearance of] the Australian Christopher Skase-type characters as criminals. . . . I'm not sure in the case of the police. Perhaps they've been exposed more in the media, yes. Perhaps the racist attitudes of Australian cops that I've always been aware of have been exposed more . . . both in fiction and in documentary-type things.

Q: How does this view you have, and the view you mentioned before of liking to think there is such a thing as law and order, relate to your perception of real-life police corruption?

A: I've always been aware that police corruption exists in real life. I haven't expected it to be otherwise, so I haven't been surprised by the exposure. I've been relieved by the exposure and an admission that it's actually existing, instead of a denial. So I welcome that. I think we have ceased to deny the existence of corruption in society.

Q: So it's interesting that you're relieved at the exposure of real-life corruption, yet at the same time you like cop shows because you like to think that there is law and order.

A: Yes. But if corruption is exposed then I am more likely to find law and order.

Q: Right, so law and order is not necessarily what the police are standing for in the first instance?

A: No. No!

'Law and order' – her main pleasure in cop shows – is thus not to be revealed by repetition of the 'doxic' taken-for-granted world of 'natural' police justice, but rather by 'exposure' and 'probing'. This combination of a preference for 'real' characterisation and plot-lines with 'probing' beneath the surface of appearances is, of course, coherent. Her moral frame turns out not to be conservative at all. It derives from the epistemologically (critical) realist valuation of probing for 'ontological depth' in order to reveal the 'deep structures' underpinning patterned activity (Tulloch *et al.*, 1998, vol. 1, p. 78). Consequently, her preference (in 'helping her handle issues of crime and fear of crime') is for 'down-to-earth documentaries' on the police. It is her belief that the media increasingly are helping us to probe and not hide corruption that gives her, she said, 'a greater sense of control of her situation'. So Angela *both* sees Gerbner's 'mean world' through her television screen *and* feels a greater control over it.

SCHEDULING PLEASURES

Thus, regarding Sparks's concern about the relationship between ritual repetition in cop series and the ideological conservatism of the 'doxic', Angela's pleasure in the ritual repetition of the genre is quite the opposite. The one police series she ritually watches is *The Bill*. For her the routine characterisation of *The Bill* allows her to relax and enjoy the series according to the realist principle that as 'the weeks have gone on and the characters have been built up, more has been added to each character'.

I like *The Bill*. I always watch *The Bill*. I like the several layers to the text, the well-rounded characters, the stories – realistic stories of ordinary people. I would like to think it's a good reflection of the police force in action and the circumstances they work under. They don't always win out, the good guy *doesn't* always win, that's acknowledged.

And perhaps because I know the characters too, it's an easy thing to watch, it's a comforting show. . . . I do like comedy crime too. I like *The Thin Blue Line* because I like the comic aspect of the police force; also the rather quaint *Hamish Macbeth* dealing with a minor incident – these still exist in society. That's comforting, the fact that minor incidents are still considered important.

As Sparks might predict, Angela does not watch police series personally to manage any direct crime fears and experiences. She enjoys cop shows in relation to 'other experiences and hazards and troubles': the probing of police corruption and racism; the 'comforting' negotiation of minor, ordinary-everyday problems; the recognition that, far from being dignified and inevitably patriarchal bastions of law and order, the police can be funny as well as corrupt.

PLEASURES (AND FEARS) OF PLACE

Sparks suggests (following Stuart Hall) that the cop series' obsession with contemporary urban environments as mean, violent and dangerous may represent a crisis in the authority of the state, even while its narrative resolutions reaffirm police authority. Angela recognises (and does not like) this particular city/urban emphasis in many cop series and other media images. She feels that not enough media emphasis is placed on her own environment and its crime problems (such as young people being attacked at the local railway station). Rather,

A: a lot of emphasis is placed on the drug scenes and the drug areas like . . . Cabramatta [an outer-city Sydney suburb with a large Vietnamese population and 'notorious' according to the media for its Asian drug gangs]. . . . Then there's always an emphasis on King's Cross [Sydney's red light district] and inner Sydney. Penrith and the Western Suburbs [working class and migrant communities] cops a lot of attention too.

Q: What kind of image of those places gets conveyed?

A: There's always the image that you are going to be attacked and drugs will be forced on to you, virtually. Murder, lack of law and order or safety.

These recurrent images of city and urban areas would not stop Angela visiting these places if she needed to go there 'for some specific reason. . . . But I'm not sure that I'd then go there for pleasure. . . . So possibly there's a slight [media] influence on me there. I certainly wouldn't be attracted to these areas.'

Q: Would Redfern [an inner-city suburb of Sydney with a significant – and according to police and the media – unruly Aboriginal population] be one of these places portrayed by the media badly?

A: Oh *yes*, Redfern is badly portrayed, yes. . . . It would stop me going
       there. . . . It would be provocative I feel to walk down Eveleigh Street
       in Redfern unless I was with Aboriginal people. . . . I think that's fair
       enough. . . . I see no reason why there shouldn't be Aboriginal terri-
       tory there. So unless I'm with Aboriginal people or have some real rea-
       son to be there, I don't see why I should go there. . . . It would be
       provocative.

As we listen to Angela carefully, we realise that it is not the media image of
Redfern in itself that will prevent her going there. It is not a paleo-symbolic
effect of 'the inner city' that is determining her actions. She is not afraid of
visiting Redfern, but rather does not want to go as a white-colonial
'invader'.

Angela's sense of the media's representation of place is thus fully
informed by her realist moral frame. Angela is angered, for example, by the
fact that the local Blue Mountains media has not adequately covered the
bashings of teenagers in Katoomba station subway, while the national
media spends too much time on generating racist fears of drug wars in the
Vietnamese area of Cabramatta and Aboriginal violence in Redfern. In her
view it is the young people of the local area who are exposed to risk by
these biases (she argues that the local press is significantly biased politically).

Angela is one of Gerbner's heavy viewers of television. But her local situation is important here. As a single parent who is unable to get work locally,
Angela watches television because she cannot afford too many other enter-
tainments. Unlike Gerbner's fearful heavy viewers who imprison themselves
in electronically secured high-rise apartments and suburbs, Angela responds
to paleo-symbolic images of the inner city with recognition that poor urban
Aboriginal people have the right to local ownership rather than more
authoritarian policing (a feature of Gerbner's heavy viewers' preferences)
and displacement. She worries that the proximity of the Sydney Olympics
will enable white landlords to use police to oust the Aboriginal community
from this key inner-city suburb.

In contrast, Angela is appalled at the 'mean world' views of some of
Sydney's 'fortified enclaves' of upper-middle-class residents. Regarding
newspaper reports that the residents in the exclusive Sydney Harbour-side
suburb of Point Piper wanted to put up boom gates and surveillance cameras to control crime in their precinct after a street bashing, Angela 'found
that appalling, absolutely appalling. Fortress mentality, retreat into their
own fortress. I don't think they've got a right to retreat from the world like
that. Other people . . . have a right to use these streets, to use these spaces.'

As a result of these 'critical realist' (class, race and gender-based) critiques of Sydney's inner-city and its media representation, Angela's own
reaction to an assault on her son by a drunken Aboriginal man (while he
was travelling on the train) is embedded in a wide range of identities.

Angela's husband was African and her son is quite dark-skinned. Her fear for her son while travelling, as Sparks puts it, here ' "exceeds the information given". . . . It is deeply implicated in [her] more general sense of well-being or otherwise in the environment in which [she] finds [herself]' (1992, p. 12). That environment she sees as one where the 'ordinary people' (including Aborigines) should have more ownership. She believes, for example, that the example of Newtown (inner-city Sydney suburb with a largely mixed/migrant and student population) indicates that when you get more people on the streets, you decrease fear of crime.

> Making the streets happier places to be in. Having even just musical events, buskers. . . . In Newtown there are always people out in the streets. My friend said that people who can't sleep will get up and go for a walk, find someone to talk to. So perhaps people are more liable to make contact, commune with others. . . . That's something I've felt about being in parts of Sydney too: that, strangely for a large city, there's more of a sense of community than you will get in the Mountains. . . . Though in some suburbs of Sydney you do get people closing off and retreating to their little fortresses.

Angela, then, resists the syndrome of the generic 'mean city'. She argues instead (quite un-Romantically given her situation in the Blue Mountains) for a greater potential democracy of the streets in the city (and with it, less fear of crime) in contrast to the potential for 'fortified enclaves' in more affluent Harbour-side areas of the city. She wishes, therefore, that the media spent less time concentrating on the negative aspects of urban spaces like Cabramatta and Redfern and spent more time focusing on the positive aspects of urban spaces like Newtown. These are her comments as she talks about her son's near-violent encounter with an Aboriginal man on the train; and despite her concern about the near-bashing, she tells – with obvious pleasure – her own narrative resolution to this story. 'Another of the three Aboriginal men said to the drunken one, "Hey man, he's a brother, cool off", and they all got off and it was O.K.' For Angela the recognition of her son's colour and his acceptance as 'brother' turned the momentary risk on the train into an urban community of the best kind.

PLEASURES OF GENRE

Angela's preferences for particular police series indicate the *different kinds of emotional security* (with varying degrees of pleasure) that sub-genres within the cop show can provide. She does not, for example, agree with older people we interviewed in Angela's home town of Katoomba who used *Heartbeat* nostalgically to take them back to their past. In those days, they believed, the face-to-face presence of police on the street led to there being less crime – and fear of crime – in all city areas.

For Angela, however,

> I have this same feeling from seeing the paddy wagon patrolling
> around Katoomba [Blue Mountains], I'd get the bobby-on-the-beat
> feeling from that. They do patrol . . . and if you're out, you do see the
> police fairly regularly. . . . They're not walking the streets but *commu-
> nication* is much better, so I feel more secure about that. . . . *The Bill*
> reminds me that communications are better, we're going to have the
> police and fire and ambulance on the scene very quickly if necessary.
> . . . *Police Rescue* tends to be a different thing – it's rather nice to
> know that somewhere in the background there are policemen willing
> to swing off cliffs and save you.

Angela lives in a town perched on the edge of towering and scenic cliffs,
much visited by both bushwalkers and inexperienced tourists. So 'police rescue' becomes a regular feature of her 'landscape'.

Other police series, though, are pleasing for their uncovering of 'mystery', which for Angela is not *just* a hermeneutic puzzle. It also includes that
sense of uncovering and probing the surface of one's 'taken-for-granted',
like *The Bill* does for her to some extent. Thus, correlative with her outrage
at abuse of adult power over children is her belief that good role models for
children are those investigative media-reflexive Australian television series
(like *Media Watch* and *Four Corners*) and comic shows (like *Good News
Week*), 'which encourage young people to probe and look beyond the superficial. . . . They can be good role models in their way much better than the
Arnold Schwarzenegger sort of stuff.'

Like many of the parents that we talked with, Angela is concerned with
major issues and problems of the current social order as they concern children: violence, drugs, racism, police corruption, and so on. In particular,
though, this single parent is mainly worried about the *representation in the
media* of these social issues. Angela's social anxiety is about the mystification of these matters, and the blaming of it on 'weaker people'. Her television pleasures in relation to crime are thus greatest in those 'probing'
programmes that expose the 'real' and underlying issues 'where people
abuse their position', whether these are 'crazed' gunmen who shoot young
children or irresponsible police and media tycoons.

It is not a coincidence that she applauds the appearance of the
'Christopher Skase' type of media tycoon among the television 'baddies'
when asked her 'mean world' question. A heavy television viewer by force
of economic circumstances rather than choice, Angela is a candidate for
Gerbner's 'mean world' syndrome. She does, indeed, see a meaner world on
television nowadays. But for her this is a cause of pleasure, control and
empowerment rather than passivity (as in Gerbner). This is because the
'mean world' of television is 'probing' more and more to the reality of
power, racism and corruption that underlies appearances. Her negotiation

of her fears in relation to television and media crime is coherently and intelligibly related to this pleasure within the moral frame of 'the real'.

Conclusion

In this chapter on cop series and their audiences, we have travelled through Denzin and Lincoln's period of 'blurred genres', examining some of the ways in which different interpretive communities within media studies have understood this area. From textualist (critical Marxist to postmodern) accounts, via Gerbner and Sparks, we have arrived at local 'tales from the field'. What we find here, as we encounter Angela, is that each of us is our own ethnographer. Each of us engages not simply with the 'Other' (Angela's understanding of the Aboriginal male's assault on her son), but also negotiates reflexively with the media's paleo-symbolic and 'doxic' representations of this Other's contexts – which are often the streets of the inner city.

But these media representations, though emotionally and ideologically resonant, are not determining. We negotiate with the media via a number of circuits of communication, of which the media themselves are significant but not solitary members. The paleo-symbolic aspect of television may be, as Sparks and Kellner suggest, a potent source of diffuse anxieties. But our tales from the field suggest that there is also much pleasure to be found, reflexively, in these negotiations. As Sparks says, anxiety over risk and pleasure in controlling one's perceptions of it, are deeply – and daily – intertwined.

Methodologically, we have also shifted ground during the chapter – from a focus on textual analysis to qualitative analysis of single long interviews as 'tales from the field'. This latter kind of method, I have argued, is better at giving us access to the 'fragmentation' of the postmodern consciousness beset by 'risk' and 'simulation' while also allowing us to trace the continuing (and considerable) coherences in moral frames (as in the case of Angela) that still hark back, as Kellner rightly argues, to our embedding in modernity.

|4|

Talking about television soap opera

During the CCRR fear of crime study, in our long interview with a 16-year-old Sydney teenager, Lisa, we heard a view that was also expressed by a number of other respondents. As she discussed her viewing of 'reality genres' like the news, she said 'you don't see the ordinary events' in them. Rather, 'ordinary events' are reserved for fictional series like police shows, where they are 'not believable'.

> With child molesting it's [shown on the news] on a bigger scale – pedophilia, old men or something, rather than just like in a family situation. . . . Muggings get shown heaps on cop shows, but don't really get shown on the news very much. And the same with like family abuse or whatever, it gets shown on shows but doesn't really get on the news so much. And drug addict mothers get shown on cop shows but not really on the news. More would happen on cop shows because they're not believable.

For Lisa, these 'ordinary events' have been a familiar and long-term part of her teenage life. When she was about 11, she used to go to a girlfriend's house, where she witnessed her friend being molested by her mother's much younger boyfriend. No police were called; and Lisa's friend did not want to tell her mother because she worried that she would be sent away from home. Lisa now says, 'It was pretty bad in some ways. But it was O.K. because we like talked to each other heaps about it. But it was a bit bad not being able to tell anyone [else].'

Lisa also recalls that when she was 10 or 11 a man who pretended to be a doctor attempted to molest some of the primary school children. One day, this man followed Lisa and a friend into the toilets, and they 'freaked out and ran.' For months after that they had to always go to the toilets in pairs. Then, a couple of years later, she was robbed in an alley near Bondi Junction train station by a man who took her Reeboks. A boy she knew was also robbed of his shoes, hat and shirt. Lisa's house at Bondi was burgled twice;

and the family car was constantly being broken into or stolen. Often she and her friends were hassled for money or cigarettes at the station. And in addition, there was the problem – close to her through her older half-brother – of his drug addict mother.

So each of the things Lisa itemises in her discussion of TV dramas, news and police series – child abuse, muggings, 'drug addict mothers' – she has actually experienced. But (*pace* Gerbner and Sparks) her use of television has not helped her resolve her fears and anxieties about these matters. Cop series sometimes show child abuse, but they do not really get at the kinds of intimate things she has experienced. Rather they cover these things in a 'sensational' and 'not believable' way. Meanwhile the news frightens her because 'It shows how much is actually happening in our community . . . like passes by without us kinda even knowing or being able to stop it. So it makes it worse.'

For Lisa, the reiterated quality of television actually increases her fears. It is not 'doxic', in Bourdieu's sense, calming her terror within the ideological narrative of the 'good police' always winning. Indeed, series like *Australia's Most Wanted* actually have increased her fears because they confirm her view as to how 'dumb' the police are. 'It's brought the little hidden thought at the back of my mind right to the front' that the police cannot solve crimes, even with television's help. Moreover, her own experience of police has not been good. A friend has a policeman husband who assaults her. Another friend was hassled by a policemen when in Lisa's company near Bondi Beach after an older lady reported her for wearing a T-shirt like a short mini-skirt; and Lisa's friends, the buskers at Circular Quay in Sydney, are regularly harassed by police.

> The cops there are really mean. They *like* to harass people. The buskers, they harass them for their licences. . . . They knew [they had asked for licences the week before], and they really enjoyed it. . . . And they harass beggars and stuff. . . . They get their jollies from upsetting people.

As she has got older, Lisa has looked less and less to television of any genre to help her with 'ordinary' crimes, because: 'You experience more, whereas it kind of trivialises it on the show. . . . You get a better view of the world [through your experience]. You realise it's not like that at all, as they show it on TV shows.'

But, if Lisa does not often find ways for ordering and understanding her fears via television genres, she does *talk*, often *via* the television. For example, with her two girlfriends, Lisa has discussed major TV events like the Oklahoma bombing or the Port Arthur massacre killer Martin Bryant (who 'shouldn't be given the death penalty because he just wanted to die'). Thus she converts both major and minor TV crime events into discursive logics where she talks with her friends about the right and wrongs of punishing and releasing threatening male criminals. With her girlfriend, for example, she 'talks all the time' about a man who raped a woman to death, and that he should not be released (when there are reports on television that this might happen). Similarly she talks to her mother and stepfather about the things on the news that trouble her, and also to her neighbours at Bondi who were also 'always being robbed'. 'It does help because you kind of know that you're not the only person thinking that's pretty scary. . . . So it does help to talk, I think.' And we note that a major aspect of Lisa's anxiety at the time of the molestation incident was not being able to talk to either mother.

In the case of an older woman we interviewed in the country town of Bathurst, New South Wales, she has actually turned off any violent television since her husband died the year before and she lost the opportunity to talk. She used to watch *Australia's Most Wanted* with her husband. Now she avoids it (and all the other police shows) because it plays on her mind that things like mugging and 'home invasions' could happen to her. 'Being on your own, it's a big thing. . . . If you've got somebody to talk to, it gets it out of your system. You bottle it up when you're on your own.'

Hearing these very differently aged and situated women speaking about their TV viewing – 16-year-old Lisa in affluent middle-class areas of Sydney, and 68-year-old Anna in a rural country town – it is clear that risk as well as pleasure is an important topic of television talk. Yet most of the audience research about TV talk relates only to pleasure.

The television genre most often associated with audience 'talk' – or, more pejoratively, with 'gossip' – is soap opera. David Buckingham says in his study of the British soap opera *EastEnders* that the 'pleasure of "gossip" about a soap opera is essentially the pleasure of sharing secrets to which only "a select few" are privy' (1987, p. 64). Buckingham draws on Roland Barthes's notion of the hermeneutic code – the code that establishes puzzles, lays false clues for the viewer, and finally resolves the enigma – in explaining this 'talk' as textual pleasure. In Buckingham's view, though *EastEnders* probably uses the enigma as a means of denying information to the viewer more than other British soap operas, it has still done so quite rarely.

> While episodes normally build to a climax, it is often in these moments that information is *revealed*, rather than withheld. Viewers are left to speculate, not so much about hidden information, but about what will happen when the other characters discover what viewers themselves already know. In this sense, the hermeneutic code functions in soap opera in ways that are rather different from other genres. . . . While information is occasionally withheld, as in the cliffhanger, it is rarely withheld for long. . . . As a result, the narratives of soap opera tend to place the viewer, not in a position of relative ignorance – as in most detective stories – but in a position of knowledge.
>
> (Buckingham, 1987, pp. 63–4)

This may be one reason, then, that soap opera talk is often pleasurable, while Lisa's talk about crime on television was often fearful: soap opera viewers' *know* more – and knowledge is power (and pleasure). And yet this is also powerless knowledge because the viewer is unable to use it to change the narrative events. Buckingham argues that instead of narrative power the viewer may gain the 'pleasurable tension' of speculating 'about what would happen if the secrets were to be revealed' (1987, p. 67). The soap opera narrative frequently provides information which encourages viewers to predict future events as secrets are disclosed. Some of the pleasure, soap opera fans say, is when your predictions come true. But there is pleasure also in being occasionally surprised; and, Buckingham says, it is 'for this reason that, on occasion, the text reserves the right to bend or even break the rules' (1987, p. 69). The viewers' 'talk' (or 'gossip') about these events is therefore both pleasurable and based on fan-type competence. For example, the regular viewer knows a great deal about the 'secrets' of the show, so that even a photograph of an old-flame sitting innocently back of frame may set off a secret memory as the character on-camera enters a new relationship. In contrast, Lisa's memory of the sexual molestation incident is one of complete powerlessness. Neither did she have the power of the narrative events in the incident, nor was there a 'pleasurable tension' in 'what would happen if the secrets were revealed'. So the incident became part of her own experiential and secret narrative of risk, which television then tended to exacerbate. The soap opera fan's 'gossip' is, in comparison, less about the world 'out there', and more about the intimate complexity of individual relationships which define the genre.

This is not to devalue the 'gossip' surrounding soap opera, as has happened so often; where women who regularly watch soap opera are seen as somehow 'trivial' in relation to the 'big events' of the 'real world'. Thus news, current affairs and even police series have often been regarded (even for a long time within media studies) as more 'serious' than the soaps. Notably, 16-year-old Lisa does not even mention soap opera in her list of TV genres that could deal with the intimate risks of her early biography – and with some reason, since soap opera producers often hold back from showing incest and sexual abuse in a show designed for 'family' demographics.

But does this matter anyway? Buckingham argues that 'Far from being lulled into regarding the text as a "window on the world", viewers are aware that it is a fictional artefact which tends to work in certain ways and to obey certain rules. The text invites the viewer to play a game with the characters' lives and destinies: and viewers know that it is, in the end, just a game' (1987, p. 69).

This is, as many writers on soap opera have argued (for example, *see* Allen, 1985) a very sophisticated game where fans acquire just as much competence to read their text as a high-culture audience displays in responding to the latest *Midsummer Night's Dream*. In particular, as Charlotte Brunsdon has argued, women soap opera fans draw on a competence in the discourses of domesticity as they watch, predict and identify with the events of their favourite serials.

Yet, as we heard from Lisa and other women, we should not focus solely on this aspect of audience pleasure. A soap opera also relates to other emotions. Anxiety, fear of crime, experience of personal and domestic abuse are all areas for which people turn for 'answers' from television (sometimes in terms of their own guilty secrets), in addition to their pleasures in the hermeneutic 'guilty secrets' of soap opera. Soap operas do frequently address social issues like HIV/AIDS, drugs, domestic violence, date rape, and so on. Although they always try to present these as entertaining 'dramatic conflict' rather than moralising about 'issues' (*see* Buckingham 1987, p. 83), the repetitiveness of these health and social stories lies in the production demands of television itself. The executive producer of Australia's longest-running television drama series, the peak-rating *A Country Practice*, emphasised that when you are making several hours of television per week, you need a narrative location 'where stories come walking in your door'. The two most attractive locations for him in this respect were the police station and the hospital. He chose a hospital, and thus made a 'medical soap opera' rather than a cop series. He also situated it in the country because 'in the subconscious of every Australian there's a yearning for the country . . . to give this rat race away, buy fifty acres, go out there, milk a cow and grow our own vegetables. And I decided to tap into that subconscious by setting the serial in a country town' (Tulloch and Moran, 1986, p. 28). Thus Australia's longest running television success was born as a perceived composite of stories of risk and subconscious pleasure.

Thus the 'world out there' does *also* pull at the emotions of soap opera viewers. Buckingham quotes two of his young fans of *EastEnders* on this: Paul and Dionne.

> It shows that there is a problem, and there are people that are actually on drugs. I don't think there's any other programme that shows that sort of thing.

> It puts the wind up you. Like, I know a lot of kids that are on drugs, cocaine, the whole lot. Like when they say 'Oh, I had so many lines' and the rest of it, you think they're bullshitting you. But if you watch it on television, then you sort of think, they might not be mucking about, they might be taking it. . . . There's always this thing, it's always enticing, they're saying 'Go on, try a bit, it's not going to do you in or nothing'. . . . I've been tempted, but I ain't never done it. But watching *EastEnders*, and seeing all the drugs problems and all the rest of it, you don't want to do it.

> (1987, pp. 179–80)

Soap operas like *EastEnders* and *A Country Practice* have always been very careful to be 'responsible' in transcoding expert advice in their narratives. *A*

Country Practice had a professional nurse as a resident member of the plotting conference. Similarly, Buckingham points to the character of Dr Legg in *EastEnders* who has advised characters on a range of medical and psychological problems, such as angina, menopause, alcoholism, impotence and mental illness. In earlier research, I found that older women in particular enjoyed *A Country Practice* because its medical stories both paralleled and fortified their own caring roles, sometimes with very sick partners (Tulloch, 1989).

Buckingham indicates how this 'expert knowledge' can then be spread to other characters in the narrative, since these take up its 'talk'.

> It was in response to [Dr Legg's] suggestion that Kathy Beale became a counsellor for the Samaritans: . . . Kathy in turn has increasingly come to adopt the role of 'expert' adviser, for example condemning Dot for her bigoted and hysterical response to the threat of AIDS.
>
> (1987, p. 84)

Buckingham reveals here an interesting 'secret' about soap opera narratives themselves. Soap operas create their own 'gossip' characters, and use them very centrally in their role as the butts of 'expert knowledge' in the 'risk society'. *A Country Practice*, for example, used its town gossip, Esme Watson, quite regularly to spread the 'bigoted and hysterical' response to AIDS, as well as to other threatening diseases, psychological traumas, or social crises. It therefore marked a narrative turning point of considerable moment and visibility when Esme finally threw off her prejudices about 'catching AIDS' and came physically close to the HIV-positive central character in *A Country Practice*'s needle-sharing/AIDS story 'Sophie'.

In the rest of this chapter I will take further these two different, but important areas of soap opera viewing: audience pleasure; and audience anxiety in relation to knowledge about risk.

Soap pleasure, gender and media consumption

I mentioned in chapter 2 Pertti Alasuutari's view that Ien Ang's work has been particularly important in emphasising the non-instrumentalist aspects of soap opera pleasure. I will focus in this section on some of Ang's work because it offers a very clear view of the development of feminist television audience theory across the stages of qualitative research that Denzin and Lincoln have described. In an article with Joke Hermes, Ien Ang offers her own schematic history of the periods that Denzin and Lincoln cover (at least from the 1960s to the present). But in this case, the focus is on feminist audience theory.

Ang and Hermes begin their history of audience analysis with a book from the 1960s/early 1970s stage that Denzin and Lincoln would call 'Promethean' cultural leftist romantic: Germaine Greer's *The Female*

Eunuch (1970). Here, and in other work by Sue Sharpe (1976) and Gaye Tuchman *et al.* (1978), the mass media were seen as 'a major cause of the general reproduction of patriarchal sexual relationships' (Ang and Hermes, 1996, p. 111). Greer castigated romance novels and Sharpe and Tuchman *et al.*, criticised television genres like soap opera for their sex-role stereotypes which helped to socialise girls into passive dependent roles as housewives and mothers. This was soap opera as 'ideological effect'; in the same period as, and parallel to, the analysis of cop series' effacing of class conflict that we looked at in chapter 3.

Ang and Hermes argue that these feminist accounts were based on two unwarranted assumptions: first, that mass-media imagery consists of transparent, unrealistic and clear-cut meanings; and, second, that girls and women passively absorb these messages. They rightly point to a great deal of work in media studies which has challenged the linear and monolithic account of media as 'effect', whether on children through its diet of violence or on women via its sexist images.

The first major feminist critique of this television 'effects' tradition was in 1970s textual analysis.

> Rather than seeing media images as reflecting 'unrealistic' pictures of women, feminist scholars working within structuralist, semiotic and psychoanalytic frameworks have begun to emphasize the ways in which media representations and narratives *construct* a multiplicity of sometimes contradicting cultural definitions of femininity and masculinity, which serve as subject positions that spectators might take up in order to enter into a meaningful relationship with the texts concerned.
>
> (Ang and Hermes, 1996, p. 111)

Ang and Hermes discuss as a typically intricate and complex example of feminist work in this period Tania Modleski's analysis of the way in which soap opera texts, far from simply reflecting sexist stereotypes, 'actively produce a symbolic form of feminine identity by inscribing a specific subject position – that of the "ideal mother" – in its textual fabric' (Ang and Hermes, 1996, p. 112). But Ang and Hermes note that while feminist studies like these provided a more sophisticated analysis of the way in which soap operas 'interpellated' (Althusser's term) or 'called to' its audience, they did not usually look at the way in which actual viewers negotiated with this interpellation. As Annette Kuhn (1984) argued, textualist feminists – for instance, Laura Mulvey's path-breaking 'Visual Pleasure and Narrative Cinema' in *Screen* – tended to conflate *spectatorship* (understood as a set of subject positions constructed in and through texts) and the analysis of *social audiences* (the empirical social subjects actually watching soap operas).

Janice Radway's *Reading the Romance* was a key feminist work in shifting the terrain from textual analysis to the reading of the text in ordinary social life. Emphasising 'decoding' as socially based negotiation of the text (Hall, 1982), this line of argument, Ang and Hermes say, 'foregrounds the relevance of "ethnographic" work with and among empirical audiences' (1996, p. 113). It was taken further by Ellen Seiter *et al.*,'s 1989 study of female soap opera viewers in Oregon, USA. Here Modleski's 'ideal mother' was certainly recognised by their middle-class, college-educated respondents. But she was also strongly rejected by most of the working-class women interviewees, whose own experience conflicted 'in substantial ways with the soap opera's representation of women's problems, problems some women identified as upper or middle-class' (Seiter *et al.*, 1989, p. 241; cited in Ang and Hermes, 1996, p. 113).

As Ang and Hermes say, this work of the 1970s/1980s advanced significantly beyond the earlier feminist criticism that soap operas and romances monolithically reproduce patriarchy via 'false' images of women. On the one hand, analysis of textual mechanisms had shown them to be polyvalent, even contradictory. The multiple strands of soap opera allow, Terry Lovell has argued, audiences and producers to play between the conventions of common sense and the local knowledge of 'good sense' (Lovell *et al.*, 1981). On the other hand, qualitative and ethnographic research (like Radway's) with empirical audiences has illustrated women's active and productive role in constructing textual meanings and pleasures.

Nevertheless, Ang's own analysis of Radway's *Reading the Romance* prefigures the shift of feminist analysis into Denzin and Lincoln's fourth and fifth 'moments' of qualitative research, where the crises of representation and legitimation, authorial reflexivity, and local 'tales of the field' loom large. Ang rejects Modleski's critique of Radway's lack of 'critical distance' from her romance readers, since:

> ethnographic fieldwork among audiences – in the broad sense of engaging oneself with the unruly and heterogeneous practices and accounts of real historical viewers and readers – helps to keep our critical discourses from becoming closed texts of Truth, because it forces the researcher to come to terms with perspectives that may not be easily integrated in a smooth, finished and coherent Theory.
>
> (Ang, 1996, p. 100)

But Ang also criticises Radway for abandoning this 'self-chosen vulnerability as an ethnographer' (displayed in the early part of the book) for the 'feminist desire' of converting her romance readers to a wider political struggle by the end. Here, says Ang,

> Radway . . . represents the encounter as one that is strictly confined to the terms of a relationship between two parties with fixed identities: that of researcher/feminist and that of interviewees/romance fans. The ontological and epistemological separation between subject and object allows her to present the Smithton readers as a pre-existent 'interpretive community', a sociological entity whose characteristics and peculiarities were already there when the researcher set out to investigate.
>
> (1996, p. 101)

Ang argues that Radway's realist assumptions have blinded her to the constructivist aspect of her own enterprise as ethnographer: in other words, that her own political intervention has helped construct this 'interpretive community' in the first place.

Radway's analysis recognises symbolic resistance to patriarchy among her romance readers: as they ritually abandon their household chores to spend great amounts of time reading while husband and children are out of the house; and as they meet heroines who tame the harsh macho sides of attractive men in ways that are impossible in the women's real-life oppression by less attractive husbands. But, Ang says, in the final chapters of Radway's book, her writing has become more monologic. Here, the Smithton women are definitively relegated to the position of 'them' (Ang, 1996, p. 102) as the feminist/researcher, Radway, seeks ways to lead them away from the potentially 'disarming' impulse of romance reading and towards 'real social change' (Radway 1991, p. 213).

> 'Real' social change can only be brought about, Radway, seems to believe, if romance readers would stop reading romances and become feminist activists instead. In other words, underlying Radway's project is what Angela McRobbie has termed a 'recruitist' conception of the politics of feminist research (1982:52). . . . In short, what is therapeutic (for feminism) about *Reading the Romance* is its construction of
> ₔ romance readers as embryonic feminist.
>
> (Ang, 1996, p. 103)

Her analysis of Radway's book is an important example of Ang's emphasis on reflexivity and critical ethnographic method. She is pointing centrally here to a major concern about feminist (or other radical) 'expert knowledge' as ethnographic discourse. She rejects Radway's 'vanguardist view' for one which (following McRobbie's critique) tries not to 'underestimate the struggles for self-empowerment engaged in by "ordinary women" outside the political and ideological frameworks of the self-professed women's movement' (Ang, 1996, p. 104).

For Ang, a crucial 'lack' in Radway's narrative is around the romance readers' *pleasure*.

> The absence of pleasure *as* pleasure in *Reading the Romance* is made apparent by Radway's frequent downplaying qualifications of the enjoyment that the Smithton women have claimed to derive from their favourite genre: that it is a form of *vicarious* pleasure, that it is *only temporarily* satisfying because it is *compensatory* literature. . . . Revealed in such qualifications is a sense that the pleasure of romance reading is somehow not really real, as though there were other forms of pleasure that could be considered 'more real' because they are more 'authentic', more enduring, more veritable. . . . In line with the way in which members of the Birmingham Centre for Contemporary Cultural

Studies have interpreted youth subcultures . . . then, Radway comes to the conclusion that romance writing is a sort of 'imaginary solution' to *real*, structural problems and contradictions produced by patriarchy. . . . All this amounts to a quite functionalist explanation of romance reading, one that is preoccupied with its effects rather than its mechanisms. Consequently, pleasure as such cannot possibly be taken seriously in this theoretical framework, because the whole explanatory movement is directed towards the *ideological function* of pleasure.

(Ang, 1996, pp. 104–5)

Ang's position here is anti-realist. It is dubious of the notion that there are '*real*, structural problems and contradictions' – as assumed in Hurd *et al.*'s analysis of the cop series.

One might want to quibble with Ang's description of this kind of work as 'functionalist', since it is clear that Radway (like Hurd) is very much concerned with textual 'mechanisms' as well as with 'effects'. Nevertheless, Ang does offer her own sophisticated account of women's pleasure in soap opera in her analyses of *Dallas*. Why Ang asks should we not hope that all women get more pleasure out of identifying with Christine Cagney in the police series *Cagney and Lacey* than with Sue Ellen in *Dallas*? After all, as a professional cop Cagney resists sexual objectification by her colleagues, while Sue Ellen contributes to her own entrapment by a womanising husband she does not love; Cagney challenges the male hierarchy at work while Sue Ellen succumbs at home to the power of the oil magnet, J.R.; Cagney establishes a caring and respectful adult relationship with her 'buddy' Lacey while Sue Ellen is a 'bitch' to all around her. Further, following Gerbner, one could add that Sue Ellen is just that kind of older woman as 'witch or bitch' that female actors tend to find themselves playing once they are noticeably past the age of thirty-five.

Surely finding pleasure in Sue Ellen rather than Cagney is potentially harmful to women and girls since it 'reinforces and legitimizes masochistic feelings of powerlessness' rather than the 'strong, powerful and independent women who are able and determined to change and improve their lives, such as Christine Cagney?' (Ang, 1996, p. 92). Ang's answer of 'no' to this question depends on several layers of argument: to do with genre, narrative, the pleasure of fantasy, and multiple subjectivity.

Genre

It is important, Ang argues, to consider audience pleasure in relation to genre: Christine Cagney is a social-realist heroine of a cop series; Maddie Hayes (another woman who fights and gains respect) in *Moonlighting* is a postmodern heroine in a series that self-consciously foregrounded televisual reflexivity and parody; while Sue Ellen is the melodramatic heroine of a soap opera. Different women will find different pleasures in different television genres; and only a situated 'thick description' of particular women's everyday contexts is likely to explain why this is, and what pleasures these are.

Narrative

We also need to look at the textual features of each of these genres which help to construct their own particular pleasures. As melodrama, Ang argues, soap opera has three important formal characteristics.

- First, personal life is its 'core problematic'. In soap operas the realisation and loss of personal relationships are marked by ritualised family events like births, romances, marriages, divorces and deaths; and though social issues (like AIDS) may be a central motif in constructing these rituals, they always take on meaning from the standpoint of personal life. So while J.R.'s oil business deals might attract a wider audience (including men) to the show with their 'real world' or their cowboy/Western elements, these are always shown in the context of the well-being of his family, particularly Sue Ellen.
- Second, the soap opera plot is marked by melodramatic excess. The rapid succession of extreme storylines about kidnapping, bribery, adultery, obscure illnesses, and so on are important in melodrama not because of any referential relationship with reality, but because of the enlarged emotional impact they solicit. For example, Sue Ellen's alcoholism is a potent metaphor for a woman trapped in desperation, and her sexual affairs a potentially appealing action with which women viewers can empathise in fantasy.
- A third structural feature of soap opera is its lack of narrative resolution. *Dallas* is a never-ending story, without hope of a final, happy resolution. 'A heroine like Sue Ellen will never be able to make her own history: no matter how hard she tries, eventually the force of circumstances will be too overwhelming. She lives in the prison of an eternally conflictual present. . . . [I]nvolvement with a character like Sue Ellen is conditioned by the prior knowledge that no such happy ending will ever occur. Instead, pleasure must come from living through and negotiating with the crisis itself. To put it more precisely, many female Sue Ellen fans tended to identify with a subject position characterized by a sense of entrapment' (Ang, 1996, pp. 90–1).

Fantasy

Ang criticises much feminist theory for being over-rationalistic and instrumentalist about television and politics. Because it is often assumed that soap opera presents a stereotyped and less real version of the world of women, this approach 'can only account for the popularity of soap operas among women as something irrational. In other words, what the role/image approach tends to overlook is the large *emotional involvement* which is invested in identification with characters of popular fiction' (Ang, 1996, p. 92). Like Sparks's discussion of cop series, Ang wants to break with the notion that women's identities can be singular and 'irrational'.

In contrast to this, Ang argues that fantasy should not be seen as illusion but (following psychoanalytic theory) as a reality in itself.

> Fantasy is an imagined scene in which the fantasizing subject is the protagonist, and in which alternative, imaginary scenarios for the subject's real life are evoked. . . . I want to suggest that the pleasure of fantasy lies in its offering the subject an opportunity to take up positions which she could not assume in real life: through fantasy she can move beyond the structural constraints of everyday life and explore other, more desirable, situations, identities, lives.
>
> (Ang, 1996, pp. 92–3)

Ang's analysis here depends on a poststructural theory of identity and subjectivity.

Subjectivity

Ang rejects the notion that subjectivity is the homogenous source from which one acts, thinks and feels. Rather, viewed from her poststructuralist position, subjectivity is the product of the many meaning systems or discourses that are circulating around us, thus constructing our 'society'. 'Each individual is the site of a multiplicity of subject positions proposed to her by the discourses with which she is confronted; her identity is the precarious and contradictory result of the specific set of subject positions she inhabits at any moment in history' (Ang, 1996, p. 93).

Consequently a viewer will adopt many – sometimes contradictory – sites of subjectivity. Some of these are more socially 'legitimate' than others. But 'being a woman' is a process (rather than a static identity) whereby – especially, as Beck would say, in the individualist risk society – 'every individual woman is faced with the task of actively reinventing and redefining her femininity as required' (Ang, 1996, p. 94). Being a woman today, then, requires *working* between a range of potential identities, constructing and reconstructing them in local, situated activities. Fantasy becomes important here because it offers a private and unconstrained space to indulge in 'excess in the interstices of ordered social life where one has to keep oneself strategically under control' (Ang, 1996, p. 95). Rather than condemn many women's identification with Sue Ellen, Ang asks, 'What can be so pleasurable in imagining a fantastic scenario in one which is a self-destructive and

frustrated bitch?' (1996, p. 95). Fantasy is, on the one hand, a tacit recognition by women in their everyday life that we shape our identities but not, as
Marx said, in circumstances of our own choosing. On the other hand, fantasy allows women to indulge in feelings that 'however fleeting, can be experienced as moments of truth, of redemption, moments in which the
complexity of the task of being a woman is fully realized and accepted'
(Ang, 1996, p. 95).

Ang must still answer, however, the view of feminist critics like Modleski
(1986) and van Zoonen (1991) that to immerse oneself in the pleasures of
television is to sacrifice the critical distance of 'expert' feminist theory and
indulge in relativism and populism. She begins to answer this charge by
pointing to some of the problems associated with 'expert' analysis itself –
for example the tendency among feminist and critical theory scholars to rely
on macro-structural, sociological constructs such as social class. She points
here to apparent discrepancies between Andrea Press's analysis in *Women
Watching Television* (1991) of female audiences for *Dynasty* and Seiter *et
al.*,'s analysis of women's responses to *Dallas*. While Seiter *et al.*, found that
it was working-class women who were critical of *Dallas*'s representation of
strong female roles, Press discovered that middle-class women are more critical of *Dynasty*'s ideologies of femininity and the family.

True, different contextual factors in the research might account for this
apparent discrepancy: differences in the locality of the research, representational differences between daytime and prime-time soap opera, differences
in interview procedures, differences in theoretical emphasis in analysing the
transcripts. But again, here, Ang points to the crucial area of researcher
reflexivity in current 'fifth stage' qualitative research.

> At the very least . . . the contradiction highlights the liability of too
> easily connecting particular instances of meaning attribution to texts
> with socio-demographic background variables. Particular accounts as
> dug up in reception analysis are typically produced through
> researchers' staged conversations with a limited number of infor-
> mants, each of them marked by idiosyncratic life histories and per-
> sonal experiences. Filtering their responses – the transcripts of what
> they said during interviews – through the pregiven categories of 'work-
> ing-class' or 'middle-class' would necessarily mean a reductionist
> abstraction from the undoubtedly much more complex and contradic-
> tory nature of these women's reception of soap operas.
>
> (Ang, 1996, p. 115)

As we began to discover with Angela in the previous chapter, neither class
nor gender (nor race nor ethnicity) can ever fully contain a subject's identity,
in a poststructuralist account. 'This is not to deny that there are gender differences or gender-specific experiences and practices; it is, however, to suggest that their meanings are always relative to particular constructions in
specified contexts' (Ang, 1996, p. 118). This position brings Ang to Denzin

and Lincoln's fifth 'moment' of qualitative research, 'tales of the field', where the 'search for grand narratives will be replaced by more local, small-scale theories fitted to specific problems and specific situations' (Denzin and Lincoln, 1998, p. 22).

Tales of the field

Ang and Hermes reassert that

> poststructuralist feminist theory has powerfully questioned the essentialist and reductionist view of sexual difference underlying the assumption of fixity of gender identity (male or female). Poststructuralism asserts first of all that subjectivity is non-unitary, produced in and through the intersection of a multitude of social discourses and practices which position the individual subject in heterogeneous, overlaying and competing ways.
>
> (1996, p. 119)

Further, poststructuralist feminism emphasises that an individual's subjectivity is always in process of reproduction and transformation in a series of local situations.

To discuss more concretely how these poststructuralist perceptions relate to audience theory, Ang and Hermes usefully distinguish between gender definitions, gender positionings and gender identifications.

- *Gender definitions* circulate in culture and society by way of differently situated and empowered discourses. For example, Roman Catholic religious discourse defines woman as virgin, mother or whore; whereas radical feminist discourse defines women as victims of male exploitation. Discursive gender definitions can never be 'innocent' (or ideologically neutral), and nor are they all equally powerful. Certain discourses are more successful than others in assigning 'normal' gender vulnerabilities to women (e.g. women like to gossip, watch soap opera, escape from the 'real world', etc.); and once classified as 'normal' these are hard to break away from.
- *Gender positions* can be analysed textually, as in Ang's account of Sue Ellen and *Dallas*. To what extent are 'normal' discourses of gender inscribed in soap operas (as in Modleski's 'ideal mother') and to what extent are they resisted (as in *Cagney and Lacey*), parodied (as in *Moonlighting*) or converted into pleasurable excess (as in *Dallas*)? However, to go beyond this level of gender theory, to find to what extent discursively constructed and textually inscribed gender definitions and positions are 'taken up by concrete females and males, depends on the gender identifications made by actual subjects' (Ang and Hermes, 1996, p. 120).

- Ang and Hermes draw on the term 'investment' (Henriques *et al.*, 1984) to theorise their understanding of *gender identification*. Unlike the biological or psychological connotations of terms like 'motivation' or 'need' and the rationalistic tendency of 'choice', 'investment' engages with the subject as multiple stakeholder within localised situations of power.

> Investment suggests that people have an – often unconscious – stake in identifying with certain subject positions, including gender positions. . . . People invest in positions which confer on them relative power, although an empowering position in one context (say, in the family) can be quite disempowering in another (say, in the workplace), while in any one context a person can take up both empowering and disempowering positions at the same time.
>
> (1996, pp. 120–1)

Ang and Hermes cite here Radway's work on romances, as indicating how gender discourses based on the naturalness of sexual difference work to reproduce women's gendered subjectivity, so that their very 'declaration of independence' in reading romances simply reactivated their position within patriarchy as nurturing housewife and mother. Even the romance heroine's liberation (in transforming the 'bad' male) locks her more securely within this caring, nurturing role. 'Such an analysis highlights how one and the same practice – reading romances – can contain contradictory positionings and investments, although ultimately ending up, in Radway's analysis, in reproducing a woman's gendered subjectivity' (Ang and Hermes, 1996, p. 121).

Radway is criticised, however, for not sufficiently specifying the social circumstances in which her women performed their romance reading. In contrast, Ang and Hermes refer to Ann Gray's work (1987, 1992) for drawing attention to particular life histories in relation to women watching television. Gray shows how women with minimal education, and who had got married to get away from their parents' home, became aware, once their own children had left home, of their entrapment. Their outlet was in new investments, such as consuming 'feminine' media genres and using the VCR to tape their preferred soap operas, which they then talked about with their women friends, thus avoiding their husbands' put-downs of these shows. 'Gray's account makes clear how the apparent inevitability of the reproduction of femininity is in fact a sedimented history of previous positionings and identifications in which these women find themselves caught, although they struggle against it through new investments' (Ang and Hermes, 1996, p. 122). Women's choice of particular TV genres (like soap opera) or particular communication technologies (like video and the telephone) to 'gossip' and 'chatter' are thus accounted for by the notion of *articulation* – connoting 'a dynamic process of fixing or fitting together, which is, however, never total nor final. The concept of articulation emphasized the impossibility of fixing ultimate meanings' (Ang and Hermes, 1996, p. 123).

David Morley's study of gendered viewing habits on a working-class estate in London is seen as an example of audience consumption understood in terms of articulations, since the dominant mode of viewing where men watch the screen with full concentration while women watch distractedly as they continue with the housework (even during the evening viewing) is explained in terms of men's (but not women's) 'industrial time' and separate sites of leisure in the home. Still, Ang and Hermes argue, Morley (like Radway) does not demonstrate the articulation of (masculine) concentration and (feminine) distraction in concrete situations 'in which personal investments, social circumstances and available discourses are interconnected in specific ways within the families concerned. Articulations, in other words, are inexorably contextual' (1996, p. 123).

All of this poststructuralist theorising leads us – also inexorably – to Ang and Hermes's emphasis on local and situated 'tales of the field'. In any one localised family there may be times when women become the concentrated viewers, men the distracted ones. Daily life may be disrupted by illness, children leaving home, extramarital affairs, political upheavals, and so on, and only situated and local studies will give us access to these processes where 'existing articulations can be disarticulated' (1996, p. 124). For Ang and Hermes,

> the ethnographic turn in the study of media audiences is, given its spirit of radical contextualism and methodological situationalism . . . well suited to take on board the problematizing and investigating in which concrete situations which gender positions are taken up by which men and women, with what identificatory investments, and as a result of which specific articulations. . . . In such a context, we must accept contingency as posing the utter limit for our understanding, and historical and local specificity as the only ground upon which continuities and discontinuities in the ongoing but unpredictable articulation of gender in media consumption can be traced.
>
> (1996, pp. 124–6)

Because people living in '(post)modern societies are surrounded by an ever-present and ever-evolving media environment, they are always-already audiences of an abundance of media provisions' (Ang and Hermes, 1996, p. 126). They are also part of a whole range of routines, rituals and circuits of communication. Thus 'talk' and 'television' flow in and out from each other, and 'interpersonal' and 'mass' communication can no longer be separated.

It is no coincidence, then, that Ang and Hermes both start and end their analysis with an individual anecdote taken from Hermann Bausinger's analysis of television and daily life, where a mother who routinely avoids television sport (which her husband consumes with great concentration) ends up watching the big sports programme with her son, while her husband does not.

In unexpectedly ending up watching the sports programme, Mrs
Meier simultaneously places herself outside the gendered discourse of
'televised football is for men', and reproduces the traditional definition
of femininity in terms of emotional caretaking by using the viewing of
the game as a means of making contact with her son. It is not impossible that such accidental events will lead Mrs Meier to eventually like
football on television, thereby creating a gender-neutral zone within
the family's life with the media.

(Ang and Hermes, 1996, p. 127)

Finally, Ang and Hermes return to the political charge against them: of relativism and populism.

Doesn't postmodern particularism inevitably lead to the resignation
that all there is left viable are descriptions of particular events at particular points in time? And doesn't radical endorsement of particular-
ity and difference only serve to intensify an escalating individualism?
If we declare 'women' to be an indeterminate category, how can a feminist politics still assert itself?

(1996, p. 128)

Part of their answer to these questions is pragmatic: the fact that so many
women reject 'feminism' because it does not equate with their experience is
in itself a charge against any 'guarantee of female unity'. Equally, the more
recent acknowledgement by feminist theorists of differences between women
positioned according to class, ethnicity, generation, sexual preference and
regionality needs further extending to a 'more profound sense of gender
scepticism' (1996, p. 128). Women, in their daily life, are not trapped, Ang
and Hermes insist, in the 'prison house of gender'. They argue for the existence
of 'non-gendered or gender-neutral identifications' (1996, p. 124) when
women (and men) watch television. And, 'given the dominant culture's insistence on the all-importance of sexual difference, we might arguably want to
cherish those rare moments that women manage to escape the prison house
of gender' (1996, p. 125).

It is 'for the sake of the connections and unexpected openings situated
knowledges make possible' (Haraway, 1988, p. 590; cited in Ang and
Hermes, 1996, p. 129) that local, contextualized ethnographic studies are
important. The critical value of the production of 'situated knowledges' lies
'in their enabling of power-sensitive conversation and contestation through
comparison rather than in epistemological truth' (1996, p. 129). In the end
conversation – 'talk' – makes power contestation possible via comparison.
So women's 'talk', rather than a top-down 'expert knowledge' of feminism
establishes 'not relativism, but a politics of location' (1996, p. 129).
Returning to the 'women's genres' of romance and soap opera,

by taking the love for romantic feelings seriously as a starting point for
engagement with 'non-feminist' women, the feminist researcher might

begin to establish a 'comprehension of the self by the detour of the comprehension of the other' (Rabinow 1977, p. 5), in a confrontation with other women who may have more expertise and experience in the meanings, pleasures and dangers of romanticism than herself. What should change as a result of such an ethnographic encounter – and to my mind it is this process-oriented, fundamentally dialogic and dialectical character of knowledge acquisition that marks the distinctive critical edge of ethnography – is not only 'their' understanding of what 'we', as self-proclaimed feminists are struggling for, but, more importantly, the sense of identity that is constructed by feminism itself.

(Ang, 1996, p. 108)

'Talk' – the dialogic mode of research and inquiry – is, in this account, more 'expert' than the 'Promethean' romanticism of Germaine Greer and a generation of early feminists. Lisa's search for 'talk' in situated contexts, her use of television genres as an 'ever-proliferating set of heterogeneous and dispersed, intersecting and contradicting cultural practices' (Ang and Hermes, 1996, p. 126) leaves her closer to Ang than to Greer. And yet Lisa, like Greer, is also deeply dissatisfied with all television genres in their representation of her intimate and risky experiences as a woman. I return, finally in this chapter, to the issue of soap opera, audience anxiety and risk.

Soap, anxieties and risk

The work of Ang (and Hermes) on pleasure and TV soap operas indicates clearly the powerful and beneficial influence on audience analysis deriving from the postmodernist tradition (of Baudrillard and others) that I discussed in chapter 2. The emphasis on the release from the iron cage of 'expert' grand narratives (i.e. the rebuke of Radway), the 'flicker' of images and circuits of communication constituting women's shifting gender definitions, positions and identifications, the release of the audience subject from unity, control, narrative process and humanist agency: these are all familiar constituents of Baudrillard's 'ecstasy'.

Yet, as I have suggested, there is another aspect of 'unity' at work here. A singular emphasis on audience pleasure can lead us away from a more complex theorisation of *anxiety, risk and pleasure together*, as we began to see in Sparks's analysis of cop series. Moreover, if we speak with young people like Lisa, we find they are frequently anxious about *risk* among the 'flicker' of circuits of communication. A group of teenagers in the Blue Mountains tourist town of Katoomba told me about a murder in a local park that they had heard about via friends talk. This park, near the railway station, was a particular site where young people would meet in the evenings for under-age drinking of alcohol. Consequently, rumour of a murder there was disturbing, especially as friends of friends had supposedly found the body. No doubt there was some 'guilty secret' pleasure in the circulation of this gossip. But the teenagers we spoke with were also deeply disturbed by it – fearful for themselves, or for younger brothers and sisters. Also disturbing to the teenagers was the fact that the local newspaper had not reported this event. They were cynical about this, arguing that the local paper only printed 'good news' in case it damaged the tourist industry.

Some girls in this group also spoke of their nervousness after watching *Australia's Most Wanted*: how they would sometimes think they saw the face of a wanted man from this police series, and would look over their shoulders as they walked at night, glad for being in a group and able to talk. Another teenage girl in the group was one of the few young women we interviewed who was prepared to travel alone by train at night to Sydney. Each week she travelled to meet a friend, and said that most of the time she didn't think about any problems. But just occasionally she felt very threatened, and thought 'I don't want to be here'.

There are three things that our research has indicated about young women's anxiety over risk. The first, as my examples indicate, is that they worry about specific risks intensely at particular times – after being cued by a particular experience or perhaps a television programme. But they then generally don't think about it until another cue takes place. There is, as Ang says, no pre-given guarantee for 'female' homogeneity as 'nervous traveller'. Each of these young women adopts a multiplicity of identities, and which of these is invested in and articulated at any one time is a matter of temporal and local specificity: travelling on the train at night when confronted by a 'weird' male; walking the local streets at night after watching *Australia's Most Wanted*. At other times the pleasures – of going to see a special friend, or of watching television – are invested in more strongly.

Second, young women are acutely aware about a whole spectrum of cues ranging from minor harassments – a man staring at you or a pinch on the behind on a crowded train – to their ultimate fear of rape. One woman told us how when she was walking in the street and young men called out crude things to her from their car, it both angered and scared her. But she contained her anger because she believed that confrontation over their sexual comments was a potential path to violence and rape. As another young woman told us in describing the big difference in emotional level of being robbed on the train or being raped, 'you can always get another credit card, you can't get another body'.

Third, while fearing for their bodies sexually, young women (and men) also fear about them in terms of health. These things are not unrelated to pleasure. Sexually active young people want to know more about their bodies; and it is no coincidence that magazines for young women and teenagers have so many stories about both sexual pleasure and sexual risk. The most notable finding in research about young people's use of television and other media forms (as well as school education) in understanding HIV/AIDS

(Tulloch and Lupton, 1997) is that they want to know more about 'what *other* STDs do to your body'.

Research into television audience perceptions of risk tend to be more methodologically empirical, whereas much of Ang's emphasis on audience pleasure is textual. Even her much read study *Watching Dallas* relies on a very small number of audience letters; and moreover, with little of the reflexivity about the researcher's influence in eliciting these letters, which Ang would normally demand.

Can we, though, draw on the strengths and sophistication of Ang's textual analysis of soap opera pleasures, in examining television audience's anxiety about the 'risk society'? Given that soap opera is so often especially concerned with issues of intimate, health, life-style and familial risk, it seems surprising that more audience research has not been addressed to this area. In concluding this chapter, I will discuss briefly my approach (with Deborah Lupton) to audience readings of television HIV messages in soap opera to look at ways of incorporating Ang's interest in genre, narrative and subjectivity in this more empirical approach.

Our methodology in this research was to use seventeen focus groups of (16/17-year-old) teenagers to establish what seemed to be consensus positions on issues about HIV/AIDS, education and the media. Focus group interviews are, however, notorious for enabling dominant voices to negotiate apparent consensus. So we then used these 'apparent consensus' statements as the basis for questionnaires (drawing on the students' own comments), and administered the survey to 1005 final year students in city and rural areas of New South Wales. Out of over 60 'consensus' statements in the survey, the most endorsed was: 'We really need to learn about the symptoms of STDs; what to look for and that kind of thing.' Total agreement among girls was 95 per cent, and among boys 89 per cent. When asked 'What kinds of things about sexuality and HIV/AIDS do you think you do *not* know enough about and would like to learn more about?', both girls and boys placed 'What happens when you get other sexually transmitted diseases?' easily first, ahead of 'What happens when someone gets HIV/AIDS?' second. In contrast, *transmission* matters like 'How HIV/AIDS is spread?' and 'How to use condoms' were ranked very low in value. As both boys and girls said, they had learned 'all that stuff' long ago from TV, and school education was now just reinforcing it. They wanted to know *more* about their bodies. They argued that TV was potentially the best vehicle for showing 'What STDs really look like', And they regretted that television failed them in this major respect. Over 70 per cent of the students agreed that television did not show the infected young body in enough detail. Soft porn (let alone soap opera!) *never* engages with this aspect of sexuality.

Risks then – sexual violence, physical violence, sexually transmitted diseases – are a significant focus of invested subject positions for young people. Gender identifications are established, at specific times and in localised contexts, in risks associated with the pleasures of sexuality. So to focus only on women's pleasure in relation to soap opera and other television genres would be too partial an approach to audiences' emotional responses. Young people do – contrary to Beck, Giddens and Wynne – seek out knowledge in relation to risk and the body _both_ from 'experts' _and_ experientially (Lupton and Tulloch, 1998). Teenagers want most to learn about how HIV and STDs 'affect the body' from people-living-with-AIDS and from sexual health counsellors. These, rather than teachers (who 'learn it all from a book') and the media (which has different values, according to genre and technology) are looked to by young people to 'not beat around the bush' but show and tell them 'the basics'.

As one focus group put it:

Everyone thinks, you know, I'll never get it.
It won't happen to me.
But then you see people that's got [HIV/AIDS], and they thought the same thing, you know.

While teenagers are particularly keen to meet people living with AIDS, both documentaries and 'realistic' soap operas are also valued – especially by teenage girls – for the stories about risk. We earlier heard a female student in Buckingham's study of soap opera say, 'watching _EastEnders_, and seeing all the drugs problems and all the rest of it, you don't want to do it' (1987, pp. 179–80); and other research (Tulloch and Tulloch, 1992) has indicated that young people value soap operas for their stories about domestic violence.

It is also clear (Tulloch and Lupton, 1997) that young people use different media forms for different kinds of health risk purposes. Our survey indicated that television was valued in so far as it has the potential to give visual access to the infected body; late-night talk-back radio was valued because it provided a confidential and anonymous way of asking about STD and AIDS questions (that you were too embarrassed to admit to not knowing about in public forums); and magazines were valued (especially by girls) as domestic 'libraries' (i.e. as 'good sources of information about AIDS and STDs because you can look things up again if you need to').

Given that so many soap operas provide health information, and that some like _General Hospital_ and _A Country Practice_ have been focused around the health industry itself, what kinds of response – both in instrumental and pleasure terms – is this particular television genre most liked (and perceived as effective) for in terms of issues of risk and the body? Very little work has been done on audience responses in this area.

Certain theoretical and methodological issues are important here. First, how does soap opera's form – of multiple narratives and enigmas, and of the viewer as inscribed with long-term and privileged access to knowledge and 'secrets' – influence reception of its 'risk' stories? How does the very existence of soap opera's multiple narrative strands affect audience response to risk messages? Some soap opera writers worry that the multiple strands detract from their (often very heartfelt) health or other risk messages. Others argue that soap opera's tendency to have 'balancing stories' – where one narrative strand, in some indirect way, parallels or throws light on another – will re-enforce health and social meanings.

Second, how far do soap opera's *spectatorship* and soap opera's *social audiences* agree or differ on matters of risk. For example, the executive producer of *A Country Practice* took the same issue as concerned the *EastEnders* viewer Dionne, about the supposed lack of risk in shooting up just once; and inscribed this as a central feature of his 'Sophie' story. Did various social audiences 'read' it the same way?

Third, to what extent does the textual inscription of risk via soap opera's long-term characters improve or decrease the power of risk messages? Buckingham argues that 'soap opera is unique in providing its viewers with the opportunity to get to know characters over a long period; and it is likely that simply as a result of this familiarity we may come to regard them in a very different way from characters whom we encounter for only a short time' (1987, p. 82). The executive producer of *A Country Practice*, James Davern agreed with him and so used his most central characters for his HIV/AIDS story 'Sophie'.

Davern: You can watch a television commercial from afar and you can distance yourself. Or like when you're watching *Dallas*, you really distance yourself a little bit. It's a comic strip because you have no experience with those people. . . . But you know Alex and Terrence [lead doctors in *A Country Practice*]; they've been around for a long time; they're familiar. They're happily married, everyone has experienced what they're experiencing; they relate to them. . . . Happily married people distance themselves from AIDS; it's somebody else's problem. But it's not if it can happen to Terrence Elliott.

Does, then, the association of risk with central soap opera characters lead to audiences responding more or less powerfully than to a television public service advertisement (PSA), as Davern assumes? What about Ang's point that where soaps do address non-personal issues, these still take on meaning from the standpoint of personal life?

Fourth, what about soap opera's visual style, the 'in-your-face' close-ups, the formulaic over-the-shoulder two shots for standard 'intimacy' scenes – how do these work in relation to risk messages and audiences? Fifth – given that the 'general viewing', peak-time classification of soap operas may sometimes allow nudity but certainly never the full, explicit details of how STDs effect the body that our teenage respondents were looking to from television – is there anything of value in relation to risk for young audiences of soaps?

I have discussed all of these issues in detail elsewhere (Tulloch and Lupton, 1997; Tulloch, 1999), and will confine myself here to some theoretical and methodological points.

1. **Multiple narratives and the knowing viewer** Because the executive producer of the prime-time soap opera *A Country Practice* spent more money proportionally than the genre normally does on its writers, he attracted the best known film and television writers in Australia. These were used to writing for quicker-rhythmed film narratives. Consequently, one of these leading writers worried that there would be a loss of 'impact' in his needle sharing/HIV story, as a result of the soap opera's multiple narratives. Would 'doing a scene somewhere else about something totally different', he worried, lose his main story's momentum, or would its 'less threatening viewing' mode allow for 'a sense of audience relief' prior to them being engaged all the more powerfully (as in Hitchcock's films). At the same time, Channel 7, which screened this soap opera, had a self-perception of being a 'half-way house' between the state broadcasting service, the Australian Broadcasting Corporation, and the other 'more melodramatic' commercial channels. As a potential conduit for all viewers who switched between the ABC and these 'other commercials', Channel 7 had a strategy for retaining these channel-switchers. *A Country Practice* was designed *both* as popular soap opera (with continuing *serial* 'personal life' stories) *and* as an 'issues'-based *series*, which opened up and closed off a different issue (AIDS, teenage alcoholism, domestic violence, drugs stories, rural unemployment, youth suicide, gay sexuality, etc.) each week. As such, it had a different textual strategy from many other soaps which often introduce 'controversial' issues like gay sexuality as one (marginal) narrative among many others, and draw on market research to see whether these are popular, should be dropped, made more central and so on. *A Country Practice*, on the other hand, attracted producers who liked to play centrally between different 'issues' in the one two-episode story (say youth unemployment and youth needle-sharing/AIDS in 'Sophie'). These producers believed that one story would 'balance' another (in the sense that the 'up' ending of a youth unemployment story would offset the 'downer' stereotype of youth needle-sharing), and contextualise them (in terms of an economy of recession, and so on). To examine this complex set of industry expectations about '*spectatorship*', we showed three versions of the episode 'Sophie' to different *social audiences* of young people, with and without 'balancing stories', drawing on both qualitative (focus group) and quantitative (survey questionnaire) methods. We also addressed Buckingham's 'knowing viewer' issue by comparing audiences of *A Country Practice* regular viewers with non-viewers.

2. **Spectatorship and social audiences** For the executive producer of 'Sophie', the risk of 'shooting up just once at a party' was a major 'message' of his

needle-sharing story. But making a soap opera is an industrial process, and during this process many other HIV/AIDS (and other social) 'messages' will get added or effaced. For example, at the plotting conference it was decided that a sympathetic but deliberately anti-ageist parallel should be drawn between the father, Dr Terrence Elliott's earlier alcoholism and his daughter Sophie's current heroin addiction (it was Terrence's alcoholism which drove Sophie from home in the first place). This parallel was emphasised in the initial script, was then more-or-less lost in the studio recording, and then strongly re-inscribed at the sound dub – each as the result of different professionals' particular inflections (Tulloch and Lupton, 1997, ch. 7). Textual spectatorship, then, is a matter of a text produced as an industrial process, with many different (sometimes contradictory) professional idiolects at work. Different social audiences may then invest in a different 'AIDS message' according to different subject identifications. Two of the three versions of 'Sophie' shown to audience groups differed only on the inclusion of the audio 'sound sting' used to draw a parallel between Terrence's and Sophie's addictions; and, again, focus group interviews and surveys were used to assess any differences in response. In addition, 'before' and 'after' questions assessing various drug risks (including 'shooting-up' once at a party) were used in the survey.

3. **Soap opera's long-term characters and risk** It seems common sense to assume that tying in health and other risks with long-term characters whom audiences have got to like or 'love to hate' over a long period will have more emotional effect on viewers than a 90-second PSA about needle-sharing and HIV. To test this common sense comparison I chose apparently extreme cases: 'Sophie' (the needle-sharing/HIV story featuring the daughter of *A Country Practice*'s longest-serving and much loved central character, Dr Terrence Elliott); and the television PSAs featuring, for less than two minutes, a series of unknown people living with AIDS (PLWAs) whose faces were in shadow. In other words, these were television characters at one extreme of Davern's 'distance': unknown, unseen, and of instant, not long-term duration. We used both focus group interviews and semantic differential survey questions (which assess audience's identification with a range of binarised 'likes/dislikes' on a seven-point scale) to assess this comparison. The results would not have been expected by James Davern (Tulloch and Lupton, 1997, ch. 10). But it is important here to consider a range of contextual factors. A soap opera is an industrial product, aimed at maximum ratings. Davern's intention was to have 'one birth, one death per year' to achieve peak ratings. 'Sophie' was chosen for the peak 'death' of the year; but Sophie herself was an existing character, 'too old' to be the typical street-junkie the producers wanted (according to the series' consultant social worker-expert). Consequently, Sophie was given a younger, needle-sharing boyfriend; and their joint impact on the *serial* narrative (Terrence's recent marriage

to a much younger wife) added a complexity entirely missing from the PSAs. As an almost same-age rival to Terrence's wife Alex, Sophie was assessed (differently by boys and girls) in relation to the 'ideal mother' symbolic identity that Modleski (1982), Lovell (1981a) and others see as central to soap opera. Moreover, Sophie's relationship with Alex was a key factor in the romance/marriage/divorce 'anti-utopian' structure that Ang points to in her analysis of soap opera as melodrama. Both industrial and formal aspects of soap opera, then, complicate our common sense notions of how spectator subject positions are established through soap opera texts.

4. **Soap opera's visual style** Because 'Sophie' was the season's peak 'death' episode, it was given the unusual luxury of being a four-parter, over two weeks (four-part mini-series were drawing big ratings at the time). Therefore two directors (rather than the usual one per series 'issue') were employed. These had different training and background. One trained, the producer told us, 'BBC/ABC-style'; that is, he liked to have all his camera-angles established prior to rehearsals, allowing him to make minor adjustments for actors' needs. This shooting-style facilitated a more 'aesthetic' approach than normal in soap opera, with characters frequently positioned in deep-focus triangles rather than the familiar close-ups and over-the-shoulder two-shots. During the recording of 'Sophie', however, this director took the extremely unusual step (for him) of leaving the control room, and repositioning his cameras because a particular scene wasn't 'working'. The scene in question had the desperate Terrence telling the hospital matron that heroin should perhaps be legalised in order to break down the junkies' street economy which had trapped his daughter. It was a scene that was not originally in the script at all (it was added late by the script editor because the episode was running short) and the director originally treated it as a 'throwaway' scene – more important in his production for how it looked than what it said. However, after hearing a radio discussion about the economy of heroin use just prior to the first studio recording day, he changed his mind. He now wanted to emphasise the scene by letting his audience 'see the actor's eyes', in typical soap opera style. We could not, of course, show different audiences the two versions of this scene, because only one was recorded. But we could ask immediate 'before' and 'after' questions about legalising heroin (there was a dramatic change of opinion about this among both boys and girls), and we could compare (via 'before' and 'after' questionnaires) the reasons given by audiences for this change of view with those given in the text (the 'match' was very close). We could, then, surmise that this particular style of representing this particular 'AIDS message' was effective *in the short term* in changing young people's views. We could not assess whether any other style would have been more or less effective in doing so.

5. **Soap opera and risk** It is a familiar finding of audience research that males devalue soap opera. In relation to areas of risk, boys tend to

emphasise the importance of advertisements, while girls emphasise soap operas and personalised documentaries. After being *shown* soap operas featuring domestic violence and HIV/AIDS, however, we have found that boys can change their minds significantly (Tulloch and Lupton, 1997, ch. 10). So though soap operas will probably never show the explicit representations of STDs that many young people would like, there are other areas that both boys and girls can value soap operas for in relation to risk (Tulloch and Tulloch, 1992b).

Conclusion

This chapter has, in an important sense, moved in two contrary directions – both theoretically and methodologically.

Its initial theoretical direction was to follow Ang in rejecting the 'instrumental' focus of so much audience research for an emphasis on textual 'pleasure'. But the chapter then argues for a specific return to the instrumental (knowing more about the young body and risk) at the end. The reason for this dual emphasis was (following Sparks and Ang) to examine the industrial, textual and audience articulation of gender definitions, positions and identifications.

Methodologically, with Ang we moved away from the 'macro' and the quantitative to the fragmented, localised, contextualised micro-stories of a critical ethnography (as we had done in the previous chapter on cop series). But then at the end we refocused on quantitative ways of 'assessing' audience response. Here, my point was that in each case the quantitative survey was based on the micro-stories of producers and audiences of the soap opera text.

I will turn centrally to the issue of 'qualitative vs. quantitative' methods in the next chapter. But before I do this I want to point to the continuities across the two sections of the chapter.

Centrally, *both* rely on what Ang calls the radical contextualism of the new ethnography. Whether we look at a social audience's gender identifications or at the subject positions of spectatorship constructed in and through specific television texts, it is important to seek out the local and contextualised production of 'situated knowledge'. Ethnographies of production are as important as ethnographies of reception; and, following Alasuutari, we need to reconsider their connection. Thinking through issues of spectatorship and social audiences *within* a radically contextualised ethnography is one way of achieving a new middle-level theory of the media.

Both in the production and in the reception of television texts we find 'heterogeneous and dispersed, intersecting and contradicting cultural practices' (Ang and Hermes, 1996, p. 126). Within the production team of a soap opera we will find multiply positioned subjects, as we do among audiences – as the example of the 'BBC/ABC'-trained director who changed his camera angles after his 'intertextual' experience indicates. Neither among audiences nor among television producers are the situated discourses and articulations of gender (age, class, or race) either innocent or equally powerful – though it is probably the case that what Ang calls the 'interaction between the transnational and the indigenous' (Ang, 1996, p. 81) is more systematically tilted in production towards the 'global' than the 'local' (*despite* James Davern's tilt towards the Australian 'unconscious'). But even here, 'more nuanced accounts' (Ang, 1996, p. 81) reveal a range of subject definitions, positionings and identifications as television professionals work at making their semiotically dense texts.

Meanwhile, even Ien Ang sometimes draws on quantitative data (despite her general hostility), as when she argues the 'special significance' of her case about the 'bitch' Sue Ellen and the 'nice girl' Pamela in *Dallas*. She says that her point about women, soap opera and a tragic 'structure of feeling' is 'more pronounced in the light of the findings of a representative Dutch survey' that 'while 21.7 per cent of female viewers between 15 and 39 years mentioned Sue Ellen as their favourite *Dallas* character . . . only 5.1 per cent named Pamela as their favourite' (Ang, 1996, p. 86). But Ang would also say that while 'accurate data gathering and careful inference making remain applicable' (1996, p. 75), a radical contextualist theory must always be reflexively aware of its political role in the 'power-laden field of social discourse' (Ang, 1996, p. 76), of its provisional nature, of its 'temporary closures'.

Nowhere in audience research has this reflexivity been more absent than in the 'television, sex and violence' debates of the last half-century. I will turn to some of the implications of this in the next chapter. There, as in this and the previous chapter, we will find that Denzin and Lincoln's history of qualitative methodology is inscribed in different ways, according to the different interpretive communities (in chapter 3 frequently criminological, in chapter 4 feminist, in chapter 5 moralist and governmental) which have invested in the research debate.

|5|

From pleasure to risk:

Revisiting 'television violence'

Two positions adopted by Ien Ang as a feminist audience theorist have been extremely important; but also – if taken too singularly – problematic. The first is her emphasis on women's pleasure in television, rather than the more familiar focus (from quite different perspectives) on 'instrumental' approaches to television and audiences; for example, that television violence has bad effects on children. The second is her challenge to 'universalist' (mainly quantitative) methodologies. She focuses instead on qualitative and especially 'situated' methods that can give us more access to women's multi-subjective 'experience in the meanings, pleasures and dangers' of genres like soap opera and the romance.

Ang's work is particularly important in the context that Alasuutari describes as 'third generation' audience theory. Here, he argues, we should be concerned with what the place is 'of expert knowledge produced by media researchers . . . in reproducing or transforming the frames within which the media and "audiencing" are perceived' (1999, p. 7). As Alasuutari says:

> It is obvious that the instrumentalist perspective of mass communica-tion research on its object is not of its own making, it is in fact only echoing culturally embedded concerns about mass media. . . . There is of course really nothing wrong about addressing people's concerns with the help of systematic research, but it is also useful to ask where such concerns stem from in the culture and society. . . . Whose con-cerns are they particularly?
>
> (1999, p. 11)

'Third generation' audience theory has therefore shifted its ground from the 'effects' of television's 'bad' content on passive and susceptible audiences. But it is also moving beyond the opposite (leftist) tendency where 'Whatever researchers studied they seemed to find symbolic resistance' (1999, p. 10). Rather, there is now a greater empirical emphasis on the moral frames and hierarchies which people (and broadcasting institutions) use to legitimate what is chosen for viewing on everyday television (Alasuutari, 1999, p. 12). Turning to the 'global picture' in addition to the 'everyday', Alasuutari argues that it is because of

> the relative novelty of the contemporary 'media cultures', and the rapid development in communication technology [that] world cultures have to continuously renew the frames within which to conceive of the new 'media-scape' within which people lead their daily lives. Old and new epistemologies often live side by side, and rapid social change often causes confusion and fears.
>
> (1999, p. 17)

One of the broad differences between the different 'global' theories we discussed in chapter 2 – between recent postmodernist and risk society thinking, for example – is that one (as in Baudrillard) tends to celebrate the new frames of the 'media scape' as endless sources of pleasure in instantaneous sensual variation, and the other (as in Beck) focuses on the fears surrounding the new technologies, and the attempts by public groups that form around these fears of risk to gain voice through the media (and other public platforms). There is, in other words, an in-built tendency to the semiotics of sensuality, pleasure and ecstasy in one global theory (see again Kellner on *Miami Vice*); and towards instrumentalities of human survival in the other. Inevitably these grand theoretical differences have been reflected in competing audience theories and methodologies.

So the 'pleasure' versus 'risk' scenario that structured chapter 3 is in fact played out, as Alasuutari says, both broadly and intimately as a confusion of 'old and new epistemologies' living side by side. In this situation many levels of 'expert knowledge' also debate side by side. There are the media researchers who, as Ang warns in her critique of Radway, can often take a somewhat 'recruitist' attitude to their subjects of study. There are also the self-appointed 'experts' of the so-called 'moral majority', of which Mary Whitehouse's National Viewers and Listeners association has been the most well-known international example. It is because of the conservative ideology of these organisations, with their emphasis on the 'traditional values' of home, marriage, family, being assaulted by the depiction of 'sex, drugs and violence' on television that such issues have become a major focus for funded research, as well as for political rhetoric and interventions. In addition, there is the intensive knowledge of the 'everyday' where, as Ang says, 'other women . . . may have more expertise and experience in the meanings, pleasures and dangers of romanticism' than either the researcher or the public moralist.

It is important, of course, not to totally separate each of these levels of expertise. The researcher, as Ang, Radway and Alasuutari all argue, is also the 'everyday' woman. And Mary Whitehouse's success in representing very many 'ordinary' people's anxieties about television and its social/moral context? However, for heuristic reasons it is useful to separate them as regulatory discourses. Whitehouse has had more power to make her 'talk' enter public and political discourse than most researchers, who in turn tend to have more access to the media and public talkfests than the average person's 'lay knowledge'.

This is one reason why there are problems as well as significant advantages associated with Ang's emphasis on 'pleasure' and on qualitative research. How do we know, without some resort to generalisable methodologies, that many women do, in fact, find the pleasure the researcher says they do – either via her textual analysis of *Dallas* or by examining just 42 letter responses to her advertisement about the serial in a Dutch magazine? As we saw at the end of the last chapter, Ang herself is not beyond resorting to quantitative data to help support her argument. Moreover, surely Ang's own emphasis on the heterogenous, local and situated nature of women's subject identifications points to the need for examining much more widely other articulations and investments than 'pleasure', even within television soap opera? In our own research on fear of crime, we found that women were often articulate and knowledgable about how they negotiated different genres in terms of different kinds of pleasure and risks.

The research by Schlesinger, Dobash, Dobash and Weaver into women viewing violence has shown that a large number of women can be very anxious indeed while watching television. This is because the 'importance attributed to what was viewed was not in terms of pleasure, escape or fantasy but in terms of relevance and social importance' (Schlesinger *et al.*, 1992, p. 169). Schlesinger *et al.*,'s 'results indicate that over half those involved in the *Women Viewing Violence* project considered that the media play an important role in *increasing* their anxieties and fear of crime, and that for most women, the media play no role in *decreasing* those fears' (Schlesinger *et al.*, 1992, p. 39). Recently a number of significant audience researchers (Morley, Livingstone, etc.) have re-emphasised the importance of combined quantitative and qualitative research, and Schlesinger *et al.*,'s work is, in my view, amongst the most valuable of this kind. In this and the next chapter I will use their research to revisit the 'television violence' debate, and to broaden our focus beyond audience pleasures in soap opera and romance. I have chosen 'television violence' as a focus here because, of all expert/audience research relationships, historically it has been the most prone to the kind of functionalist/instrumentalist 'passive effects' work that Ang condemns. But research in this area does not *have* to be that way.

The Schlesinger *et al.*, research operates according to a number of theoretical and methodological principles. First, given that *Women Viewing Violence* (published in 1992) is a project conducted across Denzin and Lincoln's stages of 'blurred genres', 'crisis of legitimation' and 'local/situated' research, it is not surprising that all of these foci are important.

- As regards 'blurred genres', Schlesinger *et al.*,'s research – with its emphasis on local contextualism and 'frameworks of interpretation' rather than 'causes and effects'; on moving beyond textualist approaches and 'inscribed' subject positions; on the 'audience as active but only within determinate limits' (1992, p. 6); on feminist theory and the construction of gender identities; on the importance of race and ethnicity; and on the 'lived experience' of violence – is clearly both post-'linguistic turn' and post-'ethnographic turn' in its combination of critical theories.

- As regards the 'crises of representation and legitimation', Schlesinger *et al.,* emphasise the importance of bringing together feminist concerns with gender representation and 'the wholly separate study of domestic and sexual violence' (1992, p. 1). While noting the 'defensible logic' of the dominant tendency within feminist textualist studies of representation to 'stress the study of "women's media" or "women's genres" as the best entry point into the question of gender identity' (1992, p. 7), the researchers emphasise that it is important to go much further than a study of the pleasures women derive from romance, melodrama or soap opera. Women's situation in private and public spaces where they are systematically subject to sexual harassment and violence makes them acutely concerned about the 'real' risks in television's representation of women, wherever these are found. So while supporting the general post-1980s move towards qualitative research, Schlesinger *et al.,* argue against 'making it into an article of faith that excludes any attempt at quantification' (1992, pp. 7–8); and they draw attention to the 'combination of quantitative and qualitative methods ... currently becoming more acceptable in the study of the television audience, although this tends to be among those who lay greater emphasis on social scientific rather than on cultural studies approaches' (1992, p. 8).

- The researchers' own social scientific emphasis (in regard to the issue of 'legitimation') is to turn to the importance of providing the kind of detailed and 'developed accounts of the conduct of their investigations and how they conducted their analysis' (1992, p. 18) which in the past has been most evident in grounded theory. Thus they are meticulous in describing the pilot study and programme selection, the sample and viewing groups, the recruitment of group members, the actual conduct of the screenings and focus group discussions, the data collection instruments and analysis. For example, they discuss the method of 'funnelling' which allowed 'groups initially to determine their own agendas' (1992, p. 28) combined with standardised questions whereby 'participants are systematically faced with similar points of reference for discussion' to ensure that 'all participants were presented with the same frameworks, allowing for specific and direct comparisons to be made' (1992, p. 18). They emphasise the importance of using survey questions prior to focus group discussion, and then again after them 'in order to capture any changes in interpretation arising from the discussion' (1992, p. 27). They stress the importance of using a number of empirical strategies in the social sciences (triangulation), so that qualitative methods 'allow for more meaningful representations of what people think' (1992, p. 18), while quantitative methods 'show overall patterns' and 'may assist researchers in avoiding the temptation to present qualitative results which concentrate on only one or a few discourses and interpretive positions to the neglect of others' (1992, p. 18). They also point to the fact that women respondents commented on the 'unnatural' (albeit positive) luxury of being able to watch the various violent programmes in the project 'entire' without being interrupted by men, children and household chores. This was an intentionally contrived aspect of the research enabling women (as one mother said) to 'get each other's point of view and to actually discuss what you've seen. . . . I don't get a chance to discuss things . . . with being on my own and with my little boy' (1992, p. 27). 'Only by allowing women a space of their own', the researchers argue, 'will we be able to learn about their views' (1992, p. 17); hence focus groups were deliberately taken out of the 'normal' family situation, and were single sex. Schlesinger *et al.*, argue that by this reflexive attention to the politics as well as the 'contrived' nature of all research, and by their mix of qualitative and quantitative methods, they established viewing groups that fell 'somewhere between the tightly controlled artificiality of the psychological experiment and the naturalness of the domestic setting' (1992, p. 27).

• Schlesinger *et al.*,'s emphasis on social scientific methods (as against 'cultural studies') means that they come much closer to the postpositivist emphases on validity, generalisability and reliability (Denzin and Lincoln's 'third phase' of qualitative research) than to the 'narrativised' stories and 'tales from the field' of their 'fifth moment'. Nevertheless, the researchers' choice to compare women who have suffered significant domestic violence with women who have not done so in fact did focus the research quite centrally on the local, contextual and situated specifics of women's everyday lives and relationships. This contrast allowed the researchers to demonstrate very tellingly situated differences around experiences of violence. Thus, one middle-class woman said in response to a domestic violence episode of *EastEnders*:

I can remember when I saw it the first time, I was at a loss what to do for half an hour after the programme, really. It frightened me. You don't expect that – I've just never come up against violence from parents or from family or whatever. In that situation I suppose home is a safe haven to me, and, seeing it turn into something like that, especially in front of a child, it just frightened me, it really upset me.

(1992, pp. 91–2)

In contrast, for a woman who had experienced sustained domestic violence, the 'in front of the child' narrative was seen pragmatically and strategically. She said of the abused *EastEnders* character, 'Her reaction was instant and it was exactly the same as mine and any other woman's.

It's get the kids out of here, because I know exactly what's coming. So I thought that was perfect' (1992, pp. 92–3).

Another important principle underpinning Schlesinger *et al.*,'s research is its refusal to focus on simply one television genre (or even one programme), unlike most feminist-inspired work on pleasure. They adopt this multi-generic research strategy mainly for two reasons. The first is that the 'construction of the gender identities of women via the media needs to be understood in a context much broader than that of "women's media" alone. This is not least because femininity is constructed in relation to masculinity in a comprehensive range of media and genres' (1992, p. 7). Their first reason, then, relates to the issue of gender *representation*.

Schlesinger *et al.*,'s second reason relates to their sociological focus on the *lived experience* of violence and fear of crime. It became quickly apparent from the pilot study that women found many (but not all) genres and formats of violence created anxieties relating to their own experience. Consequently, the final choice of programmes to screen to women in the main research study depended on their having 'a significant relation to actual acts of violence committed against women' (1992, p. 20). Programmes screened differed, however, according to the following: a contrast of closed-ended narratives with open-narrative genres like soap opera; a contrast of 'real world' violence in fiction with 'factual' programmes like *Crimewatch*; a spectrum of programmes from those focusing solely on violence against women to those that represented violence as a subsidiary theme; a choice encompassing a variety of crimes of violence against women; and a representation of different female responses to violence, offering a range of views as to why women suffer violence.

In the remainder of this chapter I examine the advantages and disadvantages, similarities and differences between Schlesinger *et al.*,'s research in their work on women's responses to soap opera and Buckingham's 'single text', 'active-audience' analyses of soap opera – thus linking this chapter on 'violence' to the previous one on 'pleasure'. In the following chapter, I will compare their work on women viewing various genres of television violence with similar qualitative/quantitative research relating to children and violence. The next chapter will also move from the consideration of women viewing violence in soap opera to children viewing violence in television 'documentaries', while still keeping the comparative reference to soap opera in mind.

Two approaches to *EastEnders*

Both Schlesinger *et al.*, and Buckingham are writing about television audiences beyond the 'ethnographic turn'; and they *both* are concerned with an overemphasis on 'pleasure'. As Buckingham puts it:

The danger of defining soap opera exclusively in terms of 'pleasure' is that pleasure itself comes to be seen as a phenomenon which is beyond criticism or analysis. Yet if pleasure cannot be regarded as merely a form of escapism or delusion, it would seem equally inadequate just to celebrate it. If we are to understand the pleasures of soap opera, they cannot be seen as unitary or somehow timeless: on the contrary, they must be situated within their social and historical context.

(1987, p. 6)

This is what Buckingham seeks to do in his book. For example, he comments on the criticism of *EastEnders* from teenage boys who actually live in the East End of London, and who complain that the series does not show the 'real' crime and violence of the area: 'Like the Kray Twins . . . it's all villains, well-known people' (1987, p. 191). The boys were getting less pleasure from *EastEnders* than from series like *The Bill* because it was not 'masculine' enough, or locally detailed enough in its representations of violence. Buckingham does not, however, devalue these masculinist pleasures and displeasures as sexist fantasy. Rather,

the boys' perception and understanding of their *own* experience, and hence their judgments of what was and what was not realistic, were dependent upon their own social position as working-class men, and their attempts to define that position in positive terms. The ideology, which informed these perceptions and understandings was therefore bound up with their sense of their own identity. Their investment in an ideology of masculinity, then, was a significant aspect of their sense of identity as young men, and their attempt to find a degree of security within it. In the same way, what I have called the 'mythology' of the East End underworld was an influential part of the way in which they made sense of their own experience of living in that particular working-class neighbourhood, and attempted to construct it as 'glamorous'; and in this respect it would be mistaken to regard it merely as a romantic falsehood perpetrated by outsiders.

(Buckingham, 1987, p. 191)

Buckingham is as concerned here with the relationship between young males' pleasures and identity via television as Ang is with women's pleasures and identities in *Dallas*. In both cases there is a determination not to censor, but rather to *situate* these pleasures – even though in the East End boys' case, these are the kinds of pleasure in 'violent' male identity which might lead to some of the problems with male control experienced by many of Schlesinger *et al.*,'s women.

Schlesinger *et al.*,'s female respondents are also the tellers of situated tales; in this case arising from their actual experiences of violence. But the difference between the East End boy's use of 'represented' violence (local stories about the Kray twins, their own stories to the researchers about local murders, etc.) and the women's stories of 'actual' violence to themselves, does indicate significant differences theoretically (and therefore method-ologically) between Buckingham and Schlesinger *et al.*,'s situated accounts. These differences influenced both what they looked for and what they found in their audience research.

Theoretical differences

Buckingham's is a *processual* analysis of the soap opera audience. His book's four chapters cover sequentially:

1. creating the audience via production intentions and institutions;
2. the 'audience in the text';
3. the 'secondary' texts (like publicity, magazines, critics, reviewers, etc.) which mediate 'between the text and the audience'; and,
4. popular television's 'active audience'.

His theoretical intention is to examine the relationship between all these dif-ferent 'audiences'. So, for example, he points out that when making predic-tions of the relationship between a woman character in *EastEnders* and her supposed 'daughter', it is press coverage rather than the programme itself which fans are drawing on for this 'knowledge'. Similarly, he suggests that it is the producers' intention to avoid polemics about ethnic differences which may have lead to the lack of explicit references to ethnicity in his respondents' discussions.

This audience 'process' is not, however, conceived as a linear process of 'influence' or 'effect'. Like Schlesinger *et al.*, Buckingham explicitly rejects the 'effects' tradition of communication, which tends to assume a passive, manipulated or stupid viewer of soap opera. Rather, each stage of the indus-trial process of television making, circulation and reception makes for a *diversity* of 'readings'.

> [I]n order to retain its audience, the programme itself cannot be too prescriptive: rather than offering a single position from which it may be understood, it has to encourage a diversity of readings. The ways in which the programme is mediated, for example by marketing and by the popular press, are also likely to prevent a single, uniform interpre-tation. Finally, viewers themselves are actively engaged in negotiating meaning; while certain meanings which are perceived in the text may be refused, others may be seized upon for reasons which are quite dif-ferent from those which its producers intended.
>
> (Buckingham, 1987, p. 203)

Schlesinger *et al.*, would agree with all of this; particularly the position that rejects a dominating media (as in the American 'effects' tradition) as well as the more populist 'semiotic democracy' of 'any number of readings', which has been popular recently in cultural studies. But it is where Buckingham and Schlesinger *et al.*, go from here that differs significantly.

Buckingham's determining agenda is that of the 'active audience'. He is therefore concerned to show that soap opera audiences are not 'dupes' of the media industry; that they can distinguish between 'fiction' and 'reality'; that they play pleasurably between these two modalities; that to make their meanings they draw skilfully on a range of soap opera's formal qualities (multiple narratives, 'telling secrets', 'gossip', prediction and the process of revelation) as well as on their own everyday experience. They also work between a number of circuits of communication – production information in magazines, newspaper predictions of future events, their own talk with friends, their own regular (but critical) viewing of the series – as they constitute their pleasures and give voice to their particular ideological perspectives.

Buckingham's 'moral frame' (to use Alasuutari's term) is very clear in his use of a quotation from Dorothy Hobson. 'It is actually fun to talk about the characters in a soap opera, and yet the game that viewers play with one another is interpreted as some form of psychological disorder, when for the most part they are well aware that the game is going on' (1987, cited p. 173). One of the central 'games' of pleasure for children watching soap opera may well be, says Buckingham, their spying on, and then everyday conversation about, 'aspects of adult behaviour which are usually hidden from them' (Buckingham, 1987, p. 164) like sexuality, adultery, homosexuality and adult crime and violence. But far from suggesting anything deviant or psychologically aberrant in this 'voyeurism', Buckingham emphasises its pleasurable functionality.

> Discussing television may thus provide a relatively 'safe' way of acknowledging things which [children] are normally forbidden to talk about; as well as allowing us to look without being seen, television allows us to pass comment without fear of reprisals. In many instances [during the research interviews] these 'secrets' were discussed in tones of whispered confidentiality and barely suppressed excitement.
>
> (1987, p. 164)

At the same time as this pleasurable and functional degree of voyeurism for children, Buckingham argues that women viewers also valued *EastEnders* for its social and educational attention to 'issues' – like cot deaths, heroin, teenage pregnancy, violence. But his emphasis here is on the way in which a soap opera text that refuses to impose a single moral or ideological position on its viewers is itself positioned within a variety of moral frames by its audiences. These frames are partially determined by a viewer's age (younger viewers preferring to probe adult 'secrets' than identify with young characters), class (many viewers seeing working-class characters as 'normal' and middle-class ones as 'snobs'), gender (the girls worrying about Angie's 'weakness' and hating Den's double standards as 'a male chauvinist pig') and race (black teenagers varying in their view of the series' 'positive' or 'token' image of non-white people).

Buckingham's focus, however, is primarily not on what the text means (across however many situated moral frames), rather on 'how it *works* – that is, *how it enables viewers to produce meaning*' (1987, p. 203). Neither accepting the popular television text as an 'exercise in mass deception' nor as an 'unproblematic expression of popular expressions and desires' (1987, pp. 203–4), Buckingham is, in the end, more interested in the formal arrangements of soap opera which allow a diversity of situated audience meanings. He therefore concludes with Jane Feuer's argument that

> the emergence of soap opera as the dominant form of the 1980s may represent a response to the increasing cultural contradictions of the period. While other genres such as police series or situation comedies tend to rely more heavily on shared values and beliefs, the relative openness of the soap opera allows it to be read and enjoyed in a wider variety of ways, and thus to appeal to a more fragmented and diverse audience.
>
> (1987, p. 204)

The implicit (and valued) 'fragmented' temporality is here (as in Baudrillard or Ang) the 'post'(modern). By focusing on a single British soap opera in a particular historical situation (the 1980s period of economic decline, the Thatcherite shifting of resources from the public to the private sector, the privatising of the welfare state), Buckingham is able to draw attention to the way in which generic form is mediated within the entertainment industry and mobilised according to an audience's everyday experiences to provide both pleasures and criticisms which are not 'seen as unitary or somehow timeless' (1987, p. 6).

Schlesinger *et al.*, begin from the same emphasis on diversity – namely the 'different constructions that depend on the characteristics of specific audiences' (1992, p. 6) and the 'question of genres into which a given television programme or film may be categorised and how its discourses are organised' (1992, pp. 6–7) – but within a different methodological framework, and with different conclusions about some of the *EastEnders* audiences' moral frames. Like Buckingham, Schlesinger *et al.*, focus on key social differences like gender, ethnicity and class in tracing this diversity in interpretation. But their key focus is on the *experience* of risk. Whereas Buckingham targets a single soap opera, Schlesinger *et al.*, focus on a single issue: violence against women. So despite both researchers' emphasis on 'diversity' (in production, genre and response), this leads to significant methodological differences.

Methodological differences

Schlesinger *et al.*,'s 'everyday lives' focus is not that of the pleasures of watching television, but of fearing risk and experiencing crimes of violence.

As they say, most of the fear of crime research had been of a quantitative nature, very little of which tries to 'situate women in the specifics of their everyday lives and relationships' (1992, p. 17). Much of this quantitative work has tended to adopt a simplistic and deterministic understanding of the media in this process. For example, disparities between women's (and older people's) fear of crime and the statistical likelihood of their being victims of crime have conventionally been used to suggest that, on the one hand, these people are 'irrational' in their fear, and that on the other hand a 'sensationalist' media is the likely cause of this irrationality.

As in the case of Buckingham's concerns with conventional put-downs of soap opera audiences, this 'fear of crime' tradition overestimates the power of the media and undervalues the daily-life experience of the audience. Schlesinger *et al.*, argue that the variety (local and national) of media has tended to be ignored via a research emphasis on nationally networked television. Moreover, Stanko and others have shown that not only do official crime statistics and victim surveys under-represent violent crimes against women, but in addition women exist in a 'hostile and intimidating atmosphere' (Schlesinger *et al.*, 1992, p. 39) which directly impacts on their perception of personal safety. In other words, as we also indicated in the CCRR 'fear of crime' research (Tulloch *et al.*, 1998), statistics are blind to an entire spectrum of perceived risk which meaningfully (not 'irrationally') increases women's fear of crime. These perceived risks may be explored via a wide range of media forms and genres – hence the need to analyse much more than a single 'text'.

It is these two aspects of 'diversity' – of media genres and forms; and of women's differentially situated experience according to biography, nationality, class and ethnicity – which shaped Schlesinger *et al.*,'s research plan and methodology. While the focus of research was television, it was thought important to vary the genres that respondents watched (soap opera, documentary, televised film, and the popular crime reconstruction genre represented by *Crimewatch, UK*). Fourteen viewing groups (constituted according to differences in experience of violence, national background, ethnicity and class) spent one day watching and discussing these selected programmes.

Whereas Buckingham's major emphasis was on the *processual* relationship of different circuits of communication (leading to an analysis of the interplay of production, circulation and reception) and on how the soap opera form enables viewers to produce meaning, Schlesinger *et al.*, were more interested in how *experiential* differences (in relation to violence) and social differences (of gender, ethnicity, class, etc.) generated similar or different responses to different genres. Schlesinger *et al.*,'s approach then was fundamentally comparative (of genres, and of differentially experienced/situated audiences), while Buckingham's was formal and processual. This, as well as the different (cultural studies/sociology) disciplinary backgrounds of the researchers helps account for the very different methodological approaches taken.

It was not the actual numbers of respondents (Buckingham had 60, Schlesinger *et al.*, had 91) or of focus groups (Buckingham had 12, Schlesinger *et al.*, 14) that marked their significant difference in relation to the 'quantitative'. Beginning, like Buckingham, with focus groups, Schlesinger *et al.*, argue that outcomes of group discussions are only 'indicative . . . of certain views and lines of argument, rather than definitive'. As the authors say, 'Often . . . it is difficult for readers [of research findings] to understand *how* certain materials are chosen over others, and *why* certain quotes take precedence over those which never appear' (1992, p. 31) Three more generalising processes need to be then considered. First, these perceptions and reactions 'must be located through a wider contextual approach' (Schlesinger *et al.*, 1992, p. 17). Understanding the 'commonalities and variations in women's reading of television' requires knowledge of their biographies, particularly (in this study) their experiences of violence. Second, these biographical experiences should be understood within a wider familial and social structural framework (primarily, as this study developed, in relation to ethnicity, as class and national location were soon found to be less significant). Third, standardised measures (rather than unstructured interviews) were introduced into the focus groups so that 'we could more accurately depict and understand how cultural and social experiences shaped reactions to televised violence' (1992, p. 18).

A symptomatic result of these differences in method is evident in Buckingham's and Schlesinger *et al.*,'s analysis of ethnicity and *EastEnders*. Buckingham gives equal weight to the factors of class, race, gender and age right up to the final pages of his book, while concluding rather impressionistically that there was an absence of explicit reference to ethnicity in his respondents' discussion. Typically of his processual analysis, he argues that this might be seen as a consequence of the deliberate suppression of ethnic difference during production as the producers sought to provide a positive representation of a 'multicultural' community. In contrast, Schlesinger *et al.*, are able to demonstrate quantitatively the importance

> of the experience of violence and of ethnicity in shaping interpretations and reactions. For example, women with experience of violence were more likely to express fear of crime and to voice concern about the reporting of violence against women in the media. They were also more likely to say that they would like to see more control over the portrayal of women in the media. Two other potentially significant background variables, class and nationality, were not of major importance in shaping reactions and interpretations.
>
> (1992, p. 41)

This early quantitative finding led the authors to concentrate most of their book on ethnicity and experience of violence 'as the major determinants of varying interpretations of media representations of violence against women'

(1992, p. 42). This emphasis had two advantages: it directly linked issues of gender representation to situated experiences of violence; and it also focused the authors' attention on the relationship between experience of violence and ethnicity in their *qualitative* analysis of women's response to *EastEnders*.

> For Afro-Caribbean women, regardless of their experience of violence, the issue which dominated discussion was the programme's portrayal of the black community. Indications of the importance of this dimension have already emerged from our discussion of the quantitative findings. . . . [B]oth English Afro-Caribbean and English Asian groups sensed that the episode was not an innocent portrayal of domestic violence, but one that was attempting to pass a broader, negative, comment on mixed-race relationships . . . Afro-Caribbean women found . . . that the mixed-race relationship confused the issue of domestic violence, and that by using a black woman as a victim, the programme was distancing white society from the issue. . . . Embedded within the episode for one Afro-Caribbean group was a white man's domination of a black woman through force. This was not only domestic violence; it had the added dimension of being a racist attack.
>
> (Schlesinger *et al.*, 1992, pp. 99–100)

This relationship of quantitative with qualitative research avoids the impressionistic kind of 'on the one hand/on the other hand' comments about ethnicity and 'tokenism' in Buckingham's account. It also potentially feeds into further quantitative research, explaining Afro-Caribbean women's doubts about *EastEnders* 'doing a good job of handling social issues'.

Schlesinger *et al.*,'s approach also avoids a 'quantitative' problem raised by Buckingham. In discussing focus groups composed of black students, Buckingham says that he remains 'uneasy about making generalizations about these on the basis of a fairly small sample' (1987, p. 159). One of his 'reservations about previous research on media audiences is that it has all too often led to rather simplistic causal connections between the readings produced by certain groups and their social position: thus groups are seen to respond in particular ways *because* they are black, or female, or working-class. Furthermore, such classifications typically ignore individual's own perceptions of their social position' (1992, p. 159). Schlesinger *et al.*, make the same criticism about 'group' focused audience research, but add: 'It is not that belonging to a given social category or having had a particular experience crudely determines responses; rather, they tend to provide a discourse, or variety of discourses, for the interpretation of the wider culture, of which television is a significant part' (1992, p. 30).

By drawing on both quantitative and qualitative research together, Schlesinger *et al.*, are able to point not only to the greater salience of 'race' than 'class' or 'nationality' as group responses to television violence; but, in the specific case of the *EastEnders* 'domestic violence' episode, they are able to show how Afro-Caribbean women drew on the complicating extra discourse of 'racism' in their caution about the social value of the programme. This, then, helps to explain the further quantitative finding that Afro-Caribbean women, in contrast to both white and Asian women, found the programme much more 'disturbing' and 'offensive', and much less 'exciting' or 'entertaining'.

So while Schlesinger *et al.*, did not lose entirely the advantage of unstructured focus group discussion – since they began with open-ended questions that allowed participants to refer to whatever in the programme was most salient for them – the standardised focus group questions, combined with the quantitative survey, allowed both for comparability across groups and for a sophisticated approach to the qualitative interpretation of meaning.

Having made the case in this chapter for both a greater emphasis on anxiety about risk in audience responses (after the familiar focus on pleasure in earlier chapters) and for a combined qualitative/quantitative approach, I want next to compare two different multi-generic audience analyses that adopt a qualitative/quantitative approach, to examine in them different methodological advantages and disadvantages.

|6|

Two approaches to 'documentary'

This chapter will not attempt to summarise or critique the huge literature on 'TV violence', since this has been done many times before. What it will try to do is begin to focus on audience's symbolic resources, whether these be experiential (e.g. women's knowledge gained through lived experience of domestic violence) or mediated (e.g. children's learned narrative schemas for 'what police do', 'what workers do', etc.). 'Cognitive' approaches of this kind are not fashionable in some quarters, but in my view audience knowledge (or the lack of it) is a crucial aspect of the so-called 'semiotic democracy' of the media. To draw attention explicitly to this issue of audience knowledge (as an important aspect of human agency) I have chosen to focus on audience research relating to documentary, since this TV genre is (in the eyes of both TV producers and in public perception) especially dedicated to 'information' and knowledge flow. My focus will be to compare multi-genre audience research by Schlesinger *et al.*, and Tulloch and Tulloch (1992, 1993), while focusing mainly on the 'documentary' aspects of their work.

I will begin by going a little further into Schlesinger *et al.*,'s case study, because there are a number of similarities between these two research projects.

- First – and unusually within a cultural studies framework – both Schlesinger *et al.*, and the Tullochs combine qualitative with quantitative methodologies.
- Second, both adopt a multi-genre rather than single-programme approach. Schlesinger *et al.*, screened for their participants a soap opera, a crime reconstruction series, a fictionalised 'documentary', and a feature film which had been shown on television. The Tullochs screened for their child/teenage viewers a soap opera, a cop series, a documentary, a war series, a science fiction series, and a talk-back studio discussion.
- Third, both research projects specifically chose their television genres to revisit the 'effects of violence' debate from a media/cultural studies perspective that was concerned with issues of genre and representation.

- Fourth, both sets of researchers were aware of the problems of objectivism associated with quantitative research, and so attempted to be reflexive.
- Fifth, both research teams focused on *discourses* about violence rather than behavioural effects.

There was, however, a significant difference between the two research projects. Schlesinger *et al.*,'s research, while quantitative in part, is designed to focus on situated responses by comparing women who have or have not experienced violence. The Tullochs' approach is developmental rather than situated, in so far as they argue that when dealing with the child and teenage audience, cognitive-developmental features of discourse competence and construction are as important as cultural differences (of gender, class, etc.). In this respect their analysis of children watching television violence is closer to that of Hodge and Tripp (see chapter 7), than to Schlesinger *et al.*

Nevertheless, there are, as we have seen enough similarities between the Schlesinger *et al.*, and Tulloch projects to make comparison very worthwhile. An additional similarity in the case of the programmes that will be discussed here is that both sets of researchers chose a programme that portrayed *the use of violence by those in authority in society*.

Schlesinger *et al.*: experience as symbolic resource

The example of 'documentary' here was Roger Graef's *Closing Ranks*. This was in fact a fictionalisation of his earlier book *Talking Blues*, based upon interviews with 500 police officers in 12 different forces. Graef had already produced the acclaimed documentary series on the police, *Operation Carter* (about Regional Crime Squad No. 5), and *Police*, which, as a result of its 'fly-on-the-wall' observation of police harassment of women and suspects, had also been very controversial. Graef thus made *Closing Ranks* from the 'inside', and though it did 'not purport to be drama-documentary as such, both the characterisation and elements of the plot can be seen to be derived from the tales told by Graef's police informants – and their wives' (Schlesinger *et al.*, 1992, p. 107). Schlesinger *et al.*, also note that significant sections of their audiences treated *Closing Ranks* as 'real life' documentary; as did the panel of senior police officers and counsellors who were shown on-air discussing the programme immediately after its television screening. 'It is evident, therefore, that the film has its roots in the stresses and strains of the lives of police officers as told to its director, and in that sense it certainly has a documentary (and well documented) origin. According to the publicity for *Closing Ranks*, "The really disturbing aspect ... is that all of the events of the film are based on real incidents"' (Schlesinger *et al.*, 1992, p. 108).

Closing Ranks is about the intertwining of police corruption with domestic violence within the police force, whereas the documentary screened by the Tullochs, Ken Loach's *Which Side Are You On?*, was an 'arts' programme which emphasised support between wives and husbands during the 1984 British miners' strike. But there are intriguing comparabilities between the two programmes nevertheless. Both are by television 'auteurs' (Graef and Loach) who had created high-level controversy via their uncompromising cameras. Indeed, Loach was forced into an 'arts' format because he was finding it difficult to get support to make his 'political' documentaries for television. *Which Side Are You On?* therefore focused in part on the miners' wives' (and children's) poetry and songs, justifying the 'arts' documentary tag with this 'folksong' response, while still showing significant film footage and vox-pop accounts of police violence during the miners' strike.

A second similarity is that both Graef's and Loach's programmes were deeply embedded in the broader local/national police politics of the 1980s. As Schlesinger *et al.*, say of Graef, his

> investigations were conducted during the 1980s, a period when there was increasing controversy over such issues as police corruption and racism as well as major confrontations with the trade union movement (notably the miners' and print unions). This was also the decade that saw major inner-city riots and much concern in civil libertarian quarters about the political uses of the police by Mrs Thatcher's administration.
>
> (1992, p. 107)

It was this last feature that was the central question of Loach's work; while the political ambience of the time took Graef's programme into the issue of police violence against the anti-nuclear demonstrators at Greenham Common, and thus into the public 'protest' arena too. *Closing Ranks* draws on Graef's view that rather than there being a few 'rotten apples' in the British police force, it is sustained by a culture of violence, and this is Loach's theme also. Graef's programme, however, links this to the taboo subject of police domestic violence, while Loach's links it to an overall global–national culture of government, army, police and business control.

Schlesinger *et al.*, were unable to recruit non-white women to watch *Closing Ranks*. Consequently, the important race/ethnicity theme of their larger research project could not be developed. On the other hand, they did find greater class differences in response to this programme than most others they screened. Among the women who had not experienced violence, working-class women felt it was a realistic portrayal of how the police function and of marital relations generally, and they were sympathetic to the fate of the policeman's wife, arguing that programmes like that were of value to women watching who might be experiencing similar events. In contrast middle-class women were more shocked at the representation of the police (seeing it as less 'normal'), were less sympathetic to the policeman's wife (blaming working-class mores for both the husband's and wife's behaviour), and were less sure of the programme's value to women watching.

> Women with experience of violence offered strong reactions to *Closing Ranks*; almost all of them told us that they took the drama 'seriously' or 'very seriously' . . . and they offered immediate reactions to the drama in terms of their personal experiences.
>
> (Schlesinger *et al.*, 1992, p. 120)

A far greater percentage of these women saw 'domestic violence' as the main theme of the programme (compared with 'police corruption'); and three-quarters of them found the depiction 'realistic'. Women who had experienced violence stressed that the programme was showing that *any male* was capable of domestic violence (hence the choice of one in authority); and they repeatedly emphasised the theme of transmission of violence from generation to generation illustrated by the represented relationship between the policeman and his son. Around 70 per cent of the women who had experienced violence could identify with the characters depicted in the programme, whereas only 36 per cent of women who had not experienced violence expressed this view. The majority of the women with experience of violence had been the victims of domestic assaults, and they related significantly to the scenes of physical and mental cruelty portrayed in the programme. One feature here was that whereas a number of women with no experience of violence (particularly middle-class ones) felt that the wife was unsympathetic to her husband's sexual needs prior to his rape of her, women with experience of violence regarded her reaction as entirely understandable. Moreover, the policeman's routine degradation of his wife in front of their son was seen, by these latter women, as part of a systematic pattern of male misuse of power. Unlike the difference of view among women who had not experienced violence as to whether this graphic depiction of domestic rape by a policeman should have been shown, women who had experienced violence were quite unanimous that it should – especially because it might enable women to *talk* about their experiences (one woman in this group said it had taken her two decades to talk about it).

The strength of Schlesinger *et al.*,'s research plan in comparing *experiential* background is very evident in relation to *Closing Ranks*, as indeed elsewhere in their study. As they say, viewer responses to the various TV genres they screened demonstrated a 'patterned diversity', dependent in part on factors such as class and ethnicity, but also – and crucially – according to the relation of the violence seen to their own situated memories. 'Viewing televised violence may, for some women, involve the recreation of a painful and dangerous personal experience; for others it approximates a feared event; and for others still, it is merely the depiction of a relatively abstract and distant event' (1992, p. 164).

In fact, there are at least three strong outcomes deriving from the methodological/theoretical approach that Schlesinger *et al.*, have taken.

Their study enables them to draw attention to:

1. The systematic (quantified) diversity among viewers according to ethnicity (the Afro-Caribbean women's response to *EastEnders*, for example, via the view that this programme was making a racist comment about mixed marriages; or the Asian women's distancing of themselves from the situation of the extended group rape of a white woman in the film, *The Accused*, on the basis that their own cultural controls for gender and dress would protect them from this) and class (e.g. the middle-class womens' refusal to think badly about the police, and their negativity to the policeman's wife).
2. The fact that the clearest differentiating factor among their viewers was experience or lack of experience of violence, across all genres. Here there was the additional finding that women who had experienced violence offered more nuanced, subtle and complex interpretations of televised violence; showed greater resistance to be 'taken in' by male justifications for violence (that drew on their own family circumstances, sexual frustration, etc.); and were more demanding in their expectations of producers of these programmes. They emphasised the importance of such issues being screened – for them it was the relevance and social importance of these television representations not matters of 'pleasure' or 'fantasy' that were most salient.
3. The role of gender in the *similarities* shown by women with different experiential, class and ethnic backgrounds, so that all women showed significant fear of male violence, especially rape. 'With rape, the distinctions based on women's experience breaks down. In effect, every woman could identify with the fear of rape' (Schlesinger *et al.*, 1992, p. 166). The researchers were thus able to reconsider the supposed 'irrationality' of women, frequently expressed in fear of crime research; i.e. that it is young men who are statistically more likely to suffer violence than women; and when women do experience sexual or physical violence it is more likely to be by an intimate, even while they fear more the 'unknown stranger'. Building on the in-depth and detailed observations from their focus groups, and the differences in response to the different types of violence represented via different programme genres, Schlesinger *et al.*, could argue that if, compared with men, 'the probability is low of being attacked and raped by a stranger while on the way home at night . . . the *severity* of the attack is high' and thus 'the level of fear is likely to be much greater' (1992, p. 169).

Overall, these strengths of Schlesinger *et al.*,'s research support their own claims for the value of their combined methodology and multi-genre approach.

Selecting diverse genres of programmes aimed to show the depiction of violence in a variety of audiovisual forms, each with quite distinct contents but still thematically connected. The aim was also to present a comparison of violence against women with other forms of crime, to provide elements of ethnic and class diversity in the programmes themselves, and to offer an overall 'package' of viewing in which the type and amount of violence increased in severity. Thus the viewers might be 'eased' into increasingly difficult topics, and comparisons of response might consequently be made across both diverse programmes and viewing groups. This proved fruitful, increasing the strength of generalizations that might be made to women's reactions to violence against women on television.

(1992, p. 169)

It was 'increasing the strength of generalizations' *combined with* the advantage of tracing detailed, nuanced but patterned differences via qualitative methods that was clearly the target of Schlesinger *et al.*,'s research – as it was in the case of the Tullochs' research on children viewing violence.

As I said, the weakness of the latter's research compared with Schlesinger *et al.*,'s was the lack of a basis in the situated experience of violence. There would, of course, have been ethical problems in doing this; and it would also have probably prevented the Tullochs undertaking a quantitative study. In any case, their focus was a different one: the cognitive differences in children of different ages in understanding and interpreting the various types of television violence portrayed. There were also advantages their study had over the Schlesinger *et al.*, research which are worth indicating: particularly their greater attention to a synthesis of 'global', 'textual' and 'audience' readings of the various television genres. In contrast to both the American communication tradition of TV violence research, which focused on the powerful effects of television on passive audiences, and the cultural studies emphasis on the negotiating skills of active audiences within the 'semiotic democracy' of television, the Tullochs focused centrally on issues of power *and* agency.

Tulloch and Tulloch: 'structuration' and agency

The researchers' opening theoretical agenda was to restore what Murdock called the missing context of audience studies: 'we need to explore how cultural production and consumption are structured by wider economic and symbolic formations' (Murdock, 1989, p. 229). At the same time the researchers wanted to examine how both cultural production and consumption are agentive in recasting convention and persistent symbolic structures. Their intention was to take the familiar cultural studies notion of 'resistance' beyond audience analysis to production and textual study also.

Thus the Tullochs emphasised:

- agency in television production with relation to violence, using as their audience texts popular TV programmes which were proactive and reflexive about the issue of violence in various state agencies and institutions;
- agency in audience readings of those texts via tracing children's interpretive schemata, discourse topic saliency, understanding, evaluation and behavioural possibilities and solutions;
- structured inequalities in the distribution of symbolic resources (including situation models lodged in memory) via differences of class, gender and ethnicity which could lead to a narrowing of understanding around the dominant definitions of action in the world (including behavioural possibilities and solutions).

In particular, the Tullochs asked, even where television producers take up the issues of violence and cultural representation in alternative and oppositional ways (as Murdock encouraged), to what extent were these textual interventions understood, how were they evaluated, and what new behavioural possibilities did they offer audiences, particularly those audiences disempowered by gender, class or ethnicity at which they might be aimed?

Given this agenda, the researchers focused on television texts that drew attention to 'structure', and the (often misused) power of what Althusser called 'ideological state apparatuses': the power of the army through the ideological indoctrination of basic training, the power of the police and government against a miners' strike, the patriarchal machismo conveyed by (often violent) televised sport, the familial power of males over their wives and sons in cases of domestic violence. On the other hand, they examined 'symbolic resources' and discourses as cognitive as well as ideological 'cultural competences' – instead of separating these two areas between fields of study (e.g. where psychology deals with the 'cognitive' and sociology/cultural studies with the 'ideological').

As an example of this approach I will focus on their 'textual', and audience 'narrative schema' approach to compare briefly responses to two of the programmes they screened to children, the documentary *Which Side Are You On?* (*WSAYO*) and the soap opera, *A Country Practice* (*ACP*); the former representing police brutality to striking workers, the latter (picking up the theme of Graef's production) a husband's violence to his wife after he (but not she) fails to gain promotion at work.

The texts

A major textual focus of the research was in examining the social categorisation of the 'communities' via which the programme positioned audiences in representing conflict and institutional violence. This approach drew on the combination of social psychological and critical inquiry in Potter and Reicher's (1987) article, 'Discourses of community and conflict'. Here,

Potter and Reicher examined the linguistic representation of a British 'race riot', isolating common features of the community repertoire and indicating the markedly divergent inflection of different texts' characterisation of police involvement. The Tullochs extended this study of the relationship of structural violence and divergent accounts of community not only to audio-visual texts but to audience readings as well.

Potter and Reicher establish a 'positive' community repertoire consisting of a set of predicates (friendly, warm, happy, harmonious, close-knit, inte-grated, tight, mature, grows, evolves, acts, knows, feels) and metaphors (spatial, organic, agency). Some positive metaphors in the repertoire draw on *spatial* contexts, predicating 'community' with 'close-knit'. A second positive form of metaphor is *temporal*, where the imagery draws on evolv-ing and harmonious organic associations: 'a community is something which has a natural pace of growth'. Third, there are metaphors 'of "the commu-nity" as *agent*, with both cognitive powers (knowledge, feeling, etc.) and powers of agency: the "community" can "act" or hit back" ' (Potter and Reicher, 1987, p. 31).

The domestic violence text *(A Country Practice)* used by the Tullochs focused particularly on the metaphor of community as agent; i.e. on cogni-tive power (the *revelation* of domestic violence) enabling the power of agency, as doctors and police 'hit back'.

A Country Practice (ACP) was established as a series which, in its found-ing producer's opinion, would appeal to every Australian's dream of giving up the rat-race of the city and setting up a smallholding in the country. In this sense its appeal was designedly mythical and pastoral, gesturing to the Australian legend of bush camaraderie in contrast to a long, popular media history (Tulloch, 1981) of city meanness, pace, fragmentation and exploita-tion. But *ACP* was obviously also designed as a commercial product, a peak-viewing soap opera running at two hours per week in a series/serial format. The series aspect had a social/medical 'issues' orientation, which week by week took up (and closed off over two episodes) a particular 'prob-lem' (teenage alcoholism, Alzheimer's disease, rural unemployment, youth suicide, glue sniffing, domestic violence, AIDS, etc.). The serial aspect estab-lished the 'soapy' signature of on-going romance, marriage and marital break-up set amongst the other interpersonal relationships of a small coun-try community, with its local 'old woman gossip', its bartender, its police-man, etc. Here soap opera's 'ideal mother' (of Modleski, Seiter *et al.*: see chapter 5) can be seen to be situated in a close-knit community; in fact, the doctor's receptionist and nurse who is the wife of the local policeman. At two hours air-time per week, the series was voracious for current 'issues'; and as its founding producer pointed out, this inclined him to centre his drama in either one or other or the two locales where 'issues come walking through the door: a hospital or a police station' (Tulloch and Moran, 1986, p. 28). His choice of a hospital established the medical professional space as the focal centre of the friendly, warm, happy, harmonious, close-knit, integrated and tight 'country' community. Although the community's agency is a collective one, where all residents pull together to save walkers from bush fires, farmers from drought, and teenagers from alcoholism and unemployment, the weekly focus where the community 'acts' is the hospital. It is there that even societal problems like unemployment became, in the title of one episode, 'a health hazard'.

Further, although *ACP*'s producer chose the hospital rather than the police station as his narrative focus, police activity is in fact closely related to the hospital in two ways: first, medical problems such as the results of drunken driving or domestic violence are at the same time police problems, leading to the policeman visiting the hospital to interview patients; second, the policeman, Frank Gilroy, is married to a local nurse. As a result, it was a normal occurrence when, in the domestic violence episode used in the research, the policeman's relationship to Karen, the battered wife, was initially positioned within the hospital community. As a professional 'helper' (who instrumentalises the doctors' advice to Karen to take legal action against her husband), the policeman is very much part of the friendly, harmonious and close-knit local professional community. He is part of the intragroup, within which legal action (and medical help) is represented as neutral and unproblematical. The fact that this is, of course, a narratively constructed rather than a 'natural' position is clarified by one of the (adult) audience responses to this *ACP* text: 'Interesting that policeman is shown as sympathetic to the woman since it would appear that often the police are highly unsympathetic to victims of domestic violence.'

In this context, it is the husband, Barry, who is outside the community, even though he is part of the same family group as Karen and his son Mark. This is indicated by the fact that his actions directly negate the warm, friendly, happy, harmonious, close-knit predicates of the community. Consequently the family home becomes a place of hurt, coldness, unhappiness, distance and alienation for Karen; and it is the hospital which is her temporary home with her son. Overall, the domestic violence episode, and *ACP* generally, established a consensual world in which positive state action was progressively removing the evil face of patriarchy within the family. It is a crucial message of this episode that Barry's son, Mark (who is turning to imitative violence at school), needs to be legally separated from his father, just so that the males of the future might be different (thus addressing a crucial worry of Schlesinger *et al.*,'s audience response to *Closing Ranks*). In this sense the text is concerned with the future of the country community as well as its present.

Which Side Are You On? (*WSAYO*) is also concerned with a temporal sense of community which goes beyond its physical presence. This is conveyed by a group of miners' wives who assert that the miners are not striking for their jobs alone, but for those of their sons. 'They understand that their dad's doing it for them. I've got three boys, and I'm hoping when my kids leave school, they've got jobs.' The sense here is of a very local community extended into a future where sons work exactly as their fathers have done. Geographically, too, the community is close-knit, tight and closely integrated, as well as socially extended. The initial community is the coal-mining village which is threatened, as one woman puts it, by the sudden appearance of hundreds of policemen 'out of nowhere'. Unlike the *ACP* episode, these policemen are not part of the community, but outside it and against it. They are heavily armed with baseball bats (as still photographs reveal), with which they bash picketers, denying them medical aid, and chasing them into private homes where, according to the vox-pop narration, they crushed one woman's head between door and jamb when she resisted them entry. This detail and the refusal of medical aid was to be picked up in many of the children's summaries – a marked contrast to the medically *centred* help of the *ACP* episode, where the helpful policeman's visit to Karen's home is represented as a visit to an alien place, and his conversation with Barry is shot through the mesh of the security door, a deliberate device to mark Barry and his personal space as 'other' from the community. In this doorway scene, in contrast to the one described in *WSAYO*, it is the husband not the policeman who is outside the community.

As well as the different positioning of the police in the two texts, there is another marked difference of *WSAYO* from *ACP*. The country-based soap opera establishes a timeless (organically evolving) community embedded (in the producer's view) in every Australian's subconscious, and, as such, *pastorally* defined in opposition to 'the city'. In contrast, the village community of *WSAYO*, though local and close-knit, is positioned in the miners' 'gritty doco' vox-pop discourse at the centre of an entire industrialised nation, 'Once that colliery closes, there's whole communities die. When you attack a mining community, you attack a lot more people besides, and I believe it's time people did realise this.' As the miners explain it, the struggle against the police is part of a wider struggle against the government and 'the bosses' who are part of a military/industrial complex. Thatcher's minister responsible for coalmine closures, MacGregor, is an agent of a new economic and political order. 'Mr MacGregor's not just going to close our collieries, he's going to close a hell of a lot more work down as well' – and the miners here instance the steelworks which are reliant on coal, the railways and many other ancillary industries like engineering. Consequently, the miners' struggle is not primarily a financial one, for more pay, but against the government itself which is imposing a new post-industrial order.

As the opening sequence of the documentary makes clear (via a miner's voice-over while we watch police preventing pickets reaching their factories), the police tell the strikers that 'If you do get rid of our government, we'll be the next government, the police will be the next government.' The 'fight for the future', then, is not only for jobs within the local community. It is, more widely, a matter of class struggle against an advancing police state. Working-class folksongs and parodies of popular childrens' songs like 'The Laughing Policeman' are used by Loach to present a very divisive position. It is in these songs particularly that the need for solidarity with workers (*Which Side Are You On?*) is emphasised, but also with a wider community of resistance against the 'chap in the comical hat' (the police-man).

> If you're black or just brown,
> If you're jobless and down,
> If you speak for a world which is saner,
> If you stand up and fight
> For what is yours by right,
> If you're an anti-nuclear campaigner,
> Remember the chap in the comical hat,
> He's one of humanity's crosses.
> Wherever the trouble,
> Whatever the struggle,
> He'll be on the side of the bosses.

Whereas the community in *ACP* is defined pastorally and romantically in opposition to the city, the community of *Which Side Are You On?* is that of the oppressed pit village, defined in terms of Left politics in opposition to the post-industrial power complex of government, media, police and bosses. *ACP*, then, emerges from a producer's marketing conception of the strength of what Raymond Williams called a residual structure of feeling: in Australia a sense of country solipsism and anti-globalisation that was to be marked also in the the unexpected rise to political prominence of Pauline Hanson's One Nation Party. *WSAYO*, in contrast, is thoroughly embedded in Loach's modernist Marxist critique of Thatcherism and predicting the 'risk modernity' soon to be described by Beck.

As a radical producer working on British television, stories have not come walking through the door for Ken Loach, as they did for the producer of *A Country Practice*. Loach found it increasingly difficult in the more con-servative years of Thatcher to get his programmes to air. Some have been cancelled after being commissioned and made; others, such as his documen-tary on the British miners' strike, could only be made under the alibi of an 'Arts' programme. Loach was ostensibly putting to air 'songs and poetry' of the working class. As a result of this political and institutional strategy, Loach's documentary is formally much less accessible to schoolchildren than a conventional voice-of-god narrated documentary. The Tullochs' choice of documentary for their research project thus offered a representa-tion of police very different from the conventional narratives of cop series. The 'Arts/documentary' conjunction is a complex one which brings together documentary-style 'vox-pop' talking heads, 'news'-type footage of police violence, and filmed poetry and song. Consequently, the students had to handle an unaccustomed mix of generic styles, as well as an untypical polit-ical discourse.

Most of these difficulties would be as real for British as for Australian students. As the researchers note, the alternative kinds of television production that Murdock called for can be made more difficult for audiences to even understand (let alone 'influence their way of looking') by the institutional conditions in which they have to be made. Scheduling here is looked at very differently from Sparks' 'doxic' hypothesis; but rather as a political matter which shapes the timing and form of a television intervention, and thus the cognitive 'access' available to audiences.

The researchers' focus on analysing the 'texts' of violence thus led on into their conceptualisation of audience's narrative understandings, but within a reflexive methodological framework.

Reflexive aspects

Following Murdock, the Tullochs positioned themselves theoretically within a critical realist tradition of inquiry, with an emphasis on going beyond empiricist observation and measurement to the analysis of the 'underlying structures that organize the making and taking of meaning in everyday life' (Murdock, 1989, p. 227). Given this assumption about 'underlying structures', and also their own focus on institutionalised violence, the researchers designed their questionnaires to contain an 'underlying structure' cognitive response as well as a 'descriptive level' response. For instance, in the *A Country Practice* domestic violence episode, the husband, Barry, became extremely jealous and aggressive towards his wife as he was knocked back for promotion (in competition with a woman), while his wife, Karen, got promotion from the hospital kitchen to nurse's aid. For the strongly female-dominated production team, Karen's promotion symbolised her escape from domesticity, both at home and work; while Barry's violence resulted from a sense of inadequacy, determined profoundly by patriarchal power relations within the family. In descriptive terms, Barry did not like Karen working because (as he put it) she did not do the housework properly. But in terms of an underlying patriarchal structure, he did not like her working because it made him feel inadequate as a man, both at work and at home. In this sense, the Tullochs' multiple-choice cognitive questions, containing 'wrong' responses (e.g. 'In *WSAYO* the miners were striking for more money') and 'narratively confused' responses (e.g. 'In *WSAYO* the workers were on strike because of anger over police violence') as well as 'descriptive' and 'underlying' options were structured by their own (and in this case the producers') theoretical assumptions.

However, the Tullochs argued that they also wanted to examine school students' everyday explanatory discourses as separately as possible from the researchers' own structuring framework. Consequently, immediately after viewing the edited sequences of *ACP* and *WSAYO*, the students were asked to write a narrative account of 'what it was about'. One side of an A4 page

(18 lines) was provided for this pre-questionnaire task. It was important, the researchers argued, that this task was done before the questionnaire, because they wanted to tap into the children's everyday explanatory schemata. In asking 'what it was about', the researchers were asking students for the 'topic of discourse' or 'gist' (van Dijk, 1984) of the episode, and in doing so trying to track the text-in-memory for each student. What the researchers were trying to examine via this particular method were the differences in processing and memorising of van Dijk's notion of the 'text in full' by students of different age, class and gender. Each student's choice of discourse topic indicated the main *meaning* (as hierarchy of discourses) of the text's detailed information for her/him in the research context.

This emphasis on a particular temporal ordering of audience research methods was not to say, of course, that the students' pre-questionnaire summaries were uninfluenced by the research process. As with their questionnaire but in a different way, the researchers had to take reflexive account of their status as 'TV violence' researchers in relation to the narrative summaries too. Given the ethical requirement to obtain parental approval for children's participation in the research, many students knew that they were part of a 'TV violence' project. Sometimes (particularly at year 4 level) 'about violence' constituted an authoritative topic of discourse for these students. This 'about violence' discourse topic functioned rather like the 'topical sentences' analysed by van Dijk which provide macro-structures and thus facilitate comprehension. Particularly in the case of WSAYO, which challenged conventional 'police helper' scripts and so confused some of the younger children, the researchers' letters to parents acted like a sentence at the beginning of the texts they screened: 'This is about TV violence.' However, in most cases this was not the discourse topic chosen in assigning global coherence to the texts.

Audience's interpretive schemata

Tulloch and Tulloch chose their audience groups for ACP and WSAYO from years 4, 7 and 10 in Sydney schools (395 school students), together with a comparative sample of a few tertiary-level adult groups. These different age groups were chosen to examine developmental changes in discourse competence as well as measure class and gender differences. In their larger multi-genre study (of about 1000 students) they focused both on students' everyday interpretive discourses in relation to the salience of violence in television texts (as expressed in narrative summaries and in interviews) and on the relationship between students' socio-cognitive resources and textual meaning (as expressed in cognitive, evaluative and behavioural options via quantitative surveys).

They argued that critical theory had been noticeably absent in the area of cognitive and developmental theory, which is nevertheless a crucial area for investigation if we are to understand children's responses to television violence. Drawing attention to Hodge and Tripp's work (see chapter 7) in examining the relationship between television and linguistic development in children aged 1 to 12, they agreed with them that children should not be constituted 'as a vulnerable group' in research assumptions about television violence. But their view was that Hodge and Tripp's reliance on a Piagetian developmental framework led to a minimising of the important developments that take place during adolescence, and of the differences between adolescent and adult thinking.

- There is no space here to go far into the researchers' theoretical amalgam of psychological and sociological 'script' and narrative development concepts among children and young people (see Tulloch and Tulloch, 1992a). Suffice to say that they drew on Mandler and Johnson (1977) on story schemata, variation and story recall; Gunter (1977), Berry and Clifford (1985) on news story sequencing and understanding of central propositions; Wellman (1990) on young children's ability to explain the world through commonsense theories, in particular according to a belief/desire psychology, and on the extension from a commonsense psychology to a number of other mid-childhood and adolescence framework theories of economic, political and social processes (it is here that the Tullochs' main developmental focus lies); Collins (1983) on younger children's inability to derive implicit inferences (central to understanding variant or unusual events in the narrative); the Glasgow Media Group (Philo *et al.*, 1977) on conventional media causal chains of explanation in relation to strike action; van Dijk (1984) on the use of narrative summaries to establish the operation of children's commonsense framework theories of social action via their reduction of narrative conflict and violence to 'topics of discourse'.
- Similarly, I have only space to describe the researchers' classification of discourse topics for quantitative purposes. They isolated: (a) 'point'-less discourse topics ('I didn't understand it – it was confusing'); (b) research-led discourse topics ('it was about too much violence on TV'); (c) text-narrative-focused discourse topics, ranging from partial script/role-allocated responses ('I thought it was about police men trying to arrest men and women. I thought it was disgusting, terrible, they weren't nice at all') to full script/role allocation ('I thought it was about the police being too aggressive towards the miners that were striking'; (d) high-level propositions ('I think the employers called in the police to control the strike'); and (e) meta-textual discourse topics ('The documentary was unashamedly pro miner – no attempt to show the other side or talk to police about their view of events').
- The data from several hundred open-ended 'discourse topic' accounts and over two thousand cognitive and behavioural option surveys are too extensive even to summarise here (see Tulloch and Tulloch, 1993). But it is worth pointing to a few key findings that relate to this chapter's theme

of children's symbolic resources and the relevance of this for audience agency and power.

1. At year 4 level, police are consistently defined as 'being friends' and within the community – thus leading to considerable narrative confusion over *WSAYO*. Sometimes (at all age levels), this 'script' confusion was understood by projecting it as 'other' ('The movie was about violence in other countries') or by explaining it inter-textually via then current news footage of massed protests against Communism in Eastern Europe ('I think the video was about people protesting and communism').

2. Narrative-text-focused accounts with full script/role allocation increased markedly and systematically in years 7 and 10. Middle-class responses in this category were significantly higher than working-class in years 4 and 7. In years 7 and 10 more boys (46 per cent and 78 per cent) gave this response than girls (35 per cent and 65 per cent), though, as for class, there was a systematic increase compared with the responses in year 4 (M 18 per cent, F 16 per cent). However, the script/role-allocated responses to *WSAYO* were not, in the large majority of cases, embedded in Loach's 'class' discourse. Alternative kinds of production of the kind that Murdock calls for, seem hardly to have been understood, even at years 7 and 10. As with the previous category, students were more likely to project the contradiction between police and community on to 'otherness'.

3. It was not until the year 10 accounts that 'high level' summaries appeared which began to abstract and generalise role allocation in terms of power within either (i) social structure ('I think the employers called in the police to control the strike') or (ii) media representation (e.g. picking up on vox-pop miners' complaints about the systematic bias of the media against them: 'It was about the police and the miners and the violence against each other and how it was made to look like it was all the miners fault'). It was only in the relatively small proportion of summaries at year 10 (10 per cent WC, 10 per cent MC) which generalised to questions of power and government, or social structure and representation that Loach's oppositional discourse about the military/industrial complex and police state even begins to be mentioned. It is here that Loach's interpretation of a general 'ruling class' position in relation to the violence against the miners, and the consistent media bias against them is taken up to give coherence to a few summaries. But even these more generalised accounts did not clearly accept the full Loach position. The police 'were just trying to show the people who was boss', 'the employers called in police to control the strike' because it 'probably got out of hand', etc. At best (from Loach's point of view) there was a tiny minority of one or two students who adopted a populist position. They recognised a societal problem to do with the rights of the citizenry, generalising this concept via the specific conflict between miners and police ('It was a bit lousy of

the police because they're supposed to help the community, and they were really going round beating up everybody: all the miners and that. It's not really helping the community at all. It was interesting to see how the police are over there, how brutal they are').

4. The researchers were surprised over the almost total absence of meta-textual discussion, particularly of *Which Side Are You On?* They had expected opposition, even hostility, to Loach's strident pro-worker, anti-police documentary. This failed to appear. Most respondents accepted that what the documentary said about the police was true, even though it happened in some place 'other' than Australia (by year 10 17 per cent of respondents positioned the violence specially in England). Full script/role allocation (even of a simple 'police vs. workers' kind) did not get above 50 per cent until year 10; and a range of discourses other than Loach's were drawn on to negotiate the textual representation of 'police vs. community' in this documentary. Before students can become reflexively aware of the form of documentary – understanding documentary, in other words, as something other than a transparent window on the world – they have to understand that it presents a particular construction of events. In *Which Side Are On?* there was no attempt to an 'objective' voice-of-God comment. Instead there was a direct focus on the miners themselves, their wives, the pickets who had encountered the police violence. In particular, miners and their wives were presented speaking with considerable emotional conviction as eyewitnesses to the events of violence and these are 'authenticated' by black-and-white photographic 'evidence' – of police without shoulder numbers; of young men with badly cut heads; of a policeman armed with a baseball bat, etc. From year 4 to year 10 these were accepted as the truth of the events, the only difference between ages being in the shift from very general to specific accounts of the police break-ins and their refusal to allow injured workers access to first aid. Clearly, the police here were not seen as part of the 'community'. But they remained for most students an inexplicable force, not part of Loach's military industrial complex either.

5. It was only at adult level (and, probably significantly, among a class of mature-aged Master's degree students in media studies) that some recognition appeared in responses of both government (as linked to bosses and police within a power elite) and 'government' (as textually constructed representation of villain and perpetrator of violence). But the researchers noted that even here, respondents' situationally specific investments and class identifications were active in their readings. One Master's student responded specifically to the miners' wives who were discussing structural aspects of the strike (to protect jobs for their children) as well as personal hardships. But this student either did not recognise or recall the narrative link ('for jobs') between the picketing and the miners'/wives' discourses, and consequently found the documentary lost its focus and broke down in the middle. It was clear that his understanding was based

on a situational model derived from his brief post-school experience as a miner, and probably from his class position (father a surgeon, mother a teacher and landowner) which influenced his continuing acceptance of the 'neutral police help the public' schema. 'I know about miners' strikes, I've been a miner. I've been to miners' strikes, and, often I didn't know why we were protesting. The reason we were protesting I couldn't justify, but because I was a member of the union, and the union voted in the majority . . . I had to follow that. There wasn't any violence and there was always police there, but they were just there to protect the innocent citizens that could get in the way.' The more typical response of the adult students who found the documentary 'biased' against the police was to link a 'police protecting the innocent public' schema with psychologised explanations of the police violence that they saw on the screen: 'What do they do to provoke this kind of reaction from the police? The police are only human after all, they have a breaking point, and if you push them far enough they will snap.' In the case of these adults, socio-cognitive interpretive schema and situation models (in one case as an ex-miner in another case as a refugee from Communism) combined to generate an alternative narrative to the 'lost focus' of Loach; and visual details from the text (such as a shot of a miner teasing police by strutting backwards and forwards just in front of their line of shields) were recalled in order to establish the necessary provocation, legitimating the 'only human' police reaction.

Cognitive and behavioural options

All of the data summarised thus far derived from the normally 'qualitative' measure of asking students (prior to responding to the structured survey questions) to write a page on 'what it was about'. By using van Dijk's notion of macro-propositions (topics of discourse), it was possible for the researchers to quantify the narrative schemas used by various age-groups in understanding and explaining the text. The analysis of students' narrative summaries was designed to examine how far their *commonsense* scripts, frames and narratives for social processes understood violent actions within the context of wider social organisations.

In the case of *Which Side Are You On?* a documentary which worked against both conventional police scripts and dominant media representations of industrial disputes, there was a serious question of the level of understanding of the interaction of basic social roles – particularly at year 4. But even at year 10, there was no clear description of the process of police violence against peaceful picketing which the documentary clearly outlined. Indeed, 'scabs' were only mentioned in one summary (at year 10), and here the term was wrongly attributed to the police. On the only occasion when a blue bus carrying the scabs and protectively surrounded by the police was mentioned in the summaries, it was in complete puzzlement: 'Why aren't they checking the blue bus and why are they protecting the blue bus?' (year 4 MCM).

In contrast, in 'topics of discourse' responses to *A Country Practice* there was a much greater understanding of the institutional process of domestic violence, particularly in its psychological dimension (including the generational effect on reproducing male violence), and its 'necessary' relationship with a professional community of helpers. The socio-economic factor (of male/female comparative social status through work) was less well recognised. Overall, though, the family/institutional parameters of domestic violence were well understood, with, by year 10, 93 per cent of students describing either the domestic and generational interpersonal effects or the importance of bringing domestic violence into the open for legal action to take place.

This 'quantitative' use of narrative summaries was possible because, following van Dijk, the researchers were able to isolate, quantify and compare (according to age, as well as class and gender) children's comprehension in terms of story/role narrative schema. This was, in other words, a qualitative methodology that lent itself to quantification.

But in addition, the researchers administered a more conventional multiple-option questionnaire (embedded, as I said, in their own 'critical realist' theoretical framework), and backed up by focus group interviews to 'fill out' these survey responses. In the survey, four options of 'behavioural response' question were offered, which represented, as mentioned earlier, a 'descriptive', a 'deep structural', a narratively 'confused' and an 'incorrect' answer to a particular text-focused question. These structured questions were used to investigate students' understanding of key narrative events and their evaluation of violent actions within the text. While there is not space here to examine this part of the research in any detail, I will indicate how the responses to some of these items shed further light on students' understanding of the 'community' metaphors described earlier.

SOCIAL COHESION – SPATIAL METAPHORS

Spatial metaphors predicate 'community' as 'close-knit'. In the researchers' analysis of the texts it was argued that whereas *ACP* focused the community around the close-knit 'professional-helper' (medical/police) in-group of the hospital, *WSAYO* established the community spatially in the coal-mining village (as a close-knit representative of the broader working class) threatened by the police, who in this case were (like the husband in *ACP*) the violent outsiders.

In the *ACP* questionnaire students were asked a question as to whether 'domestics' were any of the doctor's business. This addressed the 'close-knit' factor (the degree of helping interaction) between the doctor and Karen. Across all age groups, 95 per cent of working-class students and 92 per cent of middle-class students said that the doctor should involve herself either by directly interacting with Barry and Karen on a personal basis or by starting legal action on behalf of Karen. In contrast, when shown filmed footage in *WSAYO* of massive numbers of police entering the village jeered at by workers, students were far more confused about the parameters of 'community' in this overtly 'spatial' invasion by the out-group. Across all age, gender and class groups, 39 per cent of students argued that the workers were either happy with the police being there or content that they were only doing their job. Only 32 per cent thought they were annoyed because they did not want the police in their village.

TEMPORAL METAPHORS

Both texts related temporal metaphors for 'community' to generational issues: *ACP* to the need to prevent sons reproducing their fathers' violence; *WSAYO* to the need to protect mining jobs for the workers' sons to inherit. In the *WSAYO* questionnaire students' recognition of this fundamental reason for the strike was tested by asking them whether the strike was to protect jobs, or for more money or because the police had attacked the workers, or to try to get rid of the government. The 'to protect jobs' reason given for the strike was strongly foregrounded in the documentary (via two major vox-pop sequences, one with men-as-workers and the other with women-as-mothers) but was weakly recognised by the student audience groups. There were, however, significant age and class differences in the responses (only 5 per cent of the working-class compared with 35 per cent of the middle-class students choosing the 'to protect jobs' option). In contrast 86 per cent of year 4, 78 per cent of year 7, and 67 per cent of year 10 chose either the wrong option (for more money), or the narratively confused option (since police attacked workers after, not before, they went on strike). Notably, the percentage of those who chose (what Philo *et al.*, 1977, saw as) television's dominant ('for more money') discourse about industrial stoppages actually increased between year 4 and year 10 (27 per cent to 35 per cent), probably indicating older students' greater engagement with news and current affairs' coverage of strikes.

We have already seen that in the case of *ACP* a significant proportion of narrative summaries at all age levels described the effects of Barry's domestic violence on his son. This finding was confirmed by the cognitive option questions, which showed that 99 per cent of year 10, 96 per cent of year 7 and 86 per cent of year 4 recognised that Mark's violence at school was associated with his father's violence to his mother at home. The temporal significance of the soap opera's 'show and tell' policy on domestic violence was well understood.

AGENTIVE

Metaphors for the 'community' as agent include both cognitive powers (knowledge, feeling, etc.) and powers of agency: the community can 'hit back'. The need for battered wives to tell friends and police was insisted on in significant numbers of students' *ACP* narrative summaries (even though they were only asked to say 'what it was about'), with 34 per cent of year 7 students and 31 per cent of year 10 students saying this. There were no comparable statements about the value of illustrating on television police violence to strikers in the *WSAYO* summaries. Indeed, in a specific behavioural option question about showing police violence on television, 81 per cent of year 4, 63 per cent of year 7, and 51 per cent of year 10 students either said it should not be shown, or said it was good to show it because it would discourage others from breaking the law.

Two other survey questions also showed a marked divergence between responses to the two texts. In the *ACP* questionnaire, in response to what should Karen have done when Barry was violent to her, 97 per cent of year 7, 97 per cent of year 10 students, and 68 per cent of year 4 students argued that Karen should have worked with the police to take legal action and charge Barry with assault. In contrast, responding to the question as to what the workers should have done faced with police violence, far fewer students chose the comparable 'positive non-violent' (taking legal action) option, with 21 per cent of middle-class and 13 per cent of working-class students choosing the option of combining with other unions to defeat the government. Further, whereas in the *ACP* responses only 7 per cent of year 4, 1 per cent of year 7, and 0 per cent of year 10 chose the 'appeasing violence' solution of Karen giving up her work and becoming a good housewife, 36 per cent middle-class and 14 per cent working-class year 10's, 21 per cent middle-class and 29 per cent working-class year 7's, and 9 per cent middle-class and 17 per cent working class year 4's chose the 'appeasing violence' option of the workers giving up the strike and going back to work.

UNDERSTANDING THE TEXT

Supportive evidence from Tulloch and Tulloch's cognitive and behavioural survey questions suggested that even given the structuring influence of the researchers' questionnaire to aid them, students (especially working-class students) were far less able to understand, summarise and evaluate Loach's alternative 'class' discourse than the *ACP* producers' 'feminist' one. Among the reasons for this the researchers indicated the complex audio-visual form of Loach's discourse compared with the soap opera, a difference determined in part by the different institutional positions of radical and reformist producers within the television industry. These positions were in turn influenced by these different producers' respective representation of the police as either inter- or intra-community in their texts. In one year 10 interview, for example, students said they did not understand much except that 'the workers were always complaining' and the police suddenly 'got happy and started singing' as they were marching through the village.

Not only the complex form of *WSAYO*, however, but also its contradiction of conventional scripts and schematic narratives for both police and workers led to the differences of audience response to the two programmes. Faced with confusion between their internalised scripts and the representations of workers and police offered by Loach, children opted for a range of discursive negotiations in making the text cohere. These included research-oriented discourses, displacement of the police representations as 'other', and (increasingly with age) ascribing, as the cognitive option questions indicated, the media's dominant ('for more money') causal explanations for strikes to the Loach text. Though this latter was (by year 10) a middle-class rather than working-class phenomenon, the majority of working-class students across all age groups were unable to understand the 'to secure jobs' reason given by Loach for the strikes, and were thus unable to fully relate to the spatial, temporal and agentive aspects of the working-class community established in this 'alternative' text.

Conclusion

In his audience study of television coverage of the 1984/5 British miners' strike, Philo (1990, p. 754) reaffirms the power of the media in setting agendas. Philo indicates that the influence of media and especially television was central, since it established so firmly the *issues* which came to be associated with the strike. Both Philo and Hetherington argue that in the television coverage about the causes of the strike the apparent logic of the National Coal Board's case was too readily accepted (Hetherington, 1985, p. 277). Philo adds that television's preoccupation with violent incidents during picketing, the National Coal Board's extensive advertising and public relations campaign, and the reliance of the media on the government and Coal Board as sources of information *vis-à-vis* the economics of pit closures (Philo, 1990, p. 143) produced a situation where – as Philo's qualitative study illustrates – none of his audience groups (whether sympathetic to the miners or not) was critical of the Coal Board's view of the economics of the industry.

He also found that in the case of audience members sympathetic to the miners, their cause was not promoted in terms of the miners' union argument (which found little representation in the media) about artificial subsidies underpinning the apparent cheapness of foreign coal, or the government's hidden agenda relating to a nuclear power policy. Nor did Philo's audience groups support the miners via the words of those Labour MPs who did get exposure on television, who argued the 'case that the miners were fighting for, a case for keeping coal, a case for keeping jobs, a case for protecting their communities' (Hattersley, quoted in Philo, 1990, p. 142). Rather, support for the miners among Philo's audience groups 'came down largely to blaming the police for the violence' (Philo, 1990, p. 143).

The Tullochs' data and analysis support Philo's qualitative evidence about media power, to the extent that even where alternative discourses about the economics of pit closure are produced for television, they either meet censorship difficulties or they are allowed through in a marginalised generic form. Loach's use of an 'arts' format led to an emphasis on popular genres (folk songs, poetry) and situated narratives (group discussions by workers and workers' wives) which emphasised repertoires of community and solidarity ('Which Side Are You On?') rather than providing alternative explanations of the economics of the coal industry. The folk songs and poems which accompany the situated vox-pop narratives of the documentary replaced the conventional 'voice-of-God' narrator who normally provides coherence via macro-structural propositions.

Without this meta-discourse, Loach's textual emphasis on solidarity and working-class community led to a focus on violence, but from the police side (as in the case of Philo's pro-miner audience groups). Although dominant media ideologies of 'balance' and 'neutrality' were not mobilised by the Tullochs' school students in their interpretation of the text, the lack of a clear alternative economic logic about the future of the coal industry shifted the focus of *WSAYO* from 'jobs' to 'violence' to such an extent that even adult communication students could lose sight of the narrative connection between these two discourses. In this situation, the researchers found that, despite a clear foregrounding of the 'striking for jobs' discourse in the text, only a minority of students understood this as the cause of the strike. Further, the class differences in this reading were highly significant. While the middle-class minority choosing this option was 33 per cent (compared to 40 per cent who thought the strike was because of anger over police violence), the working-class minority was only 5 per cent (compared to 58 per cent who thought the strike was the result of police violence).

The Tullochs' analysis suggested that working-class students had less understanding of the social (and societal) context of work roles particularly in relation to police work, and of the socio-economic context of social processes, than middle-class students. In particular, working-class students were more likely to attribute causes to interpersonal (and violent) confrontation than to socio-economic imbalance and conflict. They concluded that more research is needed in explaining class differences in work-role-related narrative schemata at different ages; and particularly via the narratives (in children's storybooks, television programming, hired videos, etc.) that children in different age and class groups customarily are exposed to.

Systematic class differences in consumption of 'action' genres rather than 'news stories' have frequently been noted (Hodge and Tripp, 1986, p. 176; Tulloch, 1990, p. 213); this in turn sometimes being explained (particularly in relation to boys) as representing the very limited 'claims to adulthood' that 'can be made by people who, because of the age and class structure, have very few resources' (Connell, 1983, p. 29). The Tullochs were not arguing that middle-class students understood the 'for jobs' causes of the 1984/5 strike better than the working-class students because they watched more news and current affairs – since these television genres by and large did not carry the miners' union position on pit closures anyway. But it may well be that middle-class students have more opportunity to consult other sources of information, such as the broadsheet press and 'alternative' current affairs programmes and radio. Philo concludes that this kind of access to other sources of information was a major reason for doubting conventional news agendas among his audience groups. In contrast, violent narrative causes and solutions are the convention in action videos; and it is arguable that students who choose to watch these rather than news and current affairs will look for similar 'action' causes and consequences (such as strikes as a result of police violence) in Loach's documentary when they reject the conventional 'for more money' explanation. This tendency is likely to be increased by the standard TV news emphasis on violence in the miners' strike.

While class differences in understanding social schema, narratives and processes were apparent in audience responses to *ACP*, they were not nearly so marked. Direct and indirect personal experience of the particular conflict represented does, as both Philo and Schlesinger *et al.*, found, provide symbolic resources leading to a greater understanding of everyday (as against conventional TV representation of) social interaction and violence. In the case of the domestic violence text, all students had direct experience of familial roles; some had (at least) indirect experience of domestic violence. What was notable was the very high majority level of rejection of domestic violence, with no significant variation of response in terms of class and gender. This was the result, the researchers believed, of (a) the much greater diffusion of feminist than of critical class-based analysis in society as a whole, and (b) the particular representation of the domestic violence issue which supported (rather than challenged, as in the Loach documentary) conventional scripts and narrative schemata for professional roles like police and doctors.

|7|

Cartoons:

Modality and methodology

In the mid-1980s – post-linguistic turn and in the middle of the 'ethnographic' shift of audience studies – Bob Hodge and David Tripp wrote what was arguably the richest socio-cognitive analysis of the television audience of that time, and certainly the most path-breaking study of the child audience of cartoons. I will start with an extract of audience discussion from their book, *Children and Television*, as a way of illustrating the range of methodological, conceptual and theoretical values they achieved at a moment when audience research was beginning to turn more dominantly to feminist emphases on pleasure.

Let me first set their audience research scene. Five children are sitting in a circle with a female interviewer. There are two girls (Kristie and Michelle) and three boys (Adrian, Craig and Stephen). They have just watched a five-minute sequence of the television cartoon *Fangface*. This is a cartoon about a baby werewolf, Fangs (who changes when the moon or image of the moon 'shines' on him), and his three daring teenager friends: one girl (Kim) and two boys (Biff and Pugsie), who together 'find danger, excitement and adventure'. In the particular episode the children have seen, a monster called The Heap (who is really a professor sacked from the university for inventing a ray that transforms men into monsters) attacks other academics and steals scientific equipment. Fangs and his friends go to the rescue of the one remaining professor and his young daughter. They save them from The Heap's cave in the mountain, and, after a chase, turn The Heap back into the bad professor, who is led off into captivity at the end.

As they discuss this episode of *Fangface* with the interviewer, the children are being recorded by a video camera. From this focus group discussion, Hodge and Tripp isolate the following extract.

Int: Mm. Can you all speak up a bit. You don't need to whisper. What sort of people do you think they were? [Looks round group, focuses on Kristie.]

Kristie: Adventurous [All children look at interviewer. Kristie leans back slightly.]

Int: Mm. Can, let's take say, the girl, Kim [Stephen looks across to Kristie. Adrian and Craig exchange glances, and smile.] What sort of person do you think she was?

Adrian: Hmm. A smart person. [Grins.] She thinks she . . . she thought she knew all the answers, nearly. [Adrian looks at interviewer, smiling. Craig also smiles, looks at interviewer. Stephen looks ahead, then at Adrian and smiles. Kristie looks at Adrian. Michelle smiles and looks at interviewer.]

Int: Mm. Anything else?

Adrian: 'Cos she thought she was . . . they would have another adventure. [Adrian looks at interviewer. Stephen and Craig look down. Michelle looks at interviewer. Kristie looks at Adrian.]

Int: Mm.

Kristie: Um, she was always ready to have an adventure. She already thought of the not obvious clues. [Kristie looks at interviewer. Michelle looks at interviewer. Adrian and Craig look at interviewer. Stephen looks at Kristie, then down.]

Int: Mm. [Pause.]

I will now begin to unpack Hodge and Tripp's analysis of this conversation by contextualising it in terms of the overall methodology and theory of their research study.

Methodology

It will be obvious from the quoted extract that Hodge and Tripp attempt to do more than most audience researchers of this period by describing *the body language and eyeline* of the children as they talk, and which their video-recording method has made accessible. The researchers are reflexive about this method, arguing that by standardised quantitative criteria, their own research

> seems sadly impure and contaminated. It has grown mainly from a situation where a small number of children talk to an unfamiliar adult female, in unfamiliar surroundings, with a video camera recording the exchanges. Clearly these are not typical conditions for viewing or talking about television.
>
> (Hodge and Tripp, 1986, p. 143)

Nor was this method symptomatic of the current shift of 'active audience' research into 'ethnographic' accounts of the 'everyday'. But, Hodge and Tripp ask, what *is* a 'typical' everyday condition of viewing? Unless we take the view that an isolated individual sitting in front of a television is typical, never talking about her experience (either during or after viewing) and uninfluenced by any other earlier 'talk' (verbal, written or visual), then why is Hodge and Tripp's viewing situation any more artificial than any other? 'Discourse about television is itself a social force. It is a major site of mediation of television meanings, a site where television meanings fuse with other meanings into a new text to form a major interface with the world of action and belief' (1986, p. 143).

To illustrate their point, Hodge and Tripp quote an extract from another interview.

Int: Why do you think they should have put 'AO' on the cartoon?

Marnie: 'Cause, um, oh, if say a 2-year-old was watching it and they, they might have got a bit scared when they were ... when Fangface was changing.

Angela: When he swallows Pugsie [Smiles.]

Richard: Or when they hear the ow-oow [imitates howl], like that 'n they go, they go out for a camp and hear it, y'know, they get a little bit scared.

Int: So what were the things in that Fangface bit that you thought were really scary? They might scare somebody?

Angela: Oh, the thing when that, that, where, where that big monster [outlines shape with her hand] came in to come and get him, that was a bit scary ...

Marnie: Yeah [Others nod.]

Angela: In the dark, too.

Int: Why was it scary, that bit?

Richard: Didn't scare me, but you know ...

Hodge and Tripp note about this extract that while the 'Adults Only' warning notice was apparently unable to affect their initial views of the cartoon, 'as supplemented by the coercion of the interviewer it could begin to turn a funny cartoon into a horror movie' (1986, p. 65). The researchers note the way that Angela shifts position: from saying that *Fangface* should not be 'AO'; to giving a counter-instance of it being frightening, but said with a smile indicating that it was really funny, not scary; to finally giving an example that invited censorship. Hodge and Tripp do not worry that this incident is driven by the 'artificial' and 'demand' characteristics of the interview interaction. Rather, it is an example of the way in which power and language intervene in any social situation, including an audience discussion. 'The point is that language did not determine what they perceived initially, but cumulatively it determined what they said, and therefore what they will be judged to have thought by researchers, by teachers and parents, perhaps later even by themselves' (1986, p. 66). Children, they argue, are well able to maintain a number of alternative discursive positions; as here, with 'official' and 'child' positions both being 'real' to them. 'Even after further discussion the children had not necessarily changed what they thought about the cartoon, but they changed what they afterwards said about it in this situation, producing an alternative reading which coexisted with but did not supplant the initial reading' (1986, p. 65).

Yet the 'consensus' (that it was a scary cartoon) can very easily acquire 'a public force and status' (Hodge and Tripp, 1986, p. 144); not least through the publication of this reading as 'research findings'. Thus the 'official' reading is fed back into social life. As Hodge and Tripp argue, much as researchers may want to conceptualise 'what children think' about television as a set of internal mental units, the discussion children have about television always 'involves the insertion of television meanings into general ideological constructs which are not specific to television or to discussions about television' (1986, p. 144).

One of these ideological positions that Hodge and Tripp's book challenges is the notion that children are potential victims, helpless before the violent and corrupting influence of television, and thus in need of protection. But it is precisely this skewed power relationship between adults (teachers, parents, legislators, researchers, etc.) and children that the interview quoted above represents. Hodge and Tripp argue that their *Fangface* interviews 'represent discourse marked by an asymmetry of power. Thus they have things in common with other kinds of discourse with the same asymmetry, such as teacher–student or parent-child exchange' (1986, p. 144).

This reflexivity about their particular method enabled Hodge and Tripp to do two things to develop their research. First, they contrasted their focus group responses led by the interviewer with other children's discussion where they were asked to talk about television in any way they liked, with the interviewer at some distance (in a purely supervisory capacity, as the school insisted). These 'conversations [which] were much closer to normal peer group discussions' (1986, p. 144) were then compared with the *Fangface* ones. Second, in their analysis of the *Fangface* focus groups, the researchers extended their sensitivity to the relationship between power, language and television readings to the children themselves.

This is where the significant advantage of the video-recording of the interviews became evident. Hodge and Tripp could show the gender imbalance between boys and girls according to a much wider range of measures than researchers normally isolate.

- The boys dominated the verbal channel, each boy talking about twice as much as each girl, across all forms of speech.
- The boys dominated the gestural interactions, averaging nine times as many mimetic gestures as the girls – especially important as a communication code which often carries intimate and expressive 'feelings'.
- Laughter (frequently a mode of subverting 'authority' positions) was both used more by the boys and *in support of* boys' comments. 'In general the boys seem deliberately to set out to be funny, and their efforts are acknowledged. . . . Because the girls are not rewarded as much as boys for producing subversive child-meanings about television, they are in effect being socialized into . . . a more serious, adult stance in relation to television and enjoyment' (1986, p. 149).
- Whereas boys address their remarks equally to other boys and girls, girls remarks are addressed much more strongly to boys than girls. Girls pay five times as much attention to boys in the group than to girls. 'So not only are the boys granted twice the verbal space in the discussion, as well as much more access to non-verbal channels, they are also given much more importance' (1986, p. 150).

What we have here, Hodge and Tripp argue, is

> an ideology of sex roles . . . a major meaning carried by the substantive discourse about television. Arguably it is actually more pervasive and powerful in shaping behaviour and attitude than anything that was thought or said about *Fangface* as such.

The fact that all of the children's groups they analyzed reacted in similar ways 'showed the capacity of the ideological schema to generalize to new situations. It also no doubt confirmed, for the children, the applicability of the scheme, thereby reinforcing its taken-for-granted status.'

(1986, p. 151)

By way of their novel and detailed method of analytical observation then, Hodge and Tripp related in interesting ways to wider areas of the ideological analysis of television.

Issues of ideology

As I said earlier (chapter 3), 'ideology-critique' was a dominant mode of media/audience analysis in the 1970s and early 1980s; and a major influence in the area of 'television violence' and 'fear of crime' analysis in this tradition was the work of Gerbner and his colleagues. Gerbner *et al.*, had drawn attention to television's 'symbolic annihilation' of certain groups in society – primarily the non-white, non-male, non-adult and non-middle class. Hodge and Tripp point out that the cartoon *Fangface* supports Gerbner *et al.*,'s analysis, since the gender ratio of its characters is four males to one female, and its social class ratio is 4.5 : 1 in favour of the middle class, 'another striking distortion which is typical of American media productions' (Hodge and Tripp, 1986, p. 74). By way of their particular methodology, moreover, Hodge and Tripp can add greater weight to Gerbner *et al.*,'s concerns by indicating that in the various circuits of discourse surrounding television there is a similar gender bias. In other words, by way of their multi-channelled discourse methodology they add significant weight to Gerbner *et al.*,'s content analysis method and 'ideological-effect' thesis; so that the 'accumulated burden of such messages, carried in innumerable other discussions, would seem to be overwhelming' (Hodge and Tripp, 1986, p. 151).

But, like many other commentators, Hodge and Tripp also point to the somewhat weak correlation supporting Gerbner *et al.*,'s main 'cultivation thesis'; namely that a heavy television diet of biased and skewed content cultivates a vision of the world which is more like television than the real world. What explains this 'resistance' to the TV world of massive violence and biased social representations? And, given Hodge and Tripp's focus on children and television, 'are children more vulnerable than adults to this whole process?' (1986, p. 74). This brings the researchers to their central innovation as cultural audience theorists: a developmental approach to children.

Issues of child development

If for Ien Ang a major focus that differentiates research about audiences and gender is 'pleasure', for Hodge and Tripp the major distinguishing focus among child audiences is the issue of cognitive 'development' (though this, they argue, is integrally related to children's pleasure in cartoons). It is here that Hodge and Tripp most clearly indicate the importance to their research of the 'linguistic turn'. They, in fact, isolate the developmental and social importance of a number of different language forms.

- Following Basil Bernstein, they examine restricted codes (L-forms) and elaborated codes (H-forms) of language. In particular they are interested in children's development from paratactic language structures (where a 'story' is an endless succession of 'and then . . . and then' events) to the more powerful organisation of hypotactic structures, which reduce story elements at a lower level to the unity of age, gender, class, or other general options. They note, for instance, that *Tom and Jerry* is more paratactic than *Fangface* as a cartoon because the 'cat chases mouse . . . and again cat chases mouse' plot is repeated several times, rather than the more cumulative ideological development of the latter. Thus younger children – but also, they indicate via empirical research, working-class children –

may have more difficulty with more 'adult' hypotactic language structures (a finding of obvious relevance to the Tullochs' data on working-class comprehension of *Which Side Are You On?*, *see* chapter 6).

- Following Levi-Strauss and other structuralist theorists, Hodge and Tripp are interested in binary transformations within a mythical structure. Thus the syntagmatic story of *Fangface* (as boy-werewolf and friends 'together find danger and excitement and adventure' is subject to a number of nature/culture transformations. Hodge and Tripp's method of textual analysis is evident in their semiotic analysis of the redundancy-yet-ambiguity of paradigmatic structures in the opening credits of the *Fangface* text.

The sequence . . . goes from lightning to the house seen from the outside to a zoom on to the baby, inside the house, in a bassinet, and the baby protected within by both. In shot 7 the movement is repeated, starting with a shot of the moon (outside, nature) then showing the baby at the window (not threatened by nature). The baby then spins rapidly, like a whirlwind (nature) or like a machine (culture) and turns into a baby werewolf (nature). However, this werewolf is not a threatening figure. It has a cute expression, and wears a nappy (human, culture). Then, with the sound track saying 'only the sun [nature] can change him back to normal', we see a picture of the sun with alongside it the words 'Sunshine Laundry' (culture). A zoom out reveals that this picture of the sun is on a packet of soap powder in a kitchen. The 'sun' that controls Fangface, then, is not the natural sun, but a commercial appropriation of the sun, tamed for domestic purposes. In the cartoon that follows, Fangface's metamorphoses are always triggered by photographs or pictures of sun and moon, either seen accidentally by him in a kitchen or other domestic space, but more often shown to him by one of the 'three daring teenagers' who thus control him. The pattern throughout this sequence is built up of different arrangements of primary oppositions: nature–culture, human–animal. The result is not a single consistent message about the relations between the two. Sometimes nature is seen as threatening, sometimes as compatible with culture. Fangface is the focus of both ambiguity and ambivalence. He is both animal and human.

(1986, p. 28)

- Following Piaget, Connell and other theorists of child development, Hodge and Tripp argue that children progress in the structures they project, towards understanding more hypotactic, diachronic, transformational and large-scale forms. In this progression, however, nothing is superseded: later stages are not only logically dependent on earlier forms but can co-exist with them. 'Earlier stages survive because they are functional. They are the site of pleasure and the play of emotional energy. If later stages are essential for power, earlier stages are essential for desire'

(1986, p. 85). 'Power' is dependent on a competence in powerful trans-formational thinking that allows for critical abstract consciousness. This is only generally available after about age 12, and is not available to everyone. As Hodge and Tripp say, this stage – Piaget's stage of 'formal operations' – is that of 'multiple successive transformations, the abstract, hypothetical logical thought that distinguishes the scientist' or perhaps the 'top executive in a multinational' (1986, p. 81).

- A key emphasis of Hodge and Tripp's analysis is that television viewing, far from simply corrupting vulnerable children, actually gives them experience of developing transformational facility. The notion of intertextuality is combined in this analysis with a cognitive-developmental perspective. So, for example, *Fangface* has structural similarities with another cartoon *Scooby Doo*, where a cartoon dog also goes on adventures with three 'daring' teenagers. Similarly, The Heap is a recognisable transform of another popular cartoon character, The Incredible Hulk who also metamorphoses from a scientist. As Hodge and Tripp argue,

Only the colour (blue not green) and the valuation (bad not good) are different. Fangface, given his transformational relationship to The Heap, is also a transform of The Hulk. His derivation from the were-wolf myth is made explicit. His name, and his one prominent tooth, probably evoke the vampire myth. . . . Any one of the characters carries a rich set of meanings which are bundles of paradigmatic oppositions, representing categories which are basic to a cultural logic, thus giving them their continuous appeal. The effect of seeing a range of different versions of this figure is not so much to gain an entirely new but particular meaning, but more, as Levi-Strauss saw, a greater understanding of the transformational possibilities of a matrix of meanings. . . . This kind of 'understanding' is transformational power, the capacity for a major intellectual and cultural activity. It raises the question of whether, or when, or who among children can perform such operations on a show like *Fangface*, and whether humble television fare like this can stimulate the growth of these capacities.

(1986, pp. 31–2)

- Hodge and Tripp's empirical studies suggest that television does indeed help these growing capacities of children's minds, with syntagmatic and paradigmatic structures developing in complexity, and transformational capacity increasing with age. They argue that children prefer television programme types 'that are the best available for their cognitive development' (1986, p. 98): cartoons for younger and prime-time soap operas for older children. Moreover, there are class differences, with working-class children displaying more paratactic readings of cartoons, and a relative lack of transformational facility compared with middle-class children. 'Ideology-critique', they argue, must therefore take account of the mediation of cognitive and social processes. Audiences are 'not born preformed into an ideological role, but have their developing potentialities shaped and formed and constrained by experiences and institutions such as television' (1986, p. 98). As part of that second-stage 'resistance' tradition of audience research which Alasuutari (1999) criticises, Hodge and Tripp find the potential for resistance even in what they call the 'cognitive deprivation' of transformational facility among working-class children. The 'more paratactic, transformationally simpler modes of thought that working-class children deployed have their own strengths and functions. . . . They tend to represent issues in terms of black and white, not in shifting shades of grey. This may lead to more sexist thinking, in a gendered social group; but it may also lead to effective resistance to shades of grey, so that complex structures of mystification are less easy to impose' (1986, p. 98). The Tullochs research into children and teenagers watching Ken Loach's *Which Side Are You On?* suggests, however, that Hodge and Tripp may be wishfully thinking in this regard. 'Black and white thinking' in the case of their working-class young people tended to be polarised around the police/worker violence binary; and very few indeed understood the documentary's 'transformational' talk about the relationship between socio-economic/political structures and working-class jobs.

- Modality – a child's judgement about the reality status of what she or he sees – is a key aspect of cognitive development, and of Hodge and Tripp's analysis. They point out that even very young children are quite able to articulate the main 'internal' modality features of television cartoons; that is those formal features (like two-dimensional images, colour quality, drawing quality) which make them 'unreal'. By age 9 children are also very well equipped with 'external' modality markers, like the impossibility of Fangface changing into a werewolf, Fangface 'eating' Pugsie and then spitting him out whole, The Heap running incredibly fast, and so on. Children were therefore quite able to distinguish cartoon violence – and indeed TV violence more generally – from what happens in real life. 'The basis in every case was some recognition of the processes of media production – acting, pretending, use of tomato sauce, or some reference to the illusionism of actors and directors. A version of Brecht's alienation effect is, it seems, part of the normal development of modality structures in quite young children. Children were normally quite clear about the effect of weak modality: it turned something that would otherwise have been frightening into the opposite, something funny and/or exciting' (1986, p. 112). Hodge and Tripp argue that modality judgements develop with age, and that consequently the emotional charge of the 'scary bits' of *Fangface* reduce in intensity with age. The closer the message is judged to be to reality (i.e. the better the modal fit) the more it will be responded to both emotionally and cognitively (as we found with the 16-year-old Lisa in chapter 2). So, because cartoons are much weaker in modality than the news, children (like Lisa) will respond to the latter television genre more powerfully as they get older. Because younger children are likely to under-read modality cues, and therefore sometimes respond 'with an intensity surprising to adults . . . it follows that children do in fact need a diet rich in explicit fantasy – including cartoons – in order to develop a confident and discriminating modality system. They also need, and crave, an understanding of the processes of media production' (1986, p. 130).

Issues of audience readings (general)

Overall, Hodge and Tripp's empirical work leads to a number of hypotheses. They admit that these are based on 'only 42 children's responses, under specific conditions, to the first 5 minutes of a single 20-minute cartoon' (1986, p. 60). But they argue that their work with 9 to 12 year olds offers provisional clarification of the following.

1. By 9 years old, children decode television programmes with essentially the same 'grammar' as adults do.
2. Children develop a transformational competence, so that their reading of a cartoon episode goes wider than this text to see the characters, plots, situations and actions it contains as part of a wider series of abstract types. Any one episode and/or series is then read as a transformation of these wider abstract types.
3. Children's grasp of these rules is generative, so that they can project and predict new versions of programme types, and by age 12 project hypothetical counter-forms.
4. The primary meaning is carried by the main characters as synchronic syntagms (characters and objects together in the same space and time, so that a shot of a child playing near a fire may suggest danger). However, these synchronic syntagms are often ambiguous or contradictory, allowing children to read them differently.
5. Both television content and children's responses to it carry meanings at two levels: ideological (parent) and subversive (child). Since these two levels co-exist, children in any one conversation can vary between these levels (for example, on whether cartoon violence is 'good' – cf. here the Tullochs' 'research-led topic of discourse' – or whether middle-class cartoon teenagers are 'goody-good'), and under 'different conditions they may well say one thing or its opposite, and actually mean both' (1986, p. 61).
6. Of the two kinds of meaning, however, 'the emotional charge and attraction of the programme is invested in the subversive (child) meanings' (1986, p. 61).
7. Where the cartoon text seems to undervalue a type of person (e.g. girls in *Fangface*), children can compensate by a covert transformation of that

textual 'surface'. For example, the fact that The Heap has long hair in any one synchronic syntagm enables children to say they wondered at first if he was female. The following interview exchange then becomes possible.

Int: But you girls didn't want to be, uh, The Heap . . . or you didn't want to be Fangface.

Kristie: I'd like to be Fangface, wouldn't mind being Fangface. [Two boys look at her.]

Alan: The Heap's not for a girl. [The other two boys still look at Kristie.]

Kristie: But um The Heap, well, it'd be okay, but everybody would be out to get you. You'd have to be running all the time, you couldn't stay in one spot.

Hodge and Tripp note that Alan was the first to mention The Heap as potentially bisexual, but he now insists that girls must not be The Heap. Kristie, however, only renounces The Heap's role because of his status as victim. Meanwhile, Kim is the only actual girl in the cartoon whom girls can identify with. One 12 year old did so, but with reservations.

Kara: I'd be that girl, but I would do more if I was her. . . . I'd find out mysteries and then all the guys'd think you were fantastic. [Laughs to a girl friend.]

Hodge and Tripp argue here:

> The surface form of the cartoon is unfair to girls in that it offers them only one option to identify with as girls, whereas boys have a choice of six characters and four types of character (good and bad monster, mid-dle-class and lower-class male). . . . Excluded by the surface from this range of choices, girls have two options: to rewrite the possibilities of the girl's role, or to covertly identify with one of the 'male' characters, trans-forming his gender. Both these options have to go against the grain of the cartoon itself, but the cartoon gives both options a point of entry. The Heap does have long hair . . . and Kim is the controller of Fangface. She is the intellectual of the group . . . and, in part of the cartoon that these children did not see, she captures the ray gun to save the day.
>
> (1986, p. 56)

Issues of audience readings (specific)

By way of these various layers of Hodge and Tripp's analysis, we are now ready to return to their analysis of our opening focus group discussion between Kristie, Michelle, Adrian, Craig, Stephen and the interviewer.

Hodge and Tripp note that if we only took account of the *verbal content* of the exchange we would probably interpret Adrian's comment as 'wrong'. The girl in the cartoon, Kim, is humble and deferential and, in the extract they saw, is not a 'smart person' who 'knew all the answers'. But, because of the research methodology's use of video cameras, we can also assess non-textual indicators.

> In this group of children Kristie is a talkative, norm-breaking female. The total number of her utterances is 98, which is well above the masculine average. In this group only Adrian (131) exceeds her. She receives a high number of gazes from the boys (105), higher than anyone else in the group. It is not untypical that she is the first to respond to the interviewer's question. However, Adrian's comment is accompanied by a smile plus sideways glance – a signal of covert meaning. Craig also looks at the interviewer, but smiles, signifying that he shares the covert meaning and endorses it. When the interviewer asked the question they looked at each other, establishing a male common meaning. The other boy, Stephen, looked at Kristie when the interviewer asked the question. Later on he also looks at Kristie. The comment 'A smart person' then would be directed at Kristie rather than Kim.
>
> (Hodge and Tripp, 1986, p. 152)

Hodge and Tripp argue that this focus group incident indicates the way in which gender power relations can take place in the situated context of a research interview. In a discussion without the interviewer present these gender relations would have taken a different form. And, in this case, the presence of the female interviewer may well have facilitated Kristie's 'norm-breaking' behaviour. In this context, Adrian chooses deliberately to 'mis-read' the cartoon in order to target Kristie for her aberrant behaviour. Ironically, his misreading is, at one level, an anti-*sexist* one (since he makes the cartoon character Kim more powerful than she is) in order for him to reinforce a sexist ideology on the real-life girl Kristie. As the researchers say, this incident shows that the primary 'effect' of the television cartoon here is not direct influence, as passive victims are uncritically reproduced. Rather, it shows the way in which television becomes part of a *situated contest*, where renegotiation and re-affirmation of gender occurs in language, gesture and daily context. Here quantification, as a methodology, is embedded in a very sophisticated textual and qualitative analysis.

Moreover, quantification is by no means at the expense of an individual focus, as the next extract from a focus group discussion of another cartoon series, *The Muppets*, indicates.

Int: Can you tell us who you'd like to be? [To Catherine.]

Catherine: [Leaning forward and whispering.] Miss Piggy. [Others laugh. One child looks briefly at Catherine, others look at interviewer.]

Int:	Miss Piggy. Why would you like to be Miss Piggy?
Cath:	[Whispers inaudibly.]
Int:	[After pause.] Do you know why?
Cath:	No.
Int:	What sort of an animal is Miss Piggy? [All children look at interviewer: two with hands in air.]
Cath:	[Whispering.] She's a pig. [All children look at her briefly; then three turn back to the interviewer.]
Int:	She's a pig, um. Is she a nice pig? [Catherine nods. Boys exchange glances, and laugh together. Girls look at interviewer.]
Julian:	She's not a nice pig. [Moves closer to other boys. Two other boys whisper to each other and laugh. One girl looks at boys: others at interviewer.]
Int:	You don't think she's nice?
Julian:	She hits Kermit. [Emma mimes a karate chop in the air, and looks at Sharon who is looking at a boy. Boys continue to look at each other, then turn to interviewer.]
Int:	She hits Kermit. [Pause.] Let's go round the girls, because the girls haven't really told us much yet. [To Emma.] Who would you like to be?
Emma:	Miss Piggy. [Emma looks at interviewer. Rest look at Emma.]
Int:	You'd like to be Miss Piggy. Why?
Emma:	She crashes Kermit the Frog into pieces. [Karate chops the air, looking at interviewer. Others laugh, looking at Emma.]
Int:	Why do you want to crash Kermit into pieces?
Emma:	[Pause.] Well ... he is silly sometimes. [Looks away before speaking, then looks at interviewer. Girls look at each other then interviewer; as do boys.]

Hodge and Tripp comment on this extract that using traditional content-analysis we would have to see *The Muppets* as a strongly sexist show which provides a wider range of positive models for boys and a limited range of negative stereotypes of females. However, the non-verbal dimensions of the interview indicate a different picture. Here two girls identify positively with Miss Piggy, but for very different reasons. In the case of Catherine, it is crucial that the interviewer 'has created space for the girls to speak (and she has to keep that space open or the boys will fill it again)' (1986, p. 155).

Catherine is socially isolated. She typically looks at the interviewer or away rather than at her peers, and they look less often at her even when she is speaking than they do at Emma. Her two statements here (her only words in the whole interview) are clearly offered only because the interviewer requires them. She says them in the direction of the authority figure, and then she leans forward; but she speaks so quietly that the interviewer can hardly hear her, and her peers also are partly excluded. It is her quietness that alters the modality of her statement, allowing her peers to invert her meaning (from 'nice' to 'not nice'). Their laughter serves to re-interpret her utterance. . . . There is total opposition between her fantasy figure, Miss Piggy, boisterous and outgoing, and her social self, which is painfully shy and withdrawn. Miss Piggy seems to be a compensation representing what she is not, rather than a likely influence on her behaviour. We see two aspects of her self which are not integrated, and this lack of integration is related to her uneasy position in the group, isolated both from peers and authority figures, with just sufficient support from each to encourage her to collapse into silence and self-contradiction.

(1986, pp. 155–6)

In contrast in Emma's response there is more integration – both between her and her fantasy figure, and with other members of the group (the boys look at her more than any other girl in the group). She laughs a lot with the others in the group. Yet, there is a 'fissure' here also.

When the interviewer asks her why she would like to be Miss Piggy she pauses, and when she answers her voice quality changes, from energetic confidence to a more sing-song, didactic tone. It is as though, at this point, she opts out of a peer-oriented childlike sentiment to an imitation or parody of adult values.

(Hodge and Tripp, 1986, p. 157)

Hodge and Tripp note that this happened again with Emma when discussing *The Incredible Hulk*, where she says 'TV is not very good for you'. The researchers argue that the girl who indulged in karate chops as Miss Piggy now agrees with her mother. 'Both Catherine and Emma say contradictory things, which are a function of social conflict. The interview contains both power relations and solidarity relations, though the two children have quite different orientations to this common set of relationships' (1986, p. 157). Neither side of the contradictory statements, in either child, is on its own 'what the child really thinks'. Hodge and Tripp insist that each child 'really thinks both . . . reflecting tensions in the social relations of the child' (1986, p. 157).

As Ien Ang would argue, each child is working with a number of different gender investments, and Hodge and Tripp's major contribution to audience theory is on the developmental aspect of that. What is particularly valuable about their analysis is, as I have said, the rich diversity of concepts, methods, the individualised and collectivised focus, as well as the comfortable integration of all of this with cultural studies' familiar emphasis on class, gender, power and ideology. In particular, Hodge and Tripp time and again show with their interview excerpts how simplistic any theory of the 'effects' of television violence on supposedly passive viewers is. Above all, their analysis illustrates the value of combining the micro-narratives of situated discussion, reflexivity about the research process and the macro-analysis of 'ideology-critique'.

Conclusion: Televisual literacy

A number of television audience researchers within the media/cultural studies field have taken a combined quantitative/qualitative developmental approach to the child and teenager audience. We looked at Tulloch and Tulloch's research in the previous chapter and Hodge and Tripp's in this chapter. In addition there is Maire Messenger Davies's work on children's interpretations of television reality, which draws strongly on Hodge and Tripp's focus on modality. Much of this work consciously represents itself as promoting the study of 'media literacy', and challenging the 'plug-in-drug' critiques of television effects on children by cultural pessimists like Marie Winn, Neil Postman and George Gerbner. So the emphasis is on children's growing cognitive competence *by way of watching television* rather than 'a clinical diagnosis of harmful effects' (Messenger Davies, 1997, p. 43). Implicitly, also, there is an important critique in this visual literacy tradition to the 'pleasure' emphasis which became relatively hegemonic in feminist audience studies by the late 1980s.

The television literacy tradition (like the feminist one) works from the media studies position of the 'active audience', but it combines a child developmental focus with cultural studies' familiar emphasis on gender, class, ethnicity, and so on. The focus in particular is on age in the context of child development theory. All the researchers mentioned above have an interest in the development of children's story-telling schema and linguistic transformations as part of their 'active audience' analysis. Thus, for example, Messenger Davies draws on Susan Neumann's work to argue that:

> the interpretation of television stories is an active process, with many similarities to reading printed text . . . [T]he common element to both processes is the activation of 'schemata' or mental scenarios based on the readers expectations and knowledge, which guide the viewer/ reader's processing of a series of events as they unfold. . . . Schemata, according to Neumann, could include knowledge of genre and of the normal conventions of different kinds of programs, as well as knowledge of life drawn from experience. Obviously, the younger the

child and the less the child's experience of both art and life, the fewer the schemata available to be activated – or the less literate the child.

(1997, pp. 41–2)

The focus of television literacy audience research is thus both on 'art' (the generic, narrative and other formal competences that children learn; cf. Hodge and Tripp's emphasis on children's need and craving to understand the processes of television production) and on 'knowledge of life drawn from experience'. Messenger Davies, for example, used the empirical method of asking individual children viewing television excerpts to freeze the picture they were watching whenever they saw 'something that couldn't really happen in real life' to generate a number of 'art/internal' and 'life/external' categories.

Messenger Davies's research focus was on children age 6 to 11; and like Hodge and Tripp she found a developmental change in children's interest in genre (from fantasy and cartoons towards realistic representations and comedy) as they gradually acquire complex schemata of meta-recognition and meta-representation over time. Like Hodge and Tripp also, Messenger Davies points to the support her work gives to Piaget's emphasis on a marked developmental shift towards rationalism at around the age of 7 or 8. It is this 'on the threshold of adolescence' age period that draws the attention of Davies as well as Hodge and Tripp because it is then that 'children become less interested in the formal trappings of media products, and begin to be aware of the importance of representing reality realistically, thereby raising social, institutional and political implications' (Messenger Davies, 1997, p. 145). It was their interest in children's developing understanding of these social, institutional and political implications that led the Tullochs, in contrast, to focus on the *difference* between pre-adolescent and teenage children.

Clearly, there are both similarities and differences within the 'television literacy' research tradition, particularly in the emphasis on 'ideology' in some and not others. Hodge and Tripp's references to dominant ideological forms and oppositional readings reflect the time they were writing (mid-1980s) and their influence by the still powerful Marxist semiotics of Stuart Hall and the Birmingham Centre for Contemporary Cultural Studies, to which they acknowledge their debt. The Tullochs' research is also strongly influenced by 'ideology-critique'. Messenger Davies, writing a decade later than Hodge and Tripp, refers less to 'ideology' and more to the inherently 'anti-adult' tendencies in children when she discusses the 'uses of subversion'.

My own view is that children's tendency to resist adult-imposed ideologies and behaviours through their private rituals, games, fantasies, tastes, and interpretations of reality, both in life and in art, is a developmentally desirable one, and it has the evolutionary survival value of making sure that human diversity and adaptability continue.

Children's abiding preoccupation with alternative realities – with pretend games – almost from birth, suggests an extreme unwillingness to accept, untested, adult versions of what life is supposed to be about.

(1997, p. 146)

The shift here is one that Alasuutari has pointed to: from the 'politics' of ideology-critique to the 'pleasure' of non-instrumentalist analysis. The difference is also apparent between Messenger Davies's emphasis on 'prosocial messages' (finding girls more disapproving than boys over the ethics of media deception), and Hodge and Tripp's preference for 'a term such as ideology . . . over "pro-social"' (1986, p. 23). Nevertheless, there also is a marked continuity between Hodge and Tripp and Messenger Davies in the emphasis on the complexity of both popular television (including 'children's' genres, like cartoons) and the child audience's response to it. In particular, there is continuity in the central emphasis on 'modality' in the development of children's symbolic resources.

8

Watching TV videos:

Annie, Rocky *and an audience of 'one, two, or three'*

One of the (sometimes explicitly intended) outcomes among 'televisual literacy' scholars is the emphasis on 'equal', 'balanced' and 'rational' discussion of television between parents and children. Hodge and Tripp say that 'a more open and equal relationship over television could be an educative and bonding factor' (1986, p. 218); and Messenger Davies says that 'tele-literate children have both literate and tele-literate parents who help them to see the connections between TV, books, theatre and real-world experiences' (1997, p. 38).

This sense of familial harmony, balance and mutual, rational education is one that Valerie Walkerdine is deeply suspicious about. This chapter looks at some of Walkerdine's 'audience' analysis as a powerful counter-position to the various 'children, television and violence' and 'televisual literacy' work I have described. In particular, Walkerdine's work differs markedly from research into children's watching of television that mixes quantitative with qualitative methods, in so far that Walkerdine often analyses just one person 'watching' TV, and uses a contextualised psychoanalytical and poststructuralist framework to do so. At the same time, her interest in familial conflict rather than 'middle-class' harmony, and her focus on fantasy rather than the more instrumentalist interest in 'education' of Hodge, Tripp and Davies, draws her much closer to Ien Ang's interest in pleasure and gender. In addition, Walkerdine is reflexive, examining her own role as researcher in the 'reading television' process.

In focusing mainly on Walkerdine's work, this chapter also prioritises an academic analysis of the TV video audience. This, as we will see, is a very different 'take' on this issue from that of public pressure groups like the National Viewers and Listeners' Association or the Movement for Christian Democracy (Hill, 1999).

Poststructuralism and the child audience

Walkerdine's poststructuralism is centrally influenced by Foucault's analysis of the regulatory surveillance systems of modernity. Consequently, her analyses insist on the role of the state and its various professional agencies (like welfare officers, university researchers, etc.) in inscribing women and children within specific discursive practices (like analysing their watching of television videos). She proposes 'that subjects are created through their insertion into practices which are the object of regulation and that it is in and through their positionings within those practices that girls' subjectivities are constituted' (1993, p. 74).

Walkerdine positions her account historically; namely that the modern media initially formed part of state strategies for the regulation of working-class families. 'Government of the masses' in the early part of the twentieth century meant taking the mother 'out of the gin palaces and streets' and making her 'responsible for the psychic health and emotional and cognitive development of her children as well as their preparation for educational success' (1993, p. 75). Technologies of population management included medicine, welfare, law, education and the new media, since 'radio and then television . . . provided a way of getting working-class families off the dangerous streets and into the home. As Briggs relates: 'Children's Hour was conceived by Reith as "a happy alternative to the squalor of the streets and backyards" ' (quoted in Walkerdine, 1993, p. 75).

As in other areas, the mother was held responsible for the role of helping her children use the media to become mentally healthy, socially upright democratic citizens. The professional discourse of 'normal and natural' child development included the notion of mothers correctly regulating their children's media listening and watching.

> Regulation entered the home and found working-class viewing practices wanting. Concern in this area centred on the ways in which parents (read mothers) were regulating their children's viewing and, relatedly, the amount of viewing, as well as on children's exposure to sex and violence. Children had been taken off the streets, where they could be exposed to violence and to sex, both of which could lead to anti-social uprising, only to be confronted with television programmes which brought sex and violence into the living room
>
> (Walkerdine, 1993, p. 75).

Walkerdine's constant reference to 'proletarian families', 'masses', and working-class 'uprising' makes clear the political centrality of 'regulation' and social control in her ideology-critique. Her poststructuralist use of Foucault, however, is evident in her focus on professional regulatory discourses of surveillance and control; in which academic research has had a central role. In particular, Walkerdine points to psychological research, beginning with Himmelweit, Oppenheim and Vince in the 1950s, which 'expressed considerable concern about parents' regulation of their children's viewing, describing children who they felt viewed excessively as "addicts" ' (1993, p. 76). Middle-class parents were to be encouraged to continue to regulate their children's viewing responsibly, while broadcasters should regulate their programmes as suitable for unsupervised working-class children. Walkerdine adds that this 'normal family/pathological family' binary concern was 'absolutely endemic to the vast bulk of research on families and television which followed from Himmelweit, particularly within the field of social psychology' (1993, p. 76).

It is interesting to compare at this point Walkerdine's positioning of Himmelweit's research with Hodge and Tripp's, since both emphasise, reflexively, the role of academic research in societal power relations. Hodge and Tripp take a Kuhnian 'paradigm' approach to the history of the 'TV violence' debate, arguing for periods of 'normal science', in Kuhn's sense, followed by a period of paradigm crisis. 'Normal science' was represented by the 'effects' paradigm of the 1950s and 1960s, where the work of Schramm and Himmelweit *et al.*, rhetorically provided 'a reassuring competence' based on the 'confident basis' of an 'open-ended set of worthwhile projects' that television viewing 'for most children, under most conditions, would do little harm, and some good' (1986, p. 192).

> So a steadily increasing range of different responses was measured ever more precisely, controlling for another increasing range of variables based on mental, physical, or social attributes such as sex, age, IQ, class, race, viewing habits, and viewing situations. Superficially there were all the hallmarks of progress, through refinement and cumulation.
>
> (Hodge and Tripp, 1986, p. 193)

One of the causes of paradigm crisis at the time, Hodge and Tripp argue, was the new rhetorical strength of behaviourist psychology, which generated a series of classic laboratory studies through the 1960s, including Bandura's famous study where children exposed to a film of Bobo dolls being bashed then replicated this behaviour in the laboratory more than children who had not. These studies 'seemed to demonstrate, with impressive elegance and ingenuity in their experimental design, an effect that had eluded the broader grained work of pioneers like Schramm and Himmelweit' (1986, p. 193). This paradigm crisis, Hodge and Tripp argue, put 'violent effects' of television back on the agenda, and provided new academic rewards for researchers, as in the USA the Surgeon General's report, *Television and Growing Up: the impact of televised violence* (1972), opened the floodgates of research funding. A 1982 report by the US Department of Health and Human Services estimated that 90 per cent of all research publications about television's influence on behaviour had appeared in the ten years since the Surgeon General's report.

Hodge and Tripp then go on to describe a continuing series of paradigm shifts in the TV violence debate, as academics intertwined themselves with governments and the self-interested media industry. For example:

- Comstock's urge for a paradigm shift, drawing on new 'conceptual schemas' to explain the lack of definitive data coming out from the post-1972 research;
- Eysenck's renewed behaviourist assault, as he criticised the Surgeon General's report for going 'soft' on effects of television violence and sex, because of government and media corporation pressure (comparable to that of the tobacco industry in relation to cigarette advertising);
- the 'crisis of sociology' agenda of the mid-1970s, which challenged the self-confident empiricism of American and British psychology, sociology and education for refusing to take account of their own underpinning ideological assumptions;
- the importance of critical sociology and semiotics (as represented by Stuart Hall and the Birmingham CCCS), as high modality programmes like the television news began to attract research attention, and as 'political' violence (such as police to striking picketers) repositioned the 'TV violence' debate at the societal level, raising questions like 'whose interests are being served by either representing or concealing violence' (1986, p. 198).

Hodge and Tripp's 'charitable attitude' is a call for more interdisciplinary debate and co-operation in order to bridge the 'stand-off between the critical tradition and what some of its practitioners often dismissively label as the "positivistic" empiricist tradition dominant in America' (1986, p. 198). Hodge and Tripp's own study, *Children and Television*, with its sophisticated mix of (critical) qualitative and quantitative methods was, of course, an attempt to suggest ways to bridge this gap, especially by way of new theories in socio-linguistics.

Valerie Walkerdine is far more single-minded, critical and dismissive in her history of the 'TV violence' debate from Himmelweit onwards. She is especially hostile to psychological studies that relate family viewing to patterns of interaction and communication, pointing to their regulatory approaches to the child as 'human animal' and their suppression of analysis of any emotions other than the 'emotional attachments and bonds between mother and child' (1993, p. 76). The pathologised (working-class) family and the 'escapist' child viewer are, Walkerdine argues, the product of this type of television/audience research. 'Any family which has defences, or escapes, is therefore "badly adjusted to reality" and by implication, unhealthy. There is no place to consider conscious and unconscious processes, meanings and fantasies within this paradigm except in a model of ill-health' (1993, p. 77). The kinds of 'knowledges' that this academic research produces about the families watching television is, Walkerdine argues, one of the 'deeply regulative' technologies of the social, which her own research is seeking to subvert via an alternative theory and methodology.

An alternative methodology: just one 'pathological' family

Walkerdine's entire theoretical trajectory in her *Annie* audience analysis leads her to the 'Porta' family. This family was, in the eyes of various welfare agencies, 'extremely unhealthy. They in no way counted as a family who viewed or interacted in the right kind of way' (1993, p. 78) – the kind of way, in other words, that our 'visual literacy' scholars would prefer. The father, who is Maltese, abuses his working-class English wife and is having an affair with another woman. The mother is pregnant with her fourth child, and has three daughters, Melissa who is twelve, Eliana (the subject of this research) who is six, and Karen, three. Both the police, who have been called to the house several times because of the father's violence to Mrs Porta, and the educational welfare officer who is concerned with the mental health of the children see this as a 'problem' family. By middle-class psychologists' standards, their viewing patterns are also 'unhealthy', since mother and father neither watch nor discuss television with the children, and even during the research process Eliana and her sisters gave no 'serious' attention to the television video they had chosen to watch.

So, how can this be a 'serious' research study, focused as it is on just one child playing in front of one video on the television. The answer lies in Walkerdine's careful – historical and situated – contextualisation of this one child and one video:

- Walkerdine's historical description of the pathologisation of working-class families and the role of the media as 'technologies of the social' has provided the theoretical basis and context for watching the Porta family watch television.
- The situated account of Eliana playing with her sisters in front of the video, intermittently using parts of the video narrative to work through her own pains and fantasies embeds that earlier history in a very specific 'micro-narrative'.
- The account of the interaction between the researcher (Walkerdine herself) and Mrs Porta in responding to the children's comments about the video situates the researcher's descriptions reflexively within 'the uneven, power-laden field of social discourse' (Ang, 1996, pp. 75–6).
- Walkerdine's analysis of the video text, *Annie* (and its genre) focuses on the interplay of (societal) ideologies and (personal) subjectivities via the realm of fantasy.

A familiar text

Annie is an award-winning 'family' musical, which was first shown on British television in 1986. Its subject is an orphan in an institution run by a drunken working-class woman, Mrs Hannigan. Annie, a girl with lots of 'fight' who has attempted to run away several times, is rescued from the orphanage by an armaments millionaire, Daddy Warbucks. At first this is simply a cynical political exercise and publicity stunt (the story is based on President Hoover's hiring of a businessman during the depression to obtain support for a charity programme). But Annie successively charms both the millionaire's staff and then the bad-tempered Daddy Warbucks himself. She softens his hard exterior, turns him into a father figure, and makes him begin to notice his secretary Grace, who has become Annie's mother figure. Thus a quasi-family is established which, through Annie's continuing charm (this time on President Roosevelt) leads to Daddy Warbucks' enlistment in fund-raising for the New Deal. It turns out that Daddy Warbucks had grown up poor in Liverpool, so his rise to fortune is contrasted with the criminal working-class family of Miss Hannigan. Daddy Warbucks adopts Annie (after rescuing her from kidnap by the 'evil' working class), and is clearly shown to become romantically interested in Grace as a result. 'Annie has therefore attained a happy and rich family, brought together two parent figures and helped in the economic salvation of a nation gripped by deep economic depression' (1993, p. 80).

Walkerdine notes that the story of Annie is strikingly similar to many contemporary comic stories read by working-class girls. It is also similar to the Shirley Temple films which, as Charles Eckert demonstrates, focus on a poor girl who charms the rich, persuades them to love the poor, and provide charity for the unemployed during the depression. Walkerdine describes Annie (and Shirley) as a mythical figure (in Roland Barthes's sense), since

> while she is coded as working class, she actually has no past, no history, no family and no community. The way out for her is not to refind those things, but to strive to enter the bourgeoisie. She has nothing to belong to. She represents a working class ripe for transformation, in this case, the case of the female, to be achieved through marriage.
>
> (1993, p. 80)

At this point of the analysis, Walkerdine is representing a familiar form of 'Screen Theory' analysis (common in the 1970s, when Eckert did important work) by way of a central textual focus. But this is extended by her following psychoanalytical/empirical account.

Psychoanalysis and the family audience

In analysing *Annie*, Walkerdine notes that a man loves a woman only when his heart is softened by a child.

Annie therefore has a special, Oedipal place. In addition, there is the fantasy of the three contrasting mother-figures: the drunken Miss Hannigan, the criminal girlfriend, and the pure, good, unnoticed Grace. The former two are clearly coded as working class, of the streets and unsuitable parents. The little girl, by her charm, can omnipotently avoid these in favour of Grace. I want to suggest that for Annie, as for Shirley, the kind of love that she offers is to be understood as above all innocent and that this covers over and elides issues of sexuality and erotic attraction which enter only as unsavoury. There are some very powerful fantasies at work here, which provide ample sustenance for a poor girl living in an abusing family. These fantasies provide both a point of identification for Eliana and a way of reading, and perhaps in fantasy overcoming, the terrible obstacles that confront her in growing up.

(Walkerdine, 1993, p. 81)

In adopting her psychoanalytical approach to 'fantasies precisely in the life histories of the participants concerned' (1993, p. 81), Walkerdine clearly sets herself against the kind of developmental approach I discussed in the previous chapter. She argues that Eliana and her sisters 'are not shaped either in terms of stage of development, nor simply through a process of linguistic meaning-making in interaction with the text' (1993, p. 81). So much, then, for Hodge and Tripp! Rather, the sisters are 'produced in the complex family history in which the participants are already inscribed in meanings – the meanings which regulate them, the meanings through which their actions, needs, desires and fantasies are made to signify' (1993, p. 81).

Walkerdine wants to understand 'how a family produces a narrative of their circumstances, their hopes, their longings, pain and so forth.' For example, Eliana's mother and father both came to London with 'hopes and dreams, dreams which lie shattered in poverty, oppression, abuse and illness' (1993, p. 82). Via the 'pleasurable, comforting' reading of *Annie*, Eliana's 'deep pre-Oedipal feelings about her mother can be turned into dislike for a woman who it seems must deserve the beatings she is getting, and who comes between her and the deeply admired father, the father who abuses his wife' (1993, p. 82).

Watching Eliana 'watching' *Annie*

Walkerdine is in the living-room with Eliana and her sisters. The researcher is recording on audiotape, the girls are playing, the mother is in the kitchen and the father is out. The girls decide to put on a video, and they choose one bought by their father, *Annie* – a favourite which they have seen several times. The girls do not sit down to watch the video, but play with a frozen bottle of water. Walkerdine describes their interactions, Melissa going out to the kitchen where her mother scolds her and tells her she can go and live with her father. Melissa knows about the affair, and in conversation with Walkerdine, the mother claims that the father buys her daughter's support. After a brief moment of violence between the other two sisters, Eliana makes her only reference to the video. Miss Hannigan has appeared drunk on screen, and Eliana says to the researcher: 'She's supposed to be drunk, but she ain't . . . 'cos it's water.' At that point there is a noise at the front door and the children excitedly say 'It's daddy come back.' But it is not, and after a brief panic, Mrs Porta comes into the sitting room. Eliana asks her mother if she can offer the researcher a lager, and within two minutes Karen says 'mummy's drunk', which provokes a reaction from her mother: 'They say I'm drunk, but I'm not.'

Now Mrs Porta begins a long conversation with the researcher while all the children sit and watch the end of the video. She tells Walkerdine about the hardship of cleaning up after her husband, about his affair, about Melissa knowing about it, about the possibility – and fears – of a late abortion, about her loneliness and desperation, which led her to hitchhike back to Yorkshire the previous weekend to see her sister. She repeats that Melissa sticks up for her father. The video ends during this conversation, and Eliana takes off her microphone, ending the recording.

Walkerdine argues that though there is only one reference to *Annie* on the audiotape, the video plays a significant part in the family's attempts to understand and cope with its situation. Although it does not 'shape an overt discussion of the middle-class kind', the video does act as 'a relay point in producing ways of engaging with what is going on – and so am I, because my presence enables other people to address remarks to me that can be heard by other members of the household and therefore be attended to' (1993, p. 85). In particular, the children discuss their mother's drinking via the image of Miss Hannigan's drunkenness; and Mrs Porta refutes being likened to the cruel drunken mother figure via her comments to the researcher. Annie's 'escape' thus has nothing to do with the 'escapism' of moralistic interactionist researchers analysing the bad 'effects' of television viewing. On the one hand, her escape can be coded, by the children, as responding to a mother who is judged and found wanting; on the other hand, 'escape to another woman is a route that their mother claims that the father is also using' (1993, p. 85).

Walkerdine is, however, quite clear about the real-world status of this 'escape'.

[T]here is no narrative here for addressing the oppression suffered by the mother, nor of the conflict between the mother and father. There is no model for a father's cruelty that cannot be tamed by an alluring and enticing little girl. The mother does, however, use the film and my presence to provide a counter-argument to the one represented by the film and by the children's reference to her drunkenness. She not only claims that she is not drunk but goes on to talk about the difficulty of her life, her suffering and why she gets angry with Melissa's siding with her father. She thus tries to convince her children and win their support through my presence, which gives her a vehicle through which she can refute the *Annie* version of events. The father is present during this exchange, his place being metonymically held by the video of *Annie* itself. He is thus symbolically marked as the benefactor, the bearer of the gift and the bearer of the means through which their escape from this oppression might be possible.

(1993, p. 86)

So there *is* discussion around *Annie*, Walkerdine insists. It just isn't the middle-class style of sitting down and rationally debating the content and form of the programme that visual literacy scholars hope for. This is deep, heated and painful discussion. It is even the case that what the Portas discuss is sex and violence, since there is certainly a lot in the household. Yet they discuss it not in an abstracted and rationalist sense, but in terms of the conflicts and pains in their lives (1993, p. 86).

This narrative she has told – as surveillant Other – is, Walkerdine says, one of 'subjection and subjectivity'. It is not a story which the Porta family is totally free to transform; but nor is it totally determined by the factual and fictional narratives in which they are inscribed. 'Watching television differently cannot solve their problems, the complex psychic effects of dealing with oppression, the complex mixing of conscious and unconscious, psychic and social' (1993, p. 87). But at least telling this story is a challenge in the regulatory sphere of academia to the long-term synergy between state and 'professional' discourses of surveillance.

A reflexive account of her own surveillant power as researcher has been a major and sophisticated feature of Valerie Walkerdine's work. In an earlier analysis of one working-class father repeatedly watching the video of *Rocky* on his television, Walkerdine describes her initial shock as her subject watches a gruesome heavyweight boxing sequence again and again. All the simple stereotypes of the working-class male and macho violence were available to her in this first shock of recognition. However, the researcher then builds up layer upon layer of analysis which complicates this picture.

- The sociological account which positions the working-class father as 'head' of his household, but far down the class power structure. This account is close to the D.H. Lawrence's *Sons and Lovers* narrative (at least as reworked in Trevor Griffiths' television version) where the violence of the father is explained but not justified in terms of his own oppression within the class system.
- The feminist account of this man's daughter's 'tomboy' agency; his ambivalence in relation to a daughter who is not 'feminine' as he might have hoped, but with the qualities of a son he might have had – and how this is worked through his – and her – TV video pleasures.

- The reflexive account which parallels and interweaves this father/daughter working-class relationship with Walkerdine's situation as a child as her own father's little 'fairy'; the similarities and differences in the two father/daughter fantasies, as Walkerdine rises out of her working-class origins to become an academic who is now surveillant of (and initially disapproving of) the other working-class father. Her father's fetishised little fairy now becomes another father's powerfully surveillant Other.

Walkerdine calls for researchers to recognise their own fantasised positions when they engage in situated research, as they seek the 'mutual knowledge' claimed by ethnography. Her emphasis on academic surveillance as one of Foucault's technologies of power is, she argues, 'an important step beyond assertions that academics should side with the oppressed, that film-makers see themselves as workers or that teachers should side with their pupils' (Walkerdine, 1985, p. 191). This kind of identification can be seen as little more than a 'wish-fulfilling denial of power', while in fact researchers are reconstituting themselves as one of Foucault's 'authors', narrating tales (about a working-class father watching *Rocky*) which ask questions, monitor repeated viewing of violence, and 'bring to light' an account of a pathologised family. It is the temporal, biographical and conceptual relationship between herself as a 'good' ('normal') working-class child fantasising a world in which she was 'small, protected and never growing up' (1985, p. 187) and the 'bad' ('pathologised'), violence-loving father that she later reconstructs through her surveillant discourse which brings together the psychoanalytical, poststructuralist and reflexively situated accounts that are so symptomatic of Walkerdine's work. Although there are features of screen theory's focus on powerfully inscribing texts in her analyses, it is the combination of psychoanalysis with a critical ethnographic focus on local micro-narratives which is Walkerdine's major contribution to audience theory. As she says, her's is a psychoanalysis which critiques its use in screen theory 'to explore the relations within a film rather than to explain the engagement with the film by viewers already inserted in a multiplicity of sites for identification' (1985, p. 168).

Reading audiences

Walkerdine's piece on *Annie* is printed in David Buckingham's edited book, *Reading Audiences*, which, published in 1993, is a good example of Denzin and Lincoln's 'fifth moment' of qualitative research – representing the 'double crisis' (of representation and legitimation). How, Denzin and Lincoln ask, 'are qualitative studies to be evaluated in the poststructural moment?' (1998, p. 22) Theories need now to be 'read in narrative terms, as "tales of the field". . . . The concept of the aloof researcher has been abandoned. . . . The search for grand narratives will be replaced by more local, small-scale theories fitted to specific problems and specific situations' (Denzin and Lincoln, 1998, p. 22).

All of the chapters in Buckingham's book are small-scale 'tales from the field'. In 'Taking sides? What young girls do with television', Chris Richards resorts to his own immediate familial situation, discussing just his two young daughters. In her analysis of *The Mahabharata* as 'sacred soap', Marie Gillespie does an ethnographic study of just one Hindu family in Southall, London. Valerie Walkerdine also studies just one family, and particularly one young girl in the family. David Buckingham talks with very few focus groups of boys in his piece on 'policing masculinity'. Gemma Moss focuses on just four 12-year-old girls in her studies of romance and teenagers' reading histories. Julian Sefton-Green focuses entirely on the 'novel' of just one Greek Cypriot teenager in his discussion of boys' liking for violent stories. Martin Barker mainly focuses on three cases studies of 'fans' of the *2000 AD* comic. And Julian Wood bases his analysis on sitting with just one group of boys watching one violent video.

We are a long way here from the quantitative studies of children and television that Walkerdine castigates in her own discipline of psychology. We are a long way even from Hodge and Tripp. 'What should we say about these three case studies?' says Martin Barker (1993, p. 176). Like Walkerdine, he is prepared to say a lot; partly because in this case Barker does use a survey questionnaire to 'identify recurrent patterns' according to gender (more girl readers are prepared to designate themselves as left-wing than boys), what other comics are read (fans of American comics are most likely to find the central Judge Dredd character in *2000 AD* right-wing), and political self-designation (left-wing readers are more likely to designate the comic's authors as left-wing too; right-wing readers enjoy comics as a 'world of secret knowledge' rather than seeing 'a subversive world'). But Barker, the only author here to discuss his quantitative data (from 250 completed questionnaires), certainly does not rely on it too far, arguing (somewhat defensively): 'It seems to me that the use of questionnaires is justified provided researchers are aware that in using them they necessarily fragment the meanings of responses.'

Mainly, Barker used his questionnaires to isolate a few 'typical' readers in relation to 'key issues' that arose from the survey: like intoxication with the medium, a recognition of 'layers' in the comic; a liking of ambiguities in its heroes and villains; its 'political' dimension; suspicion at being classed a 'fan'; and orientation to the 'future'. By way of his three case studies Barker is then able to describe the very different 'orientations' readers have to these 'key issues'. Thus

Alan is a left-wing loner, and *2000 AD* captures but also offers shape to the ambiguities of his political orientation. Of Dredd himself he admits his fascistic tendencies, but adds that 'maybe' some of these tendencies are necessary in a world as dangerous as his and ours – and Alan is one who sees Dredd's world as . . . essentially a satire on ours. It may not be going too far to say that in Alan personal and political responses combine: his personal unease at mass situations, and his political radicalism which incorporates a fear of massification find more than echoes in Dredd's world.

(1993, pp. 170–1)

Barker compares Alan with the more affluent Michael who is a 'high culture' reader of the comic, comparing it favourably with American comics read by 'Townies/Homies'; and with Mary whose pessimistic structure of feeling in relation to the future is to some extent 'overwritten by the sheer power of imagining' (Barker, 1993, p. 175).

By way of examining the situated biographies of these different fans in terms of their own political ambivalences (and 'fan' ambivalences), Barker is able to erect his own generalised 'layers' of decoding with which he challenges the 'multiple, contextually-determined and potentially infinite' (1993, p. 177) audience theories of postmodernism. His three layers are as follows:

- reading: making literal sense of texts through understanding and using the text's conventions of story-telling;
- textually demanded interpretation: the comic's overt strands of intertextuality which ask readers to make connections between Dredd's world and our own;
- intercalation into the reader's social career: thus 'Alan plans to become a writer/artist of comics, with the ambition of eventually producing something like *2000 AD* himself. . . . Already he writes and draws comics for many hours every week' (1993, p. 171). This is the 'political' engagement of a left-wing loner in contrast to Michael whose high cultural commitment to 'intelligence' involves 'a sharp demarcation of comics-reading from the sphere of work, and the future' (Barker, 1993, p. 173).

As Denzin and Lincoln say, 'in the poststructural moment' notions of generalisability and reliability become highly problematic. Nevertheless, some audience theorists in Buckingham's book still attempt to generalise by relating macro-social theories to situated micro-narratives. As we have seen, Walkerdine ties her analysis of one 'unhealthy' family to Foucault's critique of the regulatory discourses of modernity. Similarly, Barker relates his mode of discourse analysis (drawing on the new 'rhetorical' approach within social psychology) to broader issues 'of the organisation and control of production, and of our own lives, within the framework of capitalism' (1993, p. 161). Barker's attempt to refocus on class (which is shared, if less explicitly, by a number of the other contributors who focus on working-class boys) shows that some audience theorists have no difficulty in attempting to synthesise one of modernity's 'grand narratives' (Marxism) with a poststructuralist emphasis on local stories and multiple identities.

Nevertheless it is this latter emphasis – on the partial, fragmentary and local story – rather than the grand narrative which dominates Buckingham's collection. Thus:

- Richards, drawing on Chodorow and Giddens, argues for a sociological psychoanalysis in which 'gendered identity has its "origins" in particular intra-familial relations, not in "universal structures" and not just in the consumption of "cultural stereotypes" ' (1993, p. 27);
- Buckingham, following Segal, rejects sex role theory for ignoring 'the dynamic complexity and the contradictions of actual gender relations in favour of the view of individuals as unitary and wholly conformist . . . recipients of adult's attempts at socialisation' (1993, p. 90);
- Moss rejects 'ideological effects' traditions of analysis which focus on reading as a unitary activity 'which happens in the interior space of the mind' rather than conceiving of reading as a very diversified social activity embedded 'in particular moments in time, in particular social settings, involving particular participants' (1993, p. 121).
- Wood wants us to 'try and understand the dynamic, precarious, virtual uses of symbols in common culture, not understanding the everyday through popular representations, but understanding popular representations through the everyday. Video comes into play, then, in a field where social agents (in this case young people) are already creating meanings, rather than waiting to be "filled up" or merely distracted' (1993, p. 198).

Certain 'generalising' statements are common to all of the chapters in this book:

- that audiences (including young audiences) are not 'passive dupes' but agentive creators of meaning (indeed, as in Walkerdine's account, there is the general suspicion that those researchers who reduce audiences to passive dupes, or indeed to class, gender, or ethnic 'representatives', are themselves agents of modernity's professional technologies of surveillance);
- that audience response is a social practice situated in a diverse range of time/space co-ordinates and local settings;
- that discourses which 'are brought into play by the text are not infinite, nor are they equally available to all. Readers do indeed make meanings, but they do so under conditions which are not of their own choosing' (Buckingham, 1993, p. 14);
- that the 'power' of the media is not a '*possession* either of texts or of audiences, but as something which is embedded in the *relationship* between them' (Buckingham, 1993, p. 14) – as, for example, in the relationship Walkerdine discovers between the *Annie* 'middle-classing' of family and the diverse readings (of the video and talk about the video) within the Porta family;
- that generalised theoretical statements about power, gender, class, and so on cannot be 'identified in the abstract, or apportioned according to some generalised theoretical equation. On the contrary, it is very much an empirical issue that needs to be addressed in relation to specific audiences, specific media and specific social contexts of use' (Buckingham, 1993, p. 14).

Thus, in response to the approaches covered in the last chapter, child '"development" cannot adequately be understood without situating it within the social contexts and relationships in which it occurs, and which essentially bring it about. Age is, in this sense, a *social* category, not merely a biological one and it interacts with other social categories in complex and diverse ways' (Buckingham, 1993, p. 15).

Only empirical analysis, all these authors insist, will help us to understand these 'complex and diverse ways' (more than one author here, for example, regrets that the dominance of recent audience analysis by feminism has led to a lack of empirical audience studies about young boys' fantasies). But this, it is argued, is not empiricism, for two major reasons.

- First, all of these empirical accounts (as in the Walkerdine example) are consciously *generated* by theory, and this determines also the methodologies in use. So, for example, Buckingham's theoretical emphasis on the complexity and ambivalence of sex role negotiation leads not only to his particular choice of subject matter (i.e. discussion by boys and girls of television genres *for* 'boys' and *for* 'girls'), but also the methodology he employs, since brief extracts from a few, small focus groups are quite adequate to indicate his main theme: boys' anxiety in 'talk' about humiliation at the hands of other boys.
- Second, every chapter in this book partakes of Denzin and Lincoln's doubt that qualitative researchers can ever directly capture lived experience, since such experience is created in the social text that the researcher her/himself writes. Every chapter is reflexive about theory and method – especially since the subject area is young people who are consistently situated in an unequal position by parents, teachers, and researchers.

David Buckingham's anxiety here is symptomatic, when he is discussing a young boy's confusion between the use of the terms 'racism' and 'sexism'.

> [I]t should be emphasised that the issue was introduced 'spontaneously' rather than in response to a question from the interviewer. Nevertheless, as an adult, the interviewer is almost invariably identified as a kind of teacher, and his presence may well cue responses which in one way or another reflect this. In this case, I would suspect that the anti-sexist discourse derives primarily from the school, where racism and sexism (and other 'isms') are likely to be dealt with together as aspects of 'equal opportunities'. Vinh's eagerness to introduce and pursue these issues may well reflect a desire to 'please teacher'.
>
> (Buckingham, 1993, p. 95)

Different researchers in Buckingham's book coped with this anxiety in different ways methodologically. At one end of the spectrum was Marie Gillespie who spent three years with the Dhani family watching two versions of *The Mahabharata* with them. Though she admits that her presence 'obviously led them to express responses, ideas and views about which they might otherwise have remained silent' (Gillespie, 1993, p. 54), we are given to assume that these are mainly comments elaborating on their own cultural common sense for an outsider. Otherwise, 'they soon accepted me as a family member and thankfully talked to me or ignored my presence as they wished' as she herself slowly grows closer to them with her 'fondness for tea and chapatis' (1993, p. 54). At the other end of the spectrum is Martin Barker who cannot afford to meet his interviewees at all, and sends them an audiotape to record on to instead. This proves to be an accidentally innovative methodology, which Barker proceeds to theorise.

> I would now recommend it as a procedure for others – provided that they have established a contract with their respondents first. From the evidence of the tapes, each person constructed a fictional persona of me and talked to that. Because this was not interfered with by what I am actually like, or by my interrupting to ask additional questions, or by making non-verbal responses of any kind, this fictional persona had the effect of enabling people to respond to questions more fully than they themselves expected. . . . Answers come with increasing fluidity as time passes.
>
> (Barker, 1993, p. 165)

It is Barker's notion of a 'contract' with respondents and his notion of 'natural readers' that Gemma Moss has most difficulty with in her analysis of girls reading teenage romances. Barker argues elsewhere that 'a "contract" involves an agreement that a text will talk to us in ways we recognise'; and that the 'media are only capable of exerting power over audiences to the extent that there is a "contract" between texts and audience which relates to some specifiable aspect(s) of the audience's social lives' (1989, p. 261). This notion of a text/reader 'contract' relates to Barker's insistence on reintroducing the political economy of the text; the particular marketing of comics in the 1970s/1980s, for example, to specific but different kinds of male 'fan'. This diversified marketing does establish continuities for the *2000 AD's* readers – in its political ambiguity for example – which readers then fashion according to their perceptions of their own futures.

> I would argue that to readers *2000 AD*, and 'Judge Dredd in particular, balance between several incompatible orientations to the future: a conservative critique of change, fearful of mobs, crime and lawlessness; a heroic, Clint Eastwood vision of male rescuers overcoming, or at least stemming the tide of destruction which is endemic to the State as much as in society; and a radical suspicion of the police as enforcers. My readers accurately perceive the ambivalences in the comic, and opt for that relation to them which co-ordinates with their own images of their own futures.
>
> (Barker, 1993, p. 178)

What is common to all of Barker's respondents is a sense of their own marginality, which is then worked through quite different biographical histories and futures.

For Moss, this notion of a 'contract' may work for regular readers of boys comics, but is less convincing when Barker tries to apply it to girls' reading of teenage romances. First, it is 'highly problematic to assert that somewhere there is a group of girls to whom *Jackie* speaks without locking such a group into the position of hapless victims unable to act in their own best interests, before one has even heard what they might have to say' (1993, pp. 118–9). Second, to assume that the researcher can recognise the form that the 'contract' will take in advance of selecting respondents is a questionable methodological procedure designed to weed out any data that does not fit the critic's advance notion of what the 'natural audience's' relation to the text should be. Third, it misses the fact that teenage girls develop rapidly through a series of levels of reading; so that among the four girls Moss looks at (all initially thought to be readers of the Sweet Valley High romance series), one is still a regular reader, comparing these books with the boringly detailed books her mother would prefer her to read; another has begun to dip into her mother's hidden Jackie Collins best sellers, linking these 'dirty books' to her curiosity about a known adult audience; another now rejects 'soppy' romances altogether, preferring 'gory' genres; and the fourth makes differentiations between 'soppy' romance novels (the Sweet Valley High romances) and more worldly romances. Moss is rejecting here the notion of an interpretive community for teenage romances as an homogenous entity.

> I am seeking a more divergent account, capable of dealing with change as well as stasis . . . I have sought to show how the romance is always contextualised in relation to specific reading histories which may differ. . . . Whilst broadly united in terms of class and educational background, these girls' reading histories are far from homogenous and the places they construct for the romance very different. . . . The romance does not speak about a single thing. It speaks differently to the girls in this group, but those differences can only be understood in relation to other kinds of texts which it is not, other kinds of reading from which it differs.
>
> (Moss, 1993, p. 133)

Gemma Moss seems less interested than other writers in this book (like Valerie Walkerdine) in the relationship between the girls interviewed and the researcher. But, like Walkerdine, she is concerned with the issue of children as objects of regulation by adults. Moss argues that the four girls she interviewed all came from a relatively affluent background and a selective school. Thus the 'kinds of choices they make about what to read and when to read become the subject of others' approval or disapproval. Much of this is governed by the need to be doing well at reading' (1993, p. 124). This is not only a matter of set reading at school. 'Reading books in one's spare time has educational implications. It suggests making an effort to do something worthwhile. . . . Nicola doesn't report any way in which her parents try to regulate what she reads, but she does say she reads because she gets told off for watching too much TV' (1993, p. 124). Book reading becomes a key forum for the girls, where 'the kinds of books that are read become another means of judging competence. These kinds of judgements are also used by the girls against each other' (1993, p. 124). Whereas other writers talk about young teenage boys using television to negotiate their own uncertainty and humiliation in relation to imperfect bodies, the girls' debate about particular reading histories allows them both to denigrate other girls' reading and to work within their (genre and class) approved regulatory discourse.

David Buckingham found that girls were more mutually supportive than boys when talking about television. 'There was often a sense that in talking about certain aspects of television, boys were unavoidably putting themselves on the line, and rendering themselves open to ridicule and possible humiliation from their peers' (1993, p. 98). Moss, however, indicates that girls are not always mutually supportive in their 'talk'. It may simply be that young teenage girls from an upwardly mobile middle-class background choose which are the important terrains on which to 'humiliate' their peers.

Buckingham throws an additional spin on the reflexive debate in this book about adult/teenage 'talk' by describing the discussion of Madonna between a *female* interviewer and teenage boys. Buckingham has already noted in his analysis that girls are much more interested in discussing the physical attractiveness of male characters than boys are prepared to discuss positively the bodies of female characters, and that the gender of the interviewer seemed to make little difference to this. 'For boys of this age, the discussion of sexuality may well hold more dangers than pleasures, in that their own power and security are so uncertain.' (1993, p. 107) But in one interview, the female interviewer offers her own sexual challenge to the boys.

Int: It strikes me that girls are more used to expressing those sorts of things 'cause they're encouraged to, whereas boys aren't in quite that way. Not till they're a bit older.

Petros: Well, if you fancy someone like that, you keep it a secret . . . 'Cause all the boys in our class spread it . . . 'Cause there's all these sort of male sex symbols.

Int: You got it!

Sean: But there isn't really like a lady superstar like you talk about all the time.

Int: What about Madonna? Isn't she?

Petros: She's not good looking, she can just sing!

Int: Mm.

Sean: The last video's a bit . . .

Int: Raunchy?

Sean: Yeah! No, but I mean you wouldn't exactly want a girl hanging
        around you, all she was doing was drooling in your ear and stuff.
        Would you? [Interviewer laughs.]

As Buckingham says, the adult female interviewer adopts here a challenging
role in an area – the discussion of sexuality – where the boys appear distinctly vulnerable; and they respond by becoming more moralistic as the discussion continues (Peter arguing that Madonna is a hypocrite for being both
such an overtly 'raunchy' woman yet giving money to AIDS research).

> In this respect she [the interviewer] effectively forces the boys to
> 'account for themselves' and thus exposes some of the contradictions
> they might have preferred to avoid. On the other hand, however, her
> active pursuit of the topic offers a means of exercising power in the sit-
> uation. Her enthusiastic comment 'you got it' at the start of the extract
> seems to define her as a sexual being or at least as a person who is
> capable of the kind of sexual fantasies the boys seem concerned to dis-
> avow. What is unspoken here, though implicit throughout, is the boys'
> anxiety about their own lack of sexual experience – experience which
> would at one level 'confirm' their heterosexual masculinity. As in the
> classroom, 'sex talk' offers a powerful means for teachers to exert
> power over their students, by positioning them as less knowledgeable
> and experienced, and hence unavoidably as 'children'.
>
> (Buckingham, 1993, p. 110)

This is an extremely interesting extract and analysis from Buckingham, raising various questions about power and gender ethics – both during research
and in the classroom. It is, for example, inconceivable that an extract from
an interview between a male interviewer with sexual fantasies and female
teenagers around this topic would have been discussed with any kind of
approval. Similarly, as Martin Barker says, there is no equivalent for men
and boys to the kind of research on women's pleasures and fantasies discussed earlier.

> It is curious to ask why it is nigh on impossible to imagine a parallel
> study of say, soft porn, violent adventure or sports stories, arguing
> that men's pleasure in these genres is not evidence of their textual sub-
> ordination or ideological construction, rather it reveals the ways in
> which men have to negotiate with dominant constructions of mas-
> culinity – or even femininity – and through fantasy cope with the
> stresses and demands of living out those contradictions.
>
> (Barker, 1993, p. 160)

Buckingham has his own careful set of answers to this apparent 'unfairness' to men and boys. To focus on the 'suffering and self-alienation' of masculinity 'is to ignore the pleasure it entails' (1993, p. 110) and its imbrication with possibilities of power which are available even for 'vulnerable' teenage boys. As Buckingham emphasises,

> we need to consider the social and material *consequences* of 'doing masculinity'. Heterosexual male power is not simply a discursive game: the institutional, economic and physical dimensions of that power depend precisely on maintaining these discourses of 'true' masculinity. As Bronwyn Davies succinctly argues, '[p]ositioning oneself as a person within the terms made available within a particular social order also creates and sustains that social order'.
>
> (1993, p. 111)

Which is why, of course, there is a world of difference between a female interviewer (or teacher) saying 'you got it!' in relation to sexual fantasies in an interview with boys and a male interviewer doing the same in an interview with girls. Given, though, the emphasis of Buckingham and others in this book on the importance of school education, some of these extracts and examples do draw attention to the extremely complex issues of power and reflexivity that proponents of 'television literacy' often fail to address.

One major value of Buckingham's book here is that it goes beyond the kind of individual researcher/interviewee encounter we have been describing to consider reflexively broader paradigms of audience research. Buckingham concludes his book by contrasting the 'radical' *Screen* theory tradition which 'provided a definition of academic theorists and avant-garde cultural producers as a kind of vanguard party of cultural struggle' (1993, p. 207) with the more recent 'progressive' tradition which celebrates too easily the 'symbolic creativity' of audiences. In this latter version, far from 'regarding young people as "dupes" of media ideologies . . . [m]edia education is regarded as a 'validation' of aspects of students' cultures which are traditionally excluded from the school curriculum. . . . [T]he students are now the experts, while the teacher is no longer the main source of authority' (1993, p. 214). Buckingham argues that this

> insistent emphasis on 'creativity' runs the risk of understating the *routinised* nature of cultural activity, and the extent to which a great deal of media use is casual and uncommitted. Far from being characterised by enormous amounts of emotional or intellectual investment, for much of the time the media are merely a form of 'moving wallpaper' or background noise, a way of passing the time when you are too tired – or just can't be bothered – to do anything else.
>
> (1993, p. 205)

But the trick is to emphasise this routine nature of media reception without lapsing into a high cultural 'television escapism' formula; to agree both with

Moss's critique of Barker that emotionally intense creative 'contracts' are not the whole of the media audience story, but also with Barker that these contracts are important, and that they draw our attention back to the social, economic and political constitution of audiences within a capitalist society. As Buckingham concludes his book,

> Audience studies have become increasingly divorced from other forms of media analysis, and there is a considerable amount of mutual caricature. Disciplinary specialisms are inevitable, of course. Yet the urgent need at present is to attempt to reintegrate the various concerns of media research – with institutions, texts and audiences – and to acknowledge the dynamic, shifting relationship between them. As Graham Murdock has argued, 'we need to conceptualise the relations between the material and discursive organisations of culture without reducing one to the other'.
>
> (1993, p. 211)

It is because Buckingham's edited collection tends, as he puts it, to avoid 'the grand rhetoric of "cultural struggle" and the seductive generalities of theory' (1993, p. 216) but focuses in all its contributions on the 'messy complexities' of young people's lives, that it does so successfully engage with one, two or three daughters in the home here (as in Richards', Walkerdine's and Gillespie's chapters), one, two or three boys in or out of school there (as in Buckingham's, Sefton-Green's and Wood's analyses) while never shifting very far from broader 'global' preoccupations.

9

Back to class and race:

Situation comedy

In his chapter in Buckingham's *Reading Audiences*, Martin Barker says,

> I believe that audience research is being cramped by being set predominantly within a feminist framework. My argument will be that the return to a *class* perspective is crucial; that is, returning to issues of the organisation and control of production, and of our own lives, within the framework of capitalism: and the understanding of cultural form – including those of gender – as partial responses to these structures.
>
> (1993, p. 161)

In fact, the issue of class has never been entirely absent from the audience studies agenda. We have seen that Hodge and Tripp, and the Tullochs, drew attention to issues of class and symbolic resources among children. It is certainly the case that feminist theories of pleasure and fantasy have been more hegemonic in recent years. But audience analysis like Walkerdine's discussed in chapter 8 works in powerful ways to bring gender and class analysis together with reflexive understandings of both fantasy and oppression.

One might equally say, with Barker, that issues of *race/ethnicity* (with the important exception of Marie Gillespie's work) have been off the audience studies agenda; and one can further agree with Barker's main point: that too much focus on the audience separated from the 'organisation and control of production' leads to the kind of banal populism that Ang, Morris and many others have criticised.

Sut Jhally and Justin Lewis's *Enlightened Racism: The Cosby Show, Audiences, and the Myth of the American Dream*, published just before Barker's comments, responded much more fully to this class/race/ethnicity agenda, in the context of the production of one top-rating situation comedy. Jhally and Lewis's notion of 'enlightened racism' is an *effect* of class – or more exactly, of the fact that '[a]ny analysis of class structures [in the USA] is simply absent from our popular vocabulary' (1991, p. 134).

Enlightened Racism is all about risk and fantasy, and the relations between them. The authors argue that sitcoms like *The Cosby Show* work to efface the increasing society of risk by adapting the fantasy of the American dream (to include affluent blacks). This, at a time (the 1980s/1990s) when black poverty, crime, arrest and imprisonment, poor health, homelessness and inadequate education are all increasing markedly.

> It is to be expected, perhaps, that more fortunate persons cling to the self-justifying individualism that the dream promotes. One of the strangest things about the United States is that less fortunate persons do so too. The ideological dominance of the American dream is sustained by its massive presence in popular culture. The TV and film industries churn out fable after fable, reducing us to spellbound passivity.
>
> (Jhally and Lewis, 1991, p. 139)

Thus, bluntly and overtly, Jhally and Lewis perpetuate the 'radical critique' that Buckingham describes as simplistic and 'no longer as prevalent as it used to be' (i.e. 'passive victims in need of ideological salvation' (1993, p. 215)). Yet, as we saw, one of the contributors to Buckingham's book argued for a 'return' to this kind of analysis. What is going on here in Denzin and Lincoln's era of 'blurred genres' and 'dual crisis'? How, when virtually every book, chapter and article one read during the 1980s objected to audience researchers who constructed their subjects as 'passive dupes', can there be such a strong statement about an audience's 'spellbound passivity'? Had Jhally and Lewis not heard?

Hardly; in fact these are two of the more sophisticated audience analysts of the period. Might there be something too simplistic, then, not about 'radical critique' but about theories which rejected the 'passive dupe'? Or was this 'passive dupe' debate an example of what Hodge and Tripp describe as the rewriting of the media studies paradigm 'in a classic Kuhnian fashion, to create a mythic enemy, a mythic struggle and a definitive victory that established the right of the new paradigm to rule' (1986, p. 193)?

Andrea Press (writing a year earlier that Jhally and Lewis about *The Cosby Show* and other American television series) begins to answer the 'paradigm' question in her book, *Women Watching Television: Gender, Class and Generation in the American Television Experience*.

Typical of other work in the 'blurred genres' era, Press insists that the complexity of television viewing can best be understood by combining several theoretical paradigms within media studies. She draws a 'hegemony theory' from 'an essentially Gramscian-Althusserian Marxist school of mass media study, the British Cultural Studies tradition' (1991, p. 15), especially as developed at the Birmingham CCCS. She also draws on American feminism which 'in its focus on individual development and processes . . . adds to the Cultural Studies' class emphasis a deeper understanding of conscious and unconscious processes governing individual thoughts and behaviors' (1991, p. 23).

> Unlike many currently working in our field, rather than conceptualizing these two modes of response in either-or fashion, I stress the need to discuss both viewer resistance to our culture's often hegemonic messages and viewer accommodation to these messages as two integral parts of women's responses to entertainment television, both of which come into play for most women in different situations, and at different times.
>
> (1991, p. 15)

Press points to a tension in the Birmingham Centre work generally as researchers tended to examine both ideas (consciousness) and social practices. Those who investigated consciousness 'are primarily informed by a Marxist conception of ideology, which implies that at times the consciousness one investigates is "false", obscuring what is real' (1991, p. 20); and she cites as an example of this trend Paul Willis's *Learning to Labour* which shows how working-class teenagers' very act of resistance to the school led to the reproduction of an exploitative class system which they could not understand. Jhally and Lewis's 'enlightened racism' clearly falls within this strand of cultural studies too, emphasising how the absence of 'class' as a circulating discourse topic perpetuates American racism, even when blacks (in enjoying *The Cosby Show*) believe that it is challenging black 'stereotypes'. In contrast, Press argues, is the more anthropological trend of the Birmingham Centre, 'which urges one to record and understand practices rather than to evaluate them, and particularly urges one to avoid labelling specific forms of consciousness and levels of understanding as "false" or "true" ' (1991, p. 21). Much of the post-'ethnographic turn' and 'active audience' research aspired to this emphasis on situated practice.

Press rightly indicates how this tension led to an ambivalence among Birmingham researchers between an '*ideology-critique*' of the institutions (including television) and subcultures (including working-class ones) which helped reproduce capitalism, and on the other hand a *celebration* of subjective forms of resistance among 'oppressed groups'. Overall, though, Press sees a distinct conceptual focus ('social class as a basic category of social analysis' 1991, p. 21)) and a 'distinct and subtle goal' ('how active consciousness also contributes to domination in capitalist societies' (1991, p. 21)) behind the work at Birmingham.

Press's emphasis here on *active* consciousness is extremely important and well-taken; and will be significant in our discussion of Jhally and Lewis's analysis in the context of accusations of the 'passive dupe' audience. But before looking at this, there is one further paradigm-contextualising move made by Press in preparing for her own account. This is the criticism of the Birmingham research by feminists such as Angela McRobbie and Elizabeth Long for both its theoretical and methodological emphases. Theoretically, the problem for Long and McRobbie was Birmingham's over-emphasis on the subcultures of working-class males. Long summarised this feminist critique as having three main points: Birmingham's bias for 'public' rather than 'private' genres; the primacy of class over gender; and the assumption that 'resistance' is rationally expressed. Methodologically, a problem emphasised by McRobbie was the difficulty of the observer gaining access to girls' and female groups' more 'private' places (their homes, homes of friends), interpersonal spaces (often the best-friend dyad), and confidence (because of the more intimate focus of the female social world). McRobbie consequently relied on more in-depth interviews than the less personal focus groups and participant observation used by Willis and other Birmingham researchers.

In addition to the emphasis on adding gender to class as organising categories in McRobbie's work, Press also describes the importance of American feminism's emphasis on viewing as practised by individuals alone in private settings. The theoretical focus was often psychoanalytical and the conceptual focus was fantasy. Press promotes the importance in American research also of Radway's ethnographic research, but notes its weakness in the area of class, since her sample was predominantly working class. There was a tension also (as at Birmingham) between Radway's 'desire to respect and simply record the cultural practices of the women she studied, and her feminist political commitments which gave her some grounds for making negative judgements regarding the content and ultimate consequences of romance readings' (1991, p. 24). We have seen that Ien Ang has similar concerns about Radway's work.

A number of features generated by this 'paradigm debate' (or at least 'blurred genres' debate) are relevant to my discussion of Jhally and Lewis's study of *The Cosby Show*.

- The Birmingham emphasis on class and its critique by British and American feminists, leading (in both Press's and Barker's view) to there being, by the early 1990s, an *under*-emphasis on class analysis.
- The growth during this period of the near-fetish of the 'passive dupe' concept which (together with international events in the Soviet Bloc) were beginning to allow 'ideology-critique' to be lumped into the same negative category as the psychological work on audiences challenged by Walkerdine.
- The growth of poststructuralist emphases on 'multiple subjectivity' which likewise critiqued 'ideology-critique' for being too homogenising, and for forgetting that being a woman requires movement between a range of potential identities, constructing and reconstructing them in local, situated activities. Thus, for Ang, fantasy becomes important (non-instrumentalist, non-'rational' space offering somewhere private and unconstrained indulgence in 'excess in the interstices of ordered social life where one has to keep oneself strategically under control' (Ang, 1996, p. 95).

- Press's underlining of the active consciousness explored in 'ideology-critique'.

These, then, were some of the important agendas that were generating what Foucault called the 'limits of the sayable' when Lewis and Jhally researched and wrote their book.

Enlightened Racism

Part 1: *The active audience*

Two things are particularly apparent about the writing of *Enlightened Racism*. One is its lack of reflexive discussion of the relationship of researchers to their audience or, indeed, to Bill Cosby. This is, to repeat, not a matter of sophistication. Justin Lewis, for example, had already written an extensive reflexive account of issues of qualitative and quantitative methodologies in audience research in the social sciences in his book, *The Ideological Octopus*. There is some brief discussion in *Enlightened Racism* of their initially favourable and supportive attitude to *The Cosby Show*, which was overturned by their reaction to the audience interviews. But there is no mention here of how this dynamic worked through the research process itself, how Cosby moved to prevent the book being published, and so on. This is because the main intention of *Enlightened Racism* is very clear, and so are the politics of its authors. This is a Marxist account, unashamedly; and one would suspect that the authors would agree with the comment once made by Trevor Griffiths on television when, speaking about his own texts, he said: 'I'm a socialist, and I like that to be upfront in everything I do.' At one level, there is no need for the text to be reflexive in a methodological way. Its 'temporary closures', to use Ien Ang's term, are very clear indeed.

The authors trajectory (from being initially supportive to becoming highly critical of *The Cosby Show*) also determines the book's structure, as well as being signalled consistently throughout its narrative. Roughly the first half of the book is concerned with the 'success of *Cosby*', in so far that the 'case for' and the 'case against' is raised in the opening chapter and then answered, apparently supporting the 'case for' with a wealth of audience data.

Jhally and Lewis ran 52 small focus groups which, as they say, is a large number for a qualitative study. There were 23 black, 3 Hispanic and 26 white groups; and the black and white groups were subdivided by social class (given that class was a major 'variable' in their analysis). Most groups included both men and women. All interviewees had to be frequent or occasional viewers of *The Cosby Show*, and all the groups were shown one episode to help open the discussion.

Because they were going to be asking 'sensitive' questions about people's views on issues of race, gender and class, the authors chose to conduct interviews in people's homes in groups of two to six people who knew each other well: 'our main requirement was that group members should be close to one another and feel comfortable about watching television together. In an informal setting, conversation could be allowed at appropriate moments to flow freely without interruption by the interviewer' (1991, p. 10). Following Lewis's own advice about focus group research in his earlier book, the interviews were very open-ended at the beginning to 'allow the respondents the freedom to set their own agendas' (1991, p. 11). Discussion started by asking the respondents to describe the story they felt they had just been told (a similar beginning to the Tullochs' 'topic of discourse' approach discussed earlier). If discussion of issues of class, race, or gender were not forthcoming, focused questions introduced them. Jhally and Lewis found that discussion of race created the most cautious or evasive reactions (especially among white groups) and tried to meet this problem to some extent by having interviewers of the same colour as the interviewees. Questions about race were of two kinds: one about *The Cosby Show*, the other about race relations generally; and the two kinds of question about race were separated by discussion of the commercials shown during the episode. 'As it turned out, the two discussions were often very different; when analyzed, the differences were often extremely revealing' (1991, p. 12).

Despite the familiar criticism of 'ideology-critique' research for forgetting audience pleasures, Jhally and Lewis in fact focus on this as they describe the responses of their white and their black viewers.

White viewers constantly refer to the show's ability to present everyday activities realistically, and many spoke of their enjoyment of its depictions of the minutiae of family life. Some white men, for example, enjoyed the gentle fun that is poked at 'juvenile' male competitiveness (between Cliff and Dr Harmann over a basketball in the episode screened); while a white woman laughed when comparing Claire Huxtable's finding of her teenage son's girlie magazines with her own reaction. 'I remember taking them downstairs and burning them in the incinerator. . . . Now that wasn't very mature, but that was my reaction; I mean, it was totally different from hers' (1991, p. 39).

As Jhally and Lewis argue,

> These comments suggest that the series does more than pleasantly wash over its viewers; it touches them, creating feelings of involvement and intimacy. This level of identification is important because it suggests that the series has a more profound influence than a show that is passively consumed and subsequently forgotten.
>
> (1991, p. 39)

Despite their later comment about 'spellbound passivity', then, the authors are here – in the first, 'ethnographic' half of the book – emphasising the active situating of the sitcom in its audiences' daily experiences and identities. Jhally and Lewis note that one way that audiences do this is by making the characters 'real' – by, for example, psychoanalysing Theo, the teenage son ('I think he's the only son in the family and that perhaps, I think, maybe makes him more social' (1991, p. 40)). At the same time, though, often the same people would speak about enjoying the *lack* of realism in this fantasy world of an affluent, dual-professional parent black family. 'But maybe what you love about them too is that nobody wants to see repeats of what they're living. . . . It's totally a fantasy to me, a fairy tale' (1991, p. 42).

As Jhally and Lewis argue, '*The Cosby Show*' appears to have cultivated a space where fantasy and reality are allowed to merge – without suffering any philosophical qualms' (1991, p. 42). So *generational* clashes (such as Claire finding Theo's girlie magazines) were both 'real' (i.e. experienced by respondents) and enjoyable (in comparing Claire's black 'cool' with one's own 'not very mature' response) – and generational conflict is one of the central generic dramatic devices of sitcom (Tulloch, 1990, ch. 10), which helps account for their popularity. Generational interactions in *The Cosby Show* (particular styles of parental discipline) were frequently referred to with pleasure, and sometimes with nostalgia (as was the series' emphasis on the 'complete' family). But *class* issues were generally effaced, but were implicitly what respondents were often referring to as 'repeats of what they're living'. 'Here we need to pay attention to what is *left out* of the picture that makes it more attractive to white viewers. . . . The celebration of what is essentially an upper middle class lifestyle is the flip side of the rejection of a working class lifestyle' (Jhally and Lewis, 1991, p. 43).

Many white viewers emphasised that they valued the Huxtables as a *black* family, thus appearing to embrace a liberal, non-racist consciousness. However, a major finding was that this black family was first *seen* as black but then assimilated ('just like us') into a white consciousness. For example, a number of white respondents spoke of disliking other black sitcoms which showed the 'black community straying among itself' (the word 'straying' is symptomatic!) rather than 'integrated' like the Cosbys. 'It's an effortless blackness. A "nice" blackness. Unlike the not-so-nice kinds of blackness exhibited on other shows' (1991, p. 47). Still, Jhally and Lewis affirm in this first ('positive') half of their book, that the fact that 'white Americans living in a society still significantly divided along racial lines can view an explicitly black family as "just people" who have the same problems, dreams, and aspirations as themselves is a significant and progressive element in our popular culture' (1991, p. 48).

Black viewers were distinguished from white viewers by one significant discourse: focusing on black 'stereotyping'. Above all black viewers took pleasure in *The Cosby Show* as a TV programme that, after years of stereotyping, showed black people as they really were.

The level of identification of black viewers with the Huxtables is very high, and although identification occurs similarly in the white responses, its intensity for black viewers puts it on a different plane. For black respondents, the show mirrored images with which they could deeply identify. Unlike white respondents, black respondents saw themselves as personally implicated in the images they were talking about. Respondents repeatedly made statements about how they saw themselves, their fathers and mothers, their brothers and sisters, and situations from their own history in the show. Furthermore, these statements were made with an understanding that this had not happened before on television. The pleasure of black respondents and their level of emotional bonding with the Huxtables reveal not just the creative ability of the show's writers but also the frustration that black Americans had felt with past portrayals of blacks.

> (Jhally and Lewis, 1991, p. 50)

Not surprisingly, *upper-middle-class* blacks identified most closely with the Huxtables. As one daughter in an upper-middle-class black family said, 'They have nice clothes. And when I look at them I look at us. Because we're not poor. We don't live in a bad community in a ghetto somewhere.' But in fact blacks in all class positions identified with the Huxtables, finding pride and pleasure in seeing a 'good' black world portrayed on television. Despite the class differences between the affluent Huxtables and some of these black respondents, there was usually a point of identification in the narrative for them: a black woman who could identify with Claire Huxtable's relationship with Theo over the girlie magazines, a black male who saw his father in Cliff's joking but intimate lines to his kids.

Jhally and Lewis make a distinction here between white and black *perceptions of black signifiers* in the series. Whites saw as 'black' the artwork on the wall of the house, the music that is played, the political issues (like the 'freedom march' reference) that get raised occasionally. In contrast, the black respondents notice

> the language, the mannerisms, the 'tone' and 'feeling' of black life. . . .
> Raymond Williams (1961, p. 48) identified something that he called a
> 'structure of feeling' that exists in every culture, the recognition of
> which is based upon experiencing it rather than learning about it sec-
> ondhand. The responses of black audience members suggest that *The
> Cosby Show* has been able to capture this structure of feeling.
>
> (Jhally and Lewis, 1991, p. 54)

As one respondent described her sense of the show's 'blackness':

> Claire is a lawyer, you never see her use legal jargon, or whatever; she
> talks just like a black woman. I was raised by a black man and woman
> and this is how they talked, so when I close my eyes I can totally tell
> the difference. Also we have a tone to our language and it comes from

our history. It is a singing type; very melodic type of talk, or conversation that is just natural for our people. So if you are watching an all-white show, you will not hear . . . the melodic sound of the voice as you can when the Huxtables speak.

(1991, p. 55)

So, it is the 'whole environment' – even the modes of discipline – of the Huxtable household that make it black. 'I just know it's a black family, that's all. . . . For instance when she's chastising the child, you very seldom see a white person chastising a child like that. . . . But I mean blacks have been chastising their children like that ever since . . .' (1991, p. 55).

So, as Jhally and Lewis conclude this half of the book, *The Cosby Show* seems to be succeeding spectacularly: breaking down white racist prejudices; attracting black audiences with its picture of everyday-real (not stereotyped) black life; and giving a lot of pleasure to all its audiences, thus staying on air. Up to this point in the book we have a classic (and positive) 'active audience' study.

- The careful description of qualitative methodology and the 'grounded' nature of the research.
- The emphasis on differentiated audiences negotiating their meanings *and* pleasures via favourite television programmes.
- The emphasis on the biographically and locally situated 'telling of tales'.
- The introduction near the end of this section of Raymond Williams's concept of 'structure of feeling', which Williams often used very positively to describe a new sensibility of change emerging between earlier and later 'rationalistic' ideologies. For Williams 'culture' (in both 'high' and 'popular' forms) could express this sensibility of a 'culture' (as a 'whole way of life') and thus lead to an emergent consciousness of the need for change.

Everything may seem set for a further development down this 'positive' direction foreshadowed by Williams's concept, and expanded perhaps by a greater focus on gendered readings in the second half of the book. But this never happens, and by the end we are left instead with an audience of 'spellbound passivity'. How this happens is itself a significant tale of the epistemology, ontology and methodology of audience studies.

Part 2: The spellbound audience

In marked contrast to the qualitative analysis of the first half of their book, Jhally and Lewis begin the second half with quantitative data. This is not, however, quantitative data about the audience as such; and Jhally and Lewis's own qualitative/quantitative synthesis is different from the ones we have looked at earlier. This quantitative data is about the American 'risk society', from the point of view of the black community. This is the story of 'Black reality: the permanent underclass and increasing poverty'.

Drawing on *The Economic Report of the People* (1986), *Statistical Abstracts of the United States* (1990) and various other statistical sources, the authors indicate a significant decline in black people's economic position between 1975 and 1988, with 33 per cent of black families living below the poverty line by that date. 'Thus the Huxtable's lifestyle reflects the reality of only a small minority of black families. The great majority of black families, in income and housing, are at the other end of the socio-economic spectrum – and the 1980s have seen a general reversal in the economic well-being of black Americans' (1991, p. 62).

The economic rationalist policies of the Reagan–Bush years have reversed any gains that may have been made since the 1960s. Moreover,

> statistics alone do not tell the whole gloomy story of the millions of black Americans who live in the inner-city ghettos. Characterized by extreme poverty, serious and violent crime, high rates of drug addiction, permanent joblessness and welfare dependency, and dramatic increase in out-of-wedlock births and female-headed families [which are systematically poorer than male-headed ones], the central core of many American cities has been converted into a no-go area that requires constant police occupation. ... Although only 1 out of 9 people in the United States is black, in 1984 nearly 50% of those arrested for murder and non-negligent manslaughter were black, and 41% of all murder victims were black. Homicide is the leading cause of death for black Americans aged 25 to 34.
>
> (Jhally and Lewis, 1991, p. 62)

This is the *black* 'risk society', an intense inflection of Ulrich Beck's versions of 'industrial' and 'risk' modernist. Unlike Beck, Jhally and Lewis's emphasis is *class* at its foundation.

Jhally and Lewis describe three distinct periods of race relations in the United States. The first is the *preindustrial* period, coinciding with pre-Civil War slavery and the postbellum period. The second is the *industrial* period, which lasts until the end of the New Deal era. Both these periods were marked by explicit efforts by whites to strengthen economic racial domination by way of legal, political and social discrimination. Policies here were based on beliefs about black biological and cultural inferiority. In the third *modern industrial* period the state has responded to some degree to black pressure in promoting racial equality. Now it is not 'racism that explains the life chances of blacks; instead it is their class position' (1991, p. 65). In the postwar period, the factory-based economy of the inner city (where migrant blacks from the south had clustered) was dispersed to the outskirts as better transport (for the middle class) allowed the chase for cheaper land. At the same time the shift from a manufacturing base to the growth of service industries resulted in the expansion of white-collar jobs, which required higher educational levels for entry. A growth in absolute numbers of black teenagers just when employment opportunities were shifting made the economic situation of blacks even worse.

On the other hand, a mixture of economic and political factors (such as the expansion of white-collar jobs, affirmative action legislation, etc.) has created new opportunities for the black middle classes; and it is their agenda of 'freedoms' that was represented by the Civil Rights movement. The relative improvement in the conditions of the black middle class indicates that it is not solely racial oppression behind these changes. 'We can now begin to understand that it is a racially inflected class structure that has placed lower class blacks in the most disadvantaged position to compete in the present economy' (1991, p. 67). The black underclass is being hit everywhere at once, as the shift of industry, and the consequent collapse of the inner city's property and income tax base has spiralled through to lack of support for urban public schools where the population has become increasingly black as well as lower class.

Parallel to this polarisation within the black community between a tiny affluent group and a massive underemployed sector, Jhally and Lewis set their own quantitative account of television representations of black people during this same period. This data (based on the Gerbner *et al.*, Cultural Indicators Project at the Annenberg School in Philadelphia and on their own content analysis of prime-time television during one week in November 1990) indicates that on television, too, the black middle class has gained at the expense of other blacks.

> Whereas 16% of black characters were working class in the pre-Cosby era, there were none at all in the Cosby period. Putting it another way, 30% of the working class characters on television between 1971 and 1976 were black; between 1984 and 1989, none of them were. The black working class seems to have disappeared from our screens.
>
> (Jhally and Lewis, 1991, p. 59)

Moreover, 'among major minority characters, upper middle class [black] people outnumber ordinary working class people 19 to 1' (1991, p. 60). Thus while upper-middle-class black characters like the Huxtables have become relatively commonplace, working class blacks (especially in major roles) are rare on television. This amounts to a black 'embourgeoisement' on *television*, paralleled by a version of the same, for a tiny minority of people, in American society.

At this point in the argument, Jhally and Lewis construct their own variant on the 'comparative TV genres' analysis which has been a feature of some chapters of this book. But it is a significantly different one from what we have looked at so far. The authors remind us that their figures are for television drama.

> As readers will be aware, these are not the only images of blacks on U.S. television. The story on television news is very different. . . . For instance, though polls suggest that only 15% of drug users are black,

network news stories associate drugs with blacks 50% of the time. . . .
Thus two very different and conflicting stories are being told on television about black people. We cannot assume that audiences, particularly white audiences, are aware of the contradiction.

(Jhally and Lewis, 1991, p. 61)

As Jhally and Lewis argue, it is necessary to have an understanding of the
structuring aspect of black risk – in particular the combined mechanisms of
economic capital and cultural capital (in Bourdieu's sense) – to be aware of
why certain groups do systematically better than others. Blacks are at the bottom end of the scale in relation to both forms of capital; yet the American
Dream continues to propagate the notion of a land of equality of opportunity.

This is the centre of Jhally and Lewis's explanation of their 'spellbound
audience'. Just as theorists of the child audience discuss the lack of narrative
schema and social discourses in relation to understanding complex social
processes, so Jhally and Lewis are arguing that without the explanatory
framework of 'class', there is no way that American audiences can see
through what the American media (and many other discourses) 'hide and
distort. . . . We believe that Americans are unable to think clearly about race
because they cannot think clearly about class' (1991, p. 70). In place of an
explanatory chain based on an understanding of the limiting effects of the
class system, the American public is likely to fall back on a different and
much more hegemonic explanatory chain: that racism only exists at an
interpersonal level, and can be eliminated at that level.

It is in this context that the 'positive images of blacks promoted by shows
like *Cosby* have . . . distinctly negative consequences by creating a conservative and comfortable climate of opinion that allows white America to
ignore widespread racial inequality' (1991, p. 72). Few of their respondents
were (or were prepared to be in interview) overtly racist at the interpersonal
level. Rather, Jhally and Lewis draw implicitly on the notion of multiple
subjectivity to argue that white viewers were often overtly liberal in their
views about racism, while at the same time enjoying the 'enlightened racism'
of *The Cosby Show*.

But multiple subjectivity is never simply 'pleasurable' or 'democratic' in
this analysis. There are always hegemonic discourses available to enable the
negotiation of contradictory readings. For example, the working-class
whites can recognise the class differences between the Huxtables and themselves, but forget these in enjoying the 'everyday' similarities with their own
lives. 'I think you see yourself in those positions the way that show is. It
takes everyday life type of things and it's funny, because a lot of things that
happen in everyday life are funny' (1991, p. 79). Meanwhile, black audiences negotiate ambiguities and contradictions in a different way.

What is notable about our black focus group's responses is not what
was said but what remained unsaid. Just as most white respondents
found it difficult to talk about class issues, so did black respondents.

. . . Among blacks, it appears to have created a form of displacement. The absence of a notion of class results in the substitution of the notion of race: 'upper middle class' became 'white'.

(Jhally and L ewis, 1991, p. 82)

It is important to understand the methodological approach that Jhally and Lewis take to legitimate their analytical claim. Whereas earlier in the book this is based on a careful discussion of focus group methods in natural situations, and later on quantitative data revealed in 'many more statistics', at this later point of the book – where the authors *return* to their interview material – their claim to a legitimate analysis is based on discourse analysis. That is, interview conversation is laid out for the reader, and systematic 'absences' or 'contradictions' are isolated for the reader to assess. Here is an example from their explication of the 'too white' displacement.

The complaint that *The Cosby Show* is 'too white' is a consequence of this displacement [of class analysis]. Although some viewers actually endorsed this criticism, few were able to disentangle the confusion it caused. In the absence of a discourse about social class, respondents found themselves discussing the Huxtables as both black *and* white. One black woman, for example, began by praising the show *because* it was black: 'I really like it. I really do because it shows black people are not like the whites think they are. . . . I'm conscious of them being a black family and proud of them, the way they carry themselves.' Later, during the same interview, she talked about the Huxtables as sharing the characteristics of a white family: 'Well, the way they sit down at the table and when they converse with each other. See, I've worked in white homes a long time and I've learned a lot myself by working around them and the way they, their mannerisms really.'

She also pointed to the manner of disciplining the children as characteristic of the upper-middle-class white homes she worked in. . . . The similarities between the Huxtables and the white families she has worked for are based upon the commonalities of their class position, and yet this fact remains elusive. The idea that the Huxtables have adopted upper-middle-class norms has been displaced by the notion that they have become 'like white people'. Without reference to a relevant discourse, class differences become racial differences. When this respondent looks at family, language and music she sees the Huxtables as clearly black. When she looks at middle class culture she sees the Huxtables as white (1991, pp. 82–3).

At certain points in their text, Jhally and Lewis illustrate a respondent 'looking' for their key missing word: class.

A male, middle class respondent revealed a similar confusion of class and race in a moment of self-consciousness. 'I think the overall concept itself, what's wrong with showing a black family who has those kind of values? I almost said white values, but that's not the word I want. There is no monopoly on that kind of thing that's owned by white folks, but what's wrong with a family living this way?' The phrase that he wants is 'middle class values', but *middle class* is a term from a discourse he does not have access to. In its absence he reverts to the terms of the discourse he knows and that make at least some sense: black equals poor, white equals affluent. This respondent's comments are particularly interesting: he clearly *wants* to break down the equation between class and race ('there's no monopoly on that kind of thing'), but finds himself without the terminology with which to do so.

(Jhally and Lewis, 1991, p. 83)

Supporting this discursive analysis underlying the legitimacy of their inter- pretation, Jhally and Lewis offer other evidence too. For example, they point to the unpopularity with some white respondents of *Roseanne* or *thir- tysomething*, the first for being too self-consciously working class in its val- ues, the latter for being too stridently 'yuppie'. 'The main offence of *thirtysomething* was not that it showed us yuppies but that it made them appear privileged, part of an exclusive world that many people will never inhabit. With its coy realism, *thirtysomething* was killjoy television, punc- turing the myth of the American dream' (1991, p. 134). Similarly, many black respondents disliked other black sitcoms like *The Jeffersons* for show- ing the 'everyday struggle of living, I don't think people really want to see that all the time; they live it too much' (1991, p. 85). Thus black viewers could *both* see these other shows as portraying the bad, old 'stereotype' of blacks as 'trouble', *and* see it as their own real lives; just as they could *both* see *The Cosby Show* as 'real' *and* as fantasy.

> It's fun to watch some classy people do their thing.

> People really don't want to see any poverty in. . . . This is nice, it looks good and it's kind of, you accept it, they have a beautiful home, and everything is okay.

One of Jhally and Lewis's particularly interesting examples of 'contradic- tion' was in a working-class group. Here, they admit, the notion of class consciousness was not entirely lacking. But when alluded to, it still tended to get displaced. The example is interesting because of its indication of the way in which viewers can play between different television genres in cueing this 'displacement' of class. In this example, a

> woman . . . perhaps significantly, reserved her most scathing criticism for the commercials shown during the show: 'The way they make it look. . . . It really irks me. They know, they never show the family with the mother and father an alcoholic, but they show the fancy clothes, the cars, the wine coolers. . . . I mean, why don't they show the father sitting there passed out in a chair and the kids yelling for something to eat?' What is interesting about this statement is that it

was *not* made in relation to *The Cosby Show*, even though . . . [it] is even guiltier of the misrepresentations she criticizes than the commercials shown during it. This suggests that the affluent consumerism of most major TV characters has become so ordinary that viewers no longer notice it.

(Jhally and Lewis, 1991, p. 84)

Finally, Jhally and Lewis employ a quantitative legitimating measure; arguing that only one respondent (a black male) out of their 52 focus groups expressed any explicit awareness of class barriers or class structures – and even he does not like the idea of a blue-collar *Cosby Show*. 'There's part of me that says, in a way, I don't want white America to see us, you know, struggling or whatever' (1991, p. 85).

'Part of me' is part of a multiple subjectivity; and it is clear that Jhally and Lewis are perfectly comfortable with this notion; that they illustrate their different respondents negotiating in different ways between these different 'parts of me'. At the same time, though, the authors are completely clear and explicit about their critical realist epistemology. 'We have two worlds: one grounded in social reality, where social injustice is rife; one rooted in television fiction, where social and economic prosperity abound without division and discrimination' (1991, p. 87).

Jhally and Lewis's analysis makes it perfectly clear that it is both possible and coherent to combine a critical realist with a poststructuralist account, a qualitative situated analysis of localised tales with statistics, and an 'ideology-critique' with concepts of fantasy and pleasure. Not all fantasies are those of 'resistance' (as in Ang); and not all pleasure is in 'excess'. For example, Jhally and Lewis's white respondents can be both 'liberal' (on interpersonal racism) and 'conservative' (in arguing that affirmative action was only needed in the past). This has, as they say, its own insidious pleasures.

The Cosby Show strikes a deal with its white audience. It asks for an attitude that welcomes a black family onto TV screens in white homes, and in return it provides white viewers pleasure without culpability, with a picture of a comfortable, ordered world in which white people (and the nation as a whole) are absolved of any responsibility for the position of black people. . . . For many respondents in our study, the Huxtables' achievement of the American dream leads them to a world where race no longer matters. This attitude enables white viewers to combine an impeccably liberal attitude towards race with a deep-rooted suspicion of black people. . . . They reject bigotry based upon skin colour, yet they are wary of most (working class) black people. Colour difference is okay, cultural difference is not. . . . *The Cosby Show* panders to the limits of white liberalism, allowing white audiences the sanctimonious pleasure of viewing the world through rose-tinted spectacles.

(Jhally and Lewis, 1991, pp. 91, 110)

Black viewers negotiate a different contradiction, across different television genres, and circulating around the issue of risk. 'That's one thing that bothers me about black shows. Everybody's got to be, you know, cracking on everybody or putting someone down or knifing someone' (1991, p. 118). So black viewers were often extremely sophisticated in their analysis of negative visual images of blacks on news broadcasts, while being highly ambivalent about watching other black sitcoms like *227*, *Amen*, *The Jeffersons*, and *Good Times*. In contrast, *The Cosby Show* is almost universally liked. This is not just because it is a 'nice' show, without risk.

> Behind the preference for *The Cosby Show* lies a subtle interaction between race and class in the context of the American culture – displayed on television and elsewhere – in which to be working class is a sign of failing in the meritocracy. In the upwardly mobile world of popular television, it is only when black people are presented as middle class that they become normal and assimilated into the succession of images of social success. The problem with many black sitcoms is, in part, that they are *working class*. Both middle class and working class black respondents interpreted the silliness, the slapstick, the negativity, the put-downs, the stereotypes as indicators of working class life.
>
> (1991, p. 119)

Two dominant notions among black people – that they have traditionally been stereotyped on television, and that a new human respect is to be measured by status and wealth – have fused, in Jhally and Lewis's view, 'in a way that locks black people into acceptance of a system that, on the whole, works against them' (1991, p. 127). It is this Marxist view of the authors (that the only positive solution for the mass of black people is a change in the capitalist system itself) which leads them from the black discourse of risk to one of false illusion. Again, they quote the discursive contradiction in the interview text of one black middle class respondent to *The Cosby Show*.

> You know, it's always that upper middle class, upper class mentality. . . . It's just not real for me. Again, I like the show per se because it does depict blacks in a more positive way than we usually – we're not killing each other. We're not raping people. You know, we're sane, ordinary people who like the nice things in life like everybody else.

It is the effacement of a structural logic in that respondent's conjunctural use of 'again', the lack of any apparent alternative between the 'upper class mentality' that is 'just not real for me' and the risky and grisly black alternative of killing and raping people, that generates – via *The Cosby Show* – 'a necessary illusion' (1991, p. 13). But it is, at the same time, in Jhally and Lewis's account, 'cultural and political suicide' for black people to have this 'illusion'.

The Cosby Show, and others like it, diverts attention from the class-based causes of racial inequality. More than this, the series throws a veil of confusion over black people who are trying to comprehend the inequities of modern racism. It derails dissatisfaction with the system and converts it, almost miraculously, into acceptance of its values. In a culture where white people now refuse to acknowledge the existence of unequal opportunity, the political consequences of this acceptance are, for black people, disastrous.

(Jhally and Lewis, 1991, p. 127)

This is, then, the evil face of fantasy. Not Ang's fantasy as a *real* 'imagined scene' in which 'alternative, imaginary scenarios for the subject's real life are evoked.' Rather it is fantasy as illusion embedded in real structural constraints. Ang speaks against this position. 'I want to suggest that the pleasure of fantasy lies in its offering the subject an opportunity to take up positions which she could not assume in real life: through fantasy she can move beyond the structural constraints of everyday life and explore other, more desirable, situations, identities, lives' (Ang, 1996, pp. 92–3). Jhally and Lewis argue, in response, that it is precisely the feminist-individualist project of Ang's fantasy of living significantly outside structural constraints – rather than changing them – that is illusion. Against her they quote heavy statistics: of increasing numbers of killings by blacks, killings of young blacks, drugs, rapes, arrest and imprisonment, unemployment, ill health and all the other scenarios of risk which many black people seek to avoid in the pleasures of *The Cosby Show*. It is their sense of lost dignity they find there; but no less than among Paul Willis's working-class 'lads', their 'resistance' in doing so – in Jhally and Lewis's analysis – reproduces the structure that oppresses them.

This is the 'spellbound passivity' of Jhally and Lewis's account, in their view massively supported by a commercial television industry which continues to ensure that '[a]ny analysis of class structures is simply absent from our popular vocabulary' (1991, p. 134). It is precisely because Martin Barker believes that certain hegemonic strains in media and audience theory are inadvertently complicit in this elision that he calls for a 'return' to class (and economic-structural) analysis.

Women watching *Cosby*

It may seem surprising that Jhally and Lewis's return to class is not matched with a systematic emphasis on gender, particularly as the episode they showed respondents was 'about' sexism. Perhaps this confirms feminist critiques of 'Birmingham' inspired work?

In fact, there was a different reason, as Lewis discusses elsewhere (1991, pp. 168–72). Despite 'compromising moments' in its discourse of feminism (for example, it is unquestioned that it is Claire's job, not Cliff's, to make the dinner, even though both work outside the home), most respondents reproduced the episode's feminist message without prompting. 'The fact that only a few respondents failed to construct this reading indicates the prevalence (although not necessarily the power) of a contemporary feminist discourse, particularly among the middle and upper middle-class respondents' (1991, p. 169). This was not the case, however, with 'those forms of discrimination that remained unnamed' (1991, p. 172) – particularly the relationship of class to racism – which is why Jhally and Lewis focus almost entirely on this 'considerably more complicated' (Lewis 1991, p. 172) audience story in their *Cosby* book.

Andrea Press's feminist analysis of sitcoms (including *The Cosby Show*) and family television dramas in *Women Watching Television* redresses the balance. Press, however, does not ignore class, or generation and age. There is not the space in this chapter to deal extensively with Press's important book; but I would like to point to ways in which Press's emphasis especially on age and generational features of the female audience generates a different methodological approach to Jhally and Lewis, but with equally rich results.

For Press,

> The meaning of television as an institution has itself changed over the generations, and we know very little about these changes. Different generations of women have come of age at different ideological moments in our culture and at times when television itself has occupied different places and held different cultural meanings. Given these variations, do the generations [of women] receive television differently?
>
> (Press, 1991, p. 141)

Because of her interest in combining gender with class *and* age, Press did not ask her audience groups to respond to particular screenings or particular shows (as in the case of Jhally and Lewis). Rather, her feminist theory and her conceptualisation of the research in terms of generations of women led her to an open-ended long-interview method, where 'I wanted women to talk to me in their own words about the television they had watched and remembered, to tell me what came to their minds when they thought about television' (1991, p. 180). In this way television was remembered in its own history, as situated in different age group's different personal biographies. These memories then blended in some younger women's accounts with their nostalgia for the family television shows of their childhood, and their liking 'nostalgically' of postfeminist shows like *Cosby*.

Press's methodology thus made possible an integration of memory, situated biography, gender and the analysis of various television texts. This was why Press wanted to ensure 'that women themselves structure their discussions of television. I wanted to be guided by women's own rhythms when determining whether, and in what ways, television was important to them' (Press, 1991, p. 181). Press is (briefly) reflexive, admitting that 'it was inevitable that to some extent my own categories and preconceptions about what I wanted to know influenced both the interviews themselves and my subsequent interpretation of them' (1991, p. 181). But she argues overall for a sharing of women's experiences between researcher and respondent which (as seldom happens on television) ensured a shared or 'dialogic' response. It was her reflection on television's influence on her own interior life at different ages which had initially sparked her interest in the importance of television images for women at different stages of their life cycle.

This methodological accessing of women's memories generated three phases of 'feminist' sitcom texts.

1. **Prefeminist** family television represented women primarily as bound up with their families, particularly their male partners. Rarely were women seen to legitimately enter the 'male' public world, and when they did it could be the subject for popular sitcom. 'The extremely popular middle-class situation comedy *I Love Lucy* illustrates well these typical qualities of women on early television. But *I Love Lucy*, like other shows on early television, features a subtext of resistance to many of these conventions. Many plots revolve around Lucy's struggle to escape her circumscribed housewife role and enter the glamorous world of show business in which her husband works' (Press, 1991, p. 29). This is a typical example of Press's textual analysis of both 'hegemony' and 'resistance' at work, and it is matched by her audience analysis. Middle-class women tend to identify with the strong, 'independent woman' aspect of Lucy. They 'pick up on the power within the family which Lucy appropriates from her husband and on her attempts to gain more social power, generally by finding work outside the home' (1991, p. 77). In contrast to this middle-class 'feminist' figure, working-class women tend to comment negatively on her silliness and her 'feminine wiles' to get what she wants; and Press broadens this to an analysis of audience responses across a number of programmes where middle-class women accept women's sexuality as a mark of independence, while working-class women are more disapproving of it. Thus middle-class women, in Press's account, are both resistant (enjoying Lucy as breaking the gendered domestic role) and hegemonically positioned in terms of gender.

2. **Feminist** television responded to the second-wave feminism of the late 1960s/early 1970s. 'Where women's exit from the snug bonds of domesticity had been a cause for amusement, as in the situation comedies, or a source of danger, as in the dramas, women were now seen with increasing legitimacy outside the home. By the late seventies and early eighties, it was no longer unusual to see women in nontraditional positions'

(Press, 1991, p. 35). Press's (and her audiences') generic focus naturally shifts here – to cop and action-adventure series like *Cagney and Lacey, Hill Street Blues, Charlie's Angels*, or to 'work-place as family' sitcoms like *The Mary Tyler Moore Show*. Strong women characters who were both traditionally beautiful and action-leaders allowed different class (and gender) audiences to extract different pleasures from these shows. At the same time, they did not portray, Press argues, the loneliness that beset many women who tried to break into the male-dominated work place, while often having to deal with significant problems (single parent, or domestic tension over the care of the home) in their private lives as well. Whereas middle-class women are subject to 'gender-specific' hegemony (as in their response to pre-feminist shows), working-class women suffer television's 'class-specific' hegemony (in responding to the feminist period series). That is, 'working-class women are particularly vulnerable to television's presentation of the material accoutrements of middle-class life as the definition of what is normal in society. Their television watching may contribute, therefore to a degree of alienation from the reality of their own material experience and potential' (1991, p. 138). Certainly – like Jhally and Lewis's black viewers – these working-class women tended to reject the 'unreal' characterisation and settings of working-class television dramas in this period.

3. **Postfeminist** era television retains women's work identity, but not at the expense of a re-emphasised family role. 'The trend on postfeminist television is to take women out of the workplace-family and put them back in the home, in a revitalization of traditional family values that melds with a superficial acceptance of feminist perspectives concerning women and work' (Press, 1991, p. 38). *The Cosby Show* is very typical of this period, where Claire Huxtable is a lawyer but is rarely seen working or even discussing her work, and Cliff is a successful gynaecologist who always has ample time for counselling and interaction with his children. Claire is also symptomatic of the postfeminist television type of female agency, which is always at the individual level, and quite unlike the collective women's action of the feminist period *Annie* or even in prefeminist television sitcoms like *I Love Lucy*. 'Strident feminists' are unsympathetically portrayed in postfeminist television, 'commercial femininity' is promoted, and individual, *private* solutions to women's problems are typical. Claire Huxtable represents all these things. Yet many 'postfeminist' young women are finding that the impeccably 'cool' way in which Claire Huxtable manages both work and home is not so easy in real life. Thus while many of Press's older women viewers enjoy and applaud both the feminist period policewomen and the postfeminist lawyer/homemakers like Claire Huxtable, women under twenty-nine in Press's sample had a more complex response. Older women have often not had the opportunity to work, and so can find the portrayal of strong working women on television liberating. In contrast, they typically had

experience of nuclear families prior to television's portrayal of them, so often summarily dismiss family television shows. But the younger women in Press's audience have in some ways the opposite experience. Many of them have knowledge of working, and they do not respond with the same simple enthusiasm of older women to images of women working. On the other hand, 'younger women exhibit a sharply emotional and somewhat contradictory response to family television in particular' (1991, p. 169). Young women who are the products of unhappy or disrupted families respond particularly strongly to television's idealized family shows (of both the pre- and post-feminist periods), many of which they recall with nostalgia from childhood viewing. Further, 'young women of both classes are experiencing fully the newer social pressures of our postfeminist society, pressures to live up to both older ideals of women's service to their families and newer ideals of women's capacity for work of career performance and achievement equal to that of men' (1991, p. 169). Young working-class women in particular can feel very pressured by these ideals, given their often troubled backgrounds and limited opportunities.

Thus a number of young women in Press's interviews adopted the strategy of 'splitting' the feminist period images by talking about only the more feminine, relational family side ('wants to have children', 'very caring and helpful') of women like the tough, professional public defender, Joyce Davenport, in *Hill Street Blues*. Postfeminist shows like *The Cosby Show* are easier to read in terms of the family emphasis, and young women take to it very readily. In contrast, older women 'seem more inclined to identify with the parental point of view on *Cosby* and to mention the lessons they learn from the show, or its realistic portrayal of parent-child interactions, as they do in comments on older family television as well' (1991, p. 167).

Again, in comparing different age groups of women, Press emphasises the complicated mix of hegemonic and resistance discourses. Older women are traditional in their dislike of new sexual mores for women portrayed in feminist and postfeminist television, but give their attention and praise to depictions of women at work in these shows. Similarly, postfeminist television inspires in younger women 'criticism, admiration, and nostalgia, a mix in which resistance blends with an often backward-looking sentiment' (1991, p. 176).

Andrea Press's work on television audiences is a valuable integration of age, class and gender analysis, with an especially clear historical focus around feminist and postfeminist theories and representations. Like Jhally and Lewis's analysis, it is both overtly political in its adherence to its feminist-socialist position and embattled in its recognition that the 1980s (beginning with the Reagen presidency) marked a time of retreat for progressive politics and of decline in the condition of oppressed groups. Both Jhally and Lewis's and Press's works are very clearly marked by their particular *histor-*

ical moment in the particular time/space co-ordinates of 1980s USA. 'Blurred genres' there may be, in this work, but very little in the way of Denzin and Lincoln's 'crisis of legitimation'. For both these academic audience texts, legitimation of their analysis was to be found in the statistics and memories of a savagely and repressively hegemonic, but also changing, USA.

10

Foundations in encoding/decoding:

Current affairs and news

The direction of the book so far has been via current feminist analysis of pleasure and ethnographic theories of the everyday to audience studies that focus on age, ethnicity and class. This is in no way intended as a 'reactionary' return to outmoded and simplistic notions of 'ideology-critique'. But neither is it to underestimate the power and importance of theoretical narratives which, as Martin Barker says, have often been underestimated in recent times. In fact, as Andrea Press's work indicates, it is perfectly possible to combine 'hegemonic', 'resistance' and poststructuralist theories. This is a good moment, then, to return to the seminal work on current affairs audiences of David Morley.

It would be difficult to overestimate the importance for television audience studies of the publication in 1980 of David Morley's *The 'Nationwide' Audience*. Following his earlier book (with Charlotte Brunsdon), *Everyday Television: 'Nationwide' Television*, these books were the first sustained 'encoding/decoding' couplet in the Stuart Hall tradition. Because of the regular reference (especially in American work) to the Birmingham 'School' as a definitive 'source' for media and cultural studies, it is easy to forget how little of an empirical and sociological nature was published at this time of screen theory's textual hegemony.

This is not to say that the British Film Institute, publishers of *Screen*, did not also promote work that examined the structures of television. In the same series as the Morley (and Brunsdon) books, they published a book of that name by Nicholas Garnham, as well as Colin McArthur's *Television and History*, which was part of an important debate with *Screen* luminary Colin MacCabe about the 'classic realist text'. But, in my experience, this was a debate where McArthur was always somewhat on the back foot, consigned to the yesterday of those people supposedly naive enough to believe in the real. This was the period of the audience inscribed in the 'classic realist text', via a hierarchy of discourses – at the top of which was the discourse that never pronounced its name. The dominant critical emphasis was on post-Brechtian (and post-Godardian textual reflexivity); and 'realist' film and television makers like Ken Loach got little support, either from Left screen theorists or from film funding bodies like the BFI (Tulloch, 1990, ch. 4).

Meanwhile, major sociological investigations of television news by the Glasgow Media Group were also being given a hard time – not simply in the media industry itself but among screen theorists too. How many times, I wonder, did I hear at BFI seminars or read in reviews the dismissive comment that these kinds of work were 'just sociology', and thus naïve about textual processes. In this context, it came as something of a relief to see the BFI publish *Everyday Television: 'Nationwide'*, *The 'Nationwide' Audience*, and, at about the same time, sociologist Terry Lovell's sophisticated episte-mological critique of screen theory in *Pictures of Reality* (1980). I make these points not to denigrate the very important work of screen theory, but to explain the context in which Morley's *'Nationwide' Audience* was received by many teachers of media; and to explain also why it is that screen theory is Morley's own target in the book.

In his later book, *Television, Audiences and Cultural Studies* (1992), Morley was to comment on his sense ('as one trained initially as a sociolo-gist') of continuing marginality

> to the successive dominant paradigms (whether in their culturalist, structuralist, psychoanalytic, post-structural or postmodern variants) within cultural studies. Thus, from within cultural studies, the major critique of my own work has been that it is too essentialist or reduc-tionist. From my own point of view, the prime objective of the work has been to analyse processes of culture and communication within their social and material settings. I am personally much more worried by what I see as the tendency towards the 'textualization' of cultural studies.
>
> (Morley, 1992, p. 5)

Although Morley also critiques other media traditions (like functionalist sociology, 'effects' and 'uses and gratifications' approaches) in his opening chapters of *The 'Nationwide' Audience*, it is the 'textualization' of the then dominant screen theory which is his main interlocutor. Hence Morley's comment (properly informed by current screen analysis) of the inadequacy of a 'substantial body of work in sociology' because of its sociologism in attempting

> to immediately convert social categories (e.g. class) into meanings (e.g. ideological positions) without attention to the specific factors neces-sarily governing this conversion. . . . The problem, I would suggest, is how to think the relative autonomy of signifying practices (which most of the sociological theory neglects) in combination with the oper-ation of class/gender/race etc, as determinations.
>
> (Morley, 1980, p. 19)

But having dealt with 'sociologism' in his opening chapters, Morley deals with 'textualization' of screen theory in his theoretical concluding chapters (with the weight of his empirical chapters now behind him).

> It seems that media and film studies are still subject to the kind of oscillation described in Chapter 1. At one moment the field is dominated by a theory (such as 'uses and gratifications' in recent years) which holds the media to have little or no direct 'effect' on its audiences, and at the next moment the pendulum swings towards the dominance of a theory (such as that developed in *Screen* more recently) of a near total effectivity of the text, in their terms, in the 'positioning of the subject'. In order to escape from this oscillation we need to develop a theory which gives due weight to both the 'text' and the 'audience' halves of the equation.
>
> (Morley, 1980, p. 148)

This is what Morley's books clearly set out to do. Brunsdon and Morley's *Everyday Television: 'Nationwide'* was a sophisticated textual analysis of this early evening television current affairs show, pointing to the inscription of its populist discourse by way of a variety of formal modes of address. In this book, the authors (gaining much from the screen theory tradition) clearly avoided the sociologism of denying relative autonomy to the signifying practices of television.

In *The 'Nationwide' Audience* Morley approached the other 'half of the equation'. While Morley was careful to avoid ascribing a total homogeneity to screen theory, he argued (rightly in my opinion) that there was a very strong tendency in *Screen*'s interventions into film and media studies for 'a mechanistic assumption that the audience/viewer is necessarily "positioned" or placed in the programme so as to reproduce the dominant ideology. Their concern is with the (re)production of the ideological subject by the text, but the problematic is overly deterministic' (1980, p. 149). He quotes Heath and Skirrow's comment on TV as a medium where 'the viewer doesn't make his own decision what to look at: it is made for him' (1997, p. 33); and adds, 'What in the formulation of "preferred readings" is presented as a problematic attempt at the structuration of meaning for the audience is here presented as a necessary result' (1980, p. 149). Morley cites Paul Willis's (then recent) work on working-class boys' cultural opposition within the school system to indicate that people are active agents, not 'passive bearers of ideology . . . Structuralist theories of reproduction present the dominant ideology . . . as impenetrable. Everything fits too neatly. There are no cracks in the billiard ball smoothness of process' (Willis, 1978, p. 175).

Thus, Morley argued,

> if we are to speak of the reproduction of a dominant ideology, we must see that such an ideology can *only* have effectivity in articulation with the existing forms of common sense and culture of the groups to

whom it is addressed. However, this is not to argue that subordinate groups are free to produce their own cultural life and forms, or readings of dominant forms, in unlimited space. . . . Willis... argues that the subordinate groups produce their own cultures 'in a struggle with the constrictions of the available forms' (p. 124) – a process which is not 'carried' passively by . . . agents but contradictorily produced out of a differentially limited repertoire of available culture forms.

(Morley, 1980, p. 151)

A number of things are immediately apparent here:

- the post-'linguistic-turn' structuralism with which Morley is engaging;
- its 'ideology-critique' specification, so that (as Ang would note) an overwhelming instrumentalism leads directly to the analysis of ideologically 'powerful' television genres such as news and current affairs;
- the search within this 'text' and 'audience' framework for both structural (hegemonic) 'preferred readings' and a 'limited repertoire of available cultural forms' from which to resist them. Like Hall and others, Morley found this limited repertoire in Frank Parkin's notion of 'dominant', 'negotiated' and 'oppositional' codes.

Morley turned to discourse analysis to argue for a contextualised analysis. Referents (like 'the budget' in a current affairs programme) are

connected to discourses, not languages. . . . The analysis must aim to lay bare the structural factors which determine the relative power of different discursive formations in the struggle over the necessary multi-accentuality of the sign – for it is in this struggle over the construction and interpretation of signs that meaning . . . is produced. The crucial thing here is the 'insertion of texts into history via the way they are read' in specific socio-historical conditions, which in turn determine the relative power of different discursive formations. This is to recognise the determining effects of socio-historical conditions in the production of meaning.

(Morley, 1980, p. 156)

Not only was Morley challenging screen theory's 'formalism' via this appeal to history, but also by distinguishing between 'locus' (in the social formation) and 'position' (in discourse), and by arguing that a subject's locus in the social formation structures her or his range of access to discourses and ideological codes, he is also returning to a more sophisticated sociological account (pre-figuring, for example, some of the work on audiences' symbolic resources discussed in earlier chapters).

Thus while accepting the structuralist/Marxist (Althusserian) notion of 'interpellation', Morley argues:

What are important here are the relations of force of the competing discourses which attempt to 'interpellate' the subject: no one discourse or ideology can ever be assumed to have finally or fully dominated and enclosed an individual or social group. . . . For some sections of the audience the codes and meanings of the programme will correspond more or less closely to those which they already inhabit in their various institutional, political, cultural and educational engagements, and for those sections of the audience the dominant meanings and definitions encoded in the programme may well 'fit' and be accepted. For other sections of the audience the meanings and definitions encoded in a programme like *Nationwide* will jar to a greater or lesser extent with those produced by other institutions and discourses in which they are involved – trade unions or 'deviant' subcultures for example – and as a result the dominant meanings will be 'negotiated' or resisted. The crucial point to be explored is which sections of the audience have available to them what forms of 'resistance' to the dominant readings articulated through television. . . . Crucially, we are led to pose the relation of text and subject as an empirical question to be investigated, rather than as an *a priori* question to be deduced from a theory of the ideal spectator 'inscribed' in the text. It may be, as MacCabe (1976, p. 25) emphasises, that analysing a film within a determinate social moment in its relation to its audience 'has nothing to do with the counting of heads' but this is a point of methodological adequacy, not of theoretical principle.

(Morley, 1980, pp. 159–60)

It will be clear from this, that Morley was perfectly aware that in theory 'Each individual is the site of a multiplicity of subject positions proposed to her by the discourses with which she is confronted; her identity is the precarious and contradictory result of the specific set of subject positions she inhabits at any moment in history' (Ang, 1996, p. 93). Even as early as this 1980 text, Morley was adopting the 'poststructuralist position' that subjectivity is the product of the many meaning systems or discourses that are circulating around us, thus constructing our 'society'.

However, there were two problems with Morley's position in the eyes of commentators then and later. One was the emphasis on the instrumentalism of 'ideology-effect', which we have discussed. The other was that to achieve the empirical 'methodological adequacy' he sought, Morley turned to focus group interviews. This was for two reasons: because he could not afford long interviews as well; and because of the need to avoid the focus of much individually oriented research on treating subjects as 'individual atoms divorced from their social context' (1980, p. 33). Morley admitted in his book that there was some disagreement within his focus groups, but

the differences in decoding between the groups from the different categories is far greater than the level of difference and variation within the groups. This seems to confirm the validity of the original decision to use group discussions – feeling that the aim was to discover how interpretations were collectively constructed through talk and the interchange between respondents in a group situation – rather than to treat individuals as the autonomous repositories of a fixed set of individual 'opinions' isolated from their social context.

(Morley, 1980, p. 33)

In analysing his focus group audiotapes, Morley then worked at three levels:

- establishing differences in particular terms and patterns of phrase that marked groups off from each other;
- identifying patterns of argumentation and the manner of referring to evidence or formulating viewpoints as between different groups (around terms like 'common sense', 'the family', 'the nation', etc.);
- exploring the underlying cognitive or ideological premises structuring the logic of arguments in the different groups.

Overall, Morley's attempt to bring together 'text' and 'audience' took further both screen theory's focus on 'television specificity' and Birmingham work on Parkin's dominant, oppositional and negotiated codes. Morley's own conception of televisual specificity was, again, more sociological than that of screen theorists like John Ellis. He posed the concept of 'professional code' as the production site and the theoretical space where the 'specificity' of TV as a medium is to be situated. The professional code has, in his view, determinate effects in terms of a sedimented set of professional practices that define how the medium is to be used. In other words, it is not a quality of the medium as such. Though, Morley argues, this professional specificity is always articulated through ideology, its articulation is 'precisely the space in which we can speak of the relative autonomy of the media'. Hence the 'text' is positioned within the relative autonomy of specific generic values of practice working within television as a form.

As regards 'audiences', in attempting to construct a 'model in which the social subject is always seen as interpellated by a number of discourses', Morley moved beyond Parkin's 'ideal types' of 'dominant', 'negotiated' and 'oppositional' readings, arguing that these types oversimplified the number of meaning systems in play, and tended to locate each one in terms of only one source of origin. This in turn tended to be mechanically tied to class position. In contrast, Morley developed an approach which tried to explore the relationship between an audience's basic socio-demographic factors (age, gender, race and class), its involvement in cultural and institutional identifications (unions, tertiary colleges, parties, etc.), and its experience of the subject matter viewed – all as aspects explaining the extent to which decoding might vary. Consequently, his focus groups were chosen not according to factors such as class but rather institution affiliations (trainee bank managers, trade union shop stewards, further education students, university students, etc.).

Thus, after showing the same *Nationwide* programme to various groups, Morley found that though those with Conservative affiliations tended to produce dominant readings and those with Labour or socialist affiliations tended to produce negotiated or oppositional readings, these readings were themselves differentiated according to further discursive practices (related for instance to the location of audiences in different institutional discourse). Bank managers, apprentices and teacher training students were all Conservative but they varied in their degree of identification with the 'populist' dominant reading of the programme (as analysed earlier by Brunsdon and Morley) and with the particular level of 'BBC' mode of address – which for the apprentices was too serious and for the teachers not serious enough, a distinction relating to the Leavisian educational discourse of the latter. Similarly, the negotiated and oppositional decodings of trade union groups, shop stewards and black further education students – all sharing a common class position – were inflected differently by the influence of the discourses and institutions in which they were situated. 'In one case a tradition of mainstream working class populism, in another that of trade union and Labour party politics, in another the influence of black youth culture.'

Morley thus found plenty of evidence in his audience studies to support his rejection of a sociologistic tying of decodings mechanically to basic demographic factors. But he also found evidence to support his rejection of screen theorists' assumptions that a clear-cut, reflexive recognition of 'textuality' would correlate with an oppositional decoding, and non-recognition with acceptance of the dominant reading. In fact audience members' recognition of 'preferring mechanisms' was quite widespread, without this influencing the acceptance/rejection of the programme. 'Awareness of the construction by no means entails the rejection of what is constructed' – a pointed reference by Morley to screen theory's obsessive concern with avant-garde reflexivity during the 1970s. At the same time, he argues, the positioning of the subject by no means guarantees reproduction of the dominant ideology.

Inevitably, as path-breaking work in television audience analysis, Morley's work encountered problems and plenty of criticism – not least from himself (Morley, 1981). Because (like most qualitative audience analysts) he only extracts rather than reproduces the group discussions, there is no way of knowing how typical his selections are, particularly as he admits (but does not reproduce) contradictory positions within specific focus groups. Further, even the evidence of the interview selections he does publish creates problems.

For instance, the apprentice focus groups (with similar class, institutional, political and cultural locations) by no means respond similarly on every issue. Some Conservative voting groups are sympathetic to Ralph Nader, others are not; while Labour voting groups may adopt the Conservative formulation of 'he's in it for the money'. Similarly, when discussing the black groups' total alienation from the discourse of *Nationwide*,

Morley conveniently forgets one group that is not alienated. He has one all-black further education community studies (female, working-class, Labour voting or 'don't know') group that supports this contention, and another part-black, part-white further education group with the same characteristics which certainly does not. Both of these problems could be explained without contradicting Morley's main thesis – in terms of a complexity of discursive practices beyond the present level of the study. For instance, though some Labour and Conservative groups agree in rejecting Nader (while other Labour and Conservative groups agree in sympathising with him) this could be explained if we differentiated within Morley's catch-all 'apprentice populism' category.

Thus:

- Traditional upper-working-class Conservative apprentices appear to reject Nader because he is 'powerful enough to close firms down' – a perspective which evaluates Nader from a familiar anti-big government perspective;

- Labour voting apprentices seem on the other hand to reject him for his intended upward mobility and attempted entry into the ranks of the moneyed elite – a position of 'left' populism in contrast to that of 'right' populism above. The different meaning attached to 'he's in it for the money' would be an example of the multi-accentuality of the linguistic sign according to its location in different discursive practices which Morley discusses.

- Further, those Conservative apprentice groups which sympathise with Nader could conceivably be located in terms of a 'radical' or 'wet' Conservative environmentalist discourse, without this in any way weakening their adherence in the last instance to the dominant ideological positioning of the overall programme. This group for example rejects an 'environmentalist rubbish' student project, on the basis of the apprentices' pragmatic-vocational attitude to education, a discourse which devalues the university students' project shown on the programme as 'arty'. And this apprentice group also adopt the 'Nader's in it for the money' cynicism, despite their earlier suggestion that the programme is biased against him – biased in favour of industrialists and against the consumer.

- Similarly the discrepancy of one mainly black group (group 17) from the others could presumably be considered in terms of their placement within a part-white class. Morley opens the space for this by saying that black groups other than his 'critique of silence' (totally alienated) groups are in the presence of other discourses which work in parallel with those of the programme. In fact his group 25 of mainly black FE A-level sociology students are clearly in the presence of an academic discourse which enables them to respond to the programme – though via a contrary 'class' analysis, rather than 'in parallel' as Morley suggests. However, Morley does not take up this possibility with his discrepant group 17 – possibly because one of the black groups he confidently describes as totally alienated is also part white. In this rather contradictory situation, Morley ignores his black group 17 almost entirely – otherwise they would compromise his neat formulation that the differential involvement in the discourse of formal education of the teacher-training student groups can precisely account for their responses to the programme. For instance he argues that the university student 'rubbish' item is evaluated favourably by those who 'inhabit this same educational discourse', while other groups, especially black groups who are the 'most alienated from the discourse of formal education' tend to reject it as 'wasting time'. In fact, his own evidence shows that the teacher training students are by no means uniformly favourable to the 'rubbish' project, whereas both the mainly black group 17 and his 'critique of silence' all-black group 16 are reasonably favourable to the 'rubbish' project on the grounds that it is 'interesting': the latter group seeing it as 'youth centred' and therefore for them.

One could extend this analysis by considering the hegemonic practice described by Westergaard (and Hurd, see chapter 3) whereby class and racial contradictions are displaced onto 'safe' oppositions such as between 'young' and 'old' . But Morley does not do this; instead, in the case of his group 17 he ignores the problem, rather disingenuously accounting for the group's interest in Nader in terms of their 'understanding of the community studies course perspective' – an explanation he does not allow to his all-black group 16 who are disinterested in Nader yet also involved in the community studies programme at the same college. Finally, in his summary relating particular groups to dominant, negotiated and oppositional codes he slips his group 17 into the category of alienated 'critique of silence' groups, entirely incorrectly in terms of his own evidence.

The problem, then, is how to account for differences even within the plurality of discursive positions Morley has isolated. The answer, I suspect, is to allow more weight to 'homogenising' theories, such as that of hegemony, and yet at the same time (as Morley himself suggests) to isolate far more discursive sites. For instance, the effect of different apprentice groups' varying occupational aspirations (the pre-occupational tendency which sociologists of occupations have noted of novitiates adopting in advance imputed value patterns of their chosen vocation) might be considered to account for differences to Nader as between apprentices bound for large corporations and those who would enter state employment or self-employment. Morley does hypothetically ascribe differences between trade union groups to the effects of working in unions differentially placed in the public/private and productive/service sectors, but aspirational as well as experiential factors may well have been significant in the competition of discursive positions.

Morley followed David Thompson in rejecting the rather too familiar temptation among screen theorists to conflate 'empirical' and 'empiricist', and argued instead that the way ahead was a matter of 'methodological adequacy' not of 'theoretical principle'. In *The 'Nationwide' Audience*, the theoretical overview was, in my view, more 'adequate' than aspects of the methodological application. But if my comments above have seemed detailed and nit-picking, my point has not been to attack Morley's overall contribution as such, but rather the tendency among all of us who do qualitative research to rely on what David Silverman has called the anecdotal approach to the use of data. Silverman points to two problems he finds repeatedly in qualitative research: 'a tendency to select field data to fit an ideal conception (preconception) of the phenomenon' and 'a tendency to select field data which are conspicuous because they are exotic, at the expense of less dramatic (but possibly indicative) data' (1993, p. 153). Arguably, examples of both these problems are evident in my criticisms of Morley above.

However, Morley responds to these kinds of criticism in his own autocritique, 'The Nationwide Audience: a critical postscript', which takes his audience theory in valuable ways towards an account of 'pleasure'. In addition to criticisms of his emphasis on professional intentionality and his usage of 'preferred reading' in his earlier book (see Morley, 1981, pp. 3–7), Morley critiques his audience analysis in *The 'Nationwide' Audience* on both linguistic and sociological grounds.

Linguistically, Morley argues, his earlier analysis

> concentrated too much on the analysis of responses to isolated elements of particular messages, and in particular on the isolated moments of ideological resistance to particular messages. In this sense, some of the complexity of the argument of *Everyday TV* (in which we have attempted to generate the generative core of the discourse of [the programme]) simply did not receive justice in the audience research. What is defined in the programme analysis as a stylistically definable and ordered system of discourse is improperly reduced/disarticulated into the constituent elements in the audience interviews – which then provide us with evidence of responses to and interpretations of isolated 'bits' of the *NW* discourse, rather than to that discourse as an ordered system.
>
> (1981, pp. 7–8)

Consequently, while claiming an interest in the degree of fit between respondents' linguistic form (vocabularies and forms of speech) and those of the media, the main focus of the research had focused on 'the degree of fit or dissonance between the ideological problematics in play in the text and those articulated by different sections of the audience' (1981, p. 8).

Sociologically, Morley found fault with his audience work on the grounds that although

> reference is made to the effectivity of the structures of age, sex, race and class, only the latter is dealt with in anything resembling a systematic way. Race is invoked as an explanatory factor on a rather ad hoc basis, as is sex/gender; age is mentioned but not explored as a structuring factor.
>
> (1981, p. 8)

Nor does Morley prohibit the notion of going further into other areas of determination (as I have suggested above); though he argues that there is considerable empirical evidence to suggest the greater effectivity of class, gender, race and age in determining a wide range of cultural practices.

Morley also criticises his audience research on the grounds of generalisability. 'Minimally, given the small size of the sample studied, there is a problem about generalizing the conclusions of the study in any way that took for granted the representative nature of these groups – the groups could only be taken to have a potentially illustrative function.'

The most interesting part of Morley's self-critique, however, is in developing beyond 'ideology-critique' into a theory of genre and cultural competence. Here he rethinks his reliance on Parkin's schema of meaning systems and its assumption that, in television, one is dealing 'with a broadly political form of communication. The range of decoding positions hypothesised is based on the stance of the decoder with respect to the central/dominant values of the society – i.e. how near or far one is from the positions/definitions established by this "central value system" ' (1981, p. 10).

There are two problems with this assumption, in Morley's view. First, it directs attention at the more 'political' genres like news and current affairs. But any 'attempt to transpose the concept to the fictional realm, via the concept of "preferred reading" and "narrative closure" (or hierarchy of discourse) always runs the risk of reducing the fictional text to the mere vehicle of a banal substantive proposition which can then be labelled as "ideological" ' (1981, p. 6). Morley was quite aware of work that had been done for years in screen theory examining the 'tension' or 'excess' in fictional texts (for example, in Hollywood melodrama) via aspects of *mise-en-scène* or star image which operated to undercut narrative closure, and felt he had entirely underestimated this degree of textual complexity in his *Nationwide* audience work.

Second, in his 'Postscript' Morley begins to move towards a theory of pleasure, arguing for 'the necessity to recognise, in the first instance, the question of the viewers' positive or negative response to the text as a particular cultural form – do they enjoy it, feel bored by it, recognise it as at all relevant to their concerns?' (1981, p. 10). Morley is now talking of 'dealing more with the relevance/irrelevance and comprehension/incomprehension dimension of decoding rather than being directly concerned with the acceptance or rejection of substantive ideological propositions' (1981, p. 10). In particular, he argues for an extension of Bourdieu's notion of cultural competence in relation to a range of different genres from high art to soap opera. Thus, the 'ideal reader' inscribed in a text must begin to be related 'to different genres of texts, rather than in relation to individual texts' (1981, p. 12), as in most screen theory accounts.

Comparing, for instance, news or current affairs with soap opera, Morley argues:

> Each requires the viewer to be competent in certain forms of knowledge and to be familiar with certain conventions which constitute the grounds or framework within/on which particular propositions can be made. Thus, as Charlotte Brunsdon has argued, soap opera presumes, or requires, a viewer competent in the codes of personal relations in the domestic sphere. The viewer is required to have a particular form of cultural capital – in this case in the form of the ability to predict the range of possible consequences attendant upon actions in the sphere of the domestic/familial. Correspondingly, current affairs TV presumes, or requires, a viewer competent in the codes of parliamentary democracy and economics. The viewer is again required to have available particular forms of knowledge and expertise, because the assumptions/frameworks within which reports/discussions move will rarely be made explicit within the programmes. Thus, without prior access to these codes the particular content/items within the programmes will remain incomprehensible. These points can be related back to theories of structural distribution of cultural competence. . . . While the competence necessary for reading soap opera are most likely to have been acquired by those persons culturally constructed through discourses of femininity, the competences necessary for reading current affairs TV are more likely to have been acquired by those persons culturally constructed through discourses of masculinity (with the added rider that in the latter case, the other probable conditions of access to these forms of cultural competence are being white and being middle or upper-class).
>
> (1981, pp. 12–3)

Morley notes that his comments are 'only sketches' towards a broadly based theory of gender, genre and cultural competence. One of the problems with Morley's 1981 revisiting of his *Nationwide* audience research was its (admittedly sketchy) return to a homogenised relationship between social discourses, gender and genre; whereas his earlier work (in theory at least) acknowledged the intersection of a wide range of institutional, political, legal, familial and other discourses that make up our subjectivity.

On the other hand, a key continuity between Morley's position and work on audience's symbolic resources I have described in earlier chapters, also helps explain a central theoretical problem with Morley's 1981 re-assessment. This is that despite his mention of approaching a theory of gendered pleasure, this gets lost in his new emphasis on the 'comprehension/incomprehension dimension of decoding'. Why should we assume that if girls have the cultural competence to comprehend the domestic discourses of soap opera, and boys are competent in the codes of parliamentary democracy and economics, they will *enjoy* those particular forms more? If we move still further with our 'David Morley story', into the 1990s, we will understand that slippage better.

Debating the new revisionism

Between 1990 and 1996 there was an exchange between David Morley on the one hand, John Corner and James Curran on the other which is revealing. Both Curran (1990) and Corner (1991) had written articles challenging the 'new audience' research (in which Morley featured centrally) for denying media power and moving away from a concern with the political or ideological effects of television. Corner accused 'active audience' researchers of 'a form of sociological quietism . . . in which increasing emphasis on the micro-processes of viewing relations displaces . . . an engagement with the macro-structures of media and society' (1991, p. 269). He challenged the new orthodoxy of celebrating the polysemy of media products, and called for a renewed concern for textual determination. Curran argued that the 'active audience' new revisionists, in their celebration of the semiotic democracy of the text were reviving a 'discredited wisdom of the past' (1996, p. 269) that even the old pluralists had abandoned. Against the 'active audience' tradition of the 1980s, Curran cited Greg Philo's findings in relation to the British miners' strike of 1984 that 'audiences do not have an infinite repertoire of discourses to draw on in adapting TV meanings' (1996, p. 268). This limited discursive repertoire and the power of textual 'preferred meanings' meant, as Philo showed, 'that there was a clear correspondence between certain recurrent themes in TV reporting of the strike and what was understood, believed and remembered by the audience after a considerable lapse of time' (Curran, 1990, 1996, p. 268).

As Curran argued,

> the most revealing part of [Philo's] important study is the double insight it provides into the dialogue that takes place between viewers and TV news. On one hand, it highlights the variety of resources that audience subjects drew upon in resisting or negotiating TV meanings – first-hand knowledge (and, even more important, word-of-mouth relaying of first hand knowledge), class experiences, political cultures, other media accounts, sceptical dispositions towards the news media and internal processes of logic. Conversely, it also shows the way in which some people adjusted their opinions in the light of the information they received from TV, including, crucially, people who strongly

identified with the striking National Union of Mineworkers (NUM)
but who reluctantly came to accept certain anti-NUM themes in TV
reporting.

(Curran, 1996, pp. 268–9)

Morley's negotiation with these criticisms is important and revealing. He
argued that Corner 'seems to invoke a notion of the macro which is con-
ceptualized in terms of pre-given structures, rather than (to use Giddens's
(1979) phrase) "structuration", and . . . fails to see that macro structures
can only be reproduced through micro-processes. Unless one deals in a reified sense of "structure", such an entity is simply an analytical construct
detailing the patterning of an infinite number of micro-processes and events'
(Morley, 1996, p. 280). Morley equated this with a shift in critical theory
from an Althusserian structuralist notion of 'dominant ideology' to the
more 'negotiative' situation Gramsci describes as 'hegemony'.

> Corner's critique, unfortunately, seems to conflate two different issues.
> On one hand, the conceptual shift from a model of dominant ideology
> as a given structure to a processual model of hegemony (and the conse-
> quent interest in the micro aspect of macro processes) and, on the other
> hand, the substantive reworking of the field under the impact of feminist
> theory and research, decentring the former principal concerns with
> class, in favour of a concern with the articulation of structures of gender
> and class, especially in relation to the media's role in articulating the
> public/private interface. This . . . is hardly a research agenda from
> which power has slipped.
>
> (Morley, 1996, p. 281)

Significantly, Morley's reference to the feminist research agenda was much
closer to his own account of gender, cultural competence and 'private/pub-
lic' television genres than it was to the growing feminist interest in fantasy
and pleasure.

In response to Curran, as well as challenging the latter's main thrust that
the 'active audience' tradition was a 'revival' of the old American communication theory's pluralism, Morley took particular care to distinguish
between different tendencies within the so-called 'new revisionism'. He distanced himself from both the neo-pluralist work of Ang and Hermes and
(most especially) from the 'semiotic democracy' of John Fiske. Here,
Morley's rhetorical ploy emphasised continuities between himself and
Curran.

> The implicit valorization of audience pleasure, in this work, leads into
> a cultural relativism which, as Curran notes, is readily incorporated
> into a populist neo-liberal rhetoric which would abandon any concern
> with cultural values – or 'quality' television (see Brunsdon 1990). . . .
> As Curran observes (1990, p. 148) Fiske's celebration of a 'semiotic
> democracy', in which people drawn from a vast shifting range of

subcultures and groups construct their own meanings within an autonomous cultural economy, is problematic in various respects, but not least because it is readily subsumable within a conservative ideology of sovereign consumer pluralism.

(Morley, 1996, pp. 286)

Above all Morley's hostility – and this explains I think the slippage from 'pleasure' to 'comprehension' in his 1981 reprise – is against poststructuralist theories which celebrate pleasure as flux and diversity, and forget that power depends in central part on 'the presence or absence of . . . cultural resources necessary in order to make certain types of meaning, which is, ultimately, an empirical question' (1996, p. 288). It is also – in the view of Morley, Curran, Corner, Tulloch and Tulloch, Philo and other researchers I look at in this book – a materialist question. Discourses, schemas, narratives and 'logical scaffolding' (Morley, 1992, p. 181) for ordering the world are, for all these theorists, material resources which some people have acquired and some people have not; a situation which depends on one's place in the process of 'structuration' and not on individual qualities.

The debate between Morley and Curran continued into the pages of their jointly edited book *Cultural Studies and Communications* (Curran, Morley and Walkerdine, 1996), where valuable insights were traded about the political role of their own articles in the respective reading formations of Britain and the USA. As Curran said in his 'Media Dialogue: A Reply', however, both Morley and Curran agreed above all in being critical of research which overstated the power of media audiences. Both, says Curran,

point to the way in which audience autonomy is constrained potentially by two factors: signifying mechanisms in texts, and a variable degree of social access to ideas and meanings which facilitate contrary 'readings' of the media. . . . Micro analysis is not seen as an end in itself, as a postmodernist celebration of the irreducible complexity of audience responses to the richly textured meanings of the media, but rather as an aid to understanding the place of the media within an egalitarian social order.

(1996, pp. 294–5)

In the remainder of this chapter I will look at studies which have taken further this dual emphasis – on signifying mechanisms in news texts, and on differential audience access to wide ranging resources of meanings.

Behind the news

Justin Lewis's book, *The Ideological Octopus: an exploration of television and its audience* (1991) is similar in some respects to Morley's *The 'Nationwide' Audience* (1980) in that it begins with a historical overview of audience research, followed by his own empirical studies. Like Morley, Lewis is very concerned about textualist approaches; though, ten years on, he is ruder about screen theory.

> Textual analysis has, unfortunately, become alarmingly presumptu-ous. Throughout its brief history, there has been a tendency to distort the semiological endeavour, to show not what the text *could* mean, but to assert what it *does* mean. . . . The most well-known example of this indulgence is associated with the British journal *Screen*, particu-larly during the late 1970s. The journal, shielded by layers of impene-trable and awkward language, frequently granted films, programs and other discourses more power than was ever dreamed of by even the most misguided member of the 'effects' tradition. Audiences disap-peared from the construction of meaning altogether, to be replaced by a witless creature known as the 'textual subject'. The textual subject, like the unfortunate mouse in the behaviourist's experiment, was manipulated and forced (by the text's structures and strategies) to adopt particular positions. Once in position, the inexorable meaning of the message (produced with consummate wizardry by the analyst) would manifest itself.
>
> (1991, p. 34)

Morley's reflexive doubt, expressed in his 1981 'Postscript', as to whether the 'preferred reading' was 'a property of the text, the analyst or the audi-ence' (Morley, 1981, p. 6) has here been answered in no uncertain manner by Lewis, who then goes on to look at different methodologies which might give us access to audience readings of the text. This is not to say that in Lewis's analysis the text has no 'preferring' properties. It is just that they don't always work very well. This becomes very apparent in his comparison of two empirical studies, of *The Cosby Show* and a television news broad-cast.

In the case of *Cosby*, because of its traditional narrative format, and its regular discourse about sexist (but *not* racist) discrimination, Lewis antici-pated his audience would recognise its 'preferred reading', especially as the episode he showed them 'gently exposes the limitations of traditional male attitudes' (Lewis, 1991, p. 167). This proved to be the case, though – in an interesting development of Morley's 'pleasure' versus 'comprehension' agenda – this did not mean that everybody liked it. Most audience groups did, but two 'small subgroups reacted with displeasure: those women who found the show's message too weak; and men, from the opposite perspec-tive, who rejected the show's message altogether' (1991, p. 170). Interestingly, however, men who were stridently anti-feminist were happy with the show, since they found their own ('men be yourself') message in the two doctors' competitiveness over a ball game while Claire checks the roast dinner. As Lewis says, this indicates that resistive viewing can be fun and reactionary at the same time!

Lewis's analysis of audience responses to British television news establishes very clearly the relationship between texts, 'preferring' devices and 'the discourses that structured people's views of the world' (1991, p. 108). After showing respondents with different backgrounds and interests a number of *News at Ten* items, Lewis asked them to discuss each one (in so far as they could remember them) in their own terms. This 'what was each story about?' opening question was followed by a more detailed jogging of their memory to probe aspects of the story they had not included in their interpretation. This either led to an elaboration of the item or confirmed that they had missed aspects because the viewer found them incomprehensible or insignificant.

Lewis's hypothesis behind this methodology was that because each news item, unlike *Cosby*, has no traditional narrative structure, viewers' ability to recall details is very low. Though a number of analysts (e.g. Hartley, 1982) speak of the narrative structure of news, Lewis argues that individual items have a very particular structure which devalues traditional narrative's hermeneutic code (as described by Barthes, the code that establishes enigmas, teases viewers over their solution and finally resolves this 'absence'). Most television genres – drama, sport, quiz shows, advertisements – use the hermeneutic code. 'There is, however, one form of television that steadfastly refuses the temptations of narrative codes in general, and the hermeneutic code in particular. It is a form that, by abandoning narrative, abandons substantial sections of the viewer's consciousness. That form is television news' (1991, p. 129).

In this the television news item borrows its format from print journalism, where the 'important' elements are given first, and then filled out in declining order of newsworthiness. This enables the reader to scan the 'important bits' of a newspaper quickly, and a news editor to cut the story very easily (from the bottom upward). Borrowing this form, television news turns the hermeneutic code

> inside-out. History inevitably has an enigmatic quality – we do not know how the future will unfold. Television news takes this history and squeezes the sense of mystery right out of it. The main point of the story comes not at the end, but at the beginning. It is like being told the punchline before the joke.
>
> (Lewis, 1991, p. 131)

Lewis indicates that these points had not occurred to him before he began to try to make sense of the patterns that emerged from his audience study. This revealed that most respondents had considerable difficulty recalling news 'stories', and they tended to focus in discussion on discrete moments in each item – like riots of Palestinians on the West Bank. If they did not already know details of the events leading up to any item (for example, the sacking of three Palestinian mayors by the Israelis), they were very unlikely to remember anything about the historical context, *even where that information is given in the news item*. In fact, in the particular news item he showed them, the only interview was with an Israeli administrator 'justifying to foreign journalists the dismissal of the mayors' (1991, p. 133). Arguably, then, Lewis says, the item was structured around this piece of information, and two-thirds of the respondents remembered the interview. But *only one-fifth* of respondents connected this to the rioting.

> The failure to make these links had a distinct effect upon the audience. The majority built their reading of the item upon the images of violence shown in the report. Deprived of historical context, these images signified nothing of themselves. The story was, for most of the respondents, just another episode in an endless saga of violence in the Middle East. The specificities of the region's history faded into generalities about the world's 'trouble spots'. Over two-fifths of the respondents made a direct comparison to Northern Ireland . . . because the violent pictures looked the same.
>
> (Lewis, 1991, p. 133)

A residual racist discourse ('foreigners fight each other for no particular reason') filled in, Lewis argues, for the 'lost' parts of the news item. Consequently, the meaning constructed by viewers may be very different from the meaning news producers intended to convey. Another example in Lewis's study is a 'new deal at British Leyland' item, where the new productivity relationship between management and workers (replacing the 'bad old days' of strikes) was the focal point of the anchor's introduction, and the reporter on location began and ended his report with it. Yet only 16 per cent of Lewis's respondents made any reference to it as 'what the item was about', and very many in fact used the item to read it *in terms of* 'strikes at British Leyland'.

In contrast, respondents made sophisticated connections in a news item about changing US policy relating to support for an extreme right-wing candidate in the El Salvador elections. Lewis argues that the difference here was that 'the discussion of events in El Salvador related not to fragments and images but to a *narrative* logic. Even though the El Salvador item begins in the standard way by the anchor giving away the change of US policy, the

> power of the introduction to deflate the story that follows is lessened by the rather puzzling presentation: the connection between the two events (the possibility of an extreme right-wing victory and the U.S. volte face on D'Aubuisson) is unstated. While this would normally be interpreted as bad journalism, it allows Snow to rescue the narrative, and use his film report to develop it. . . . The film . . . mysteriously moves to a shot of Snow standing by three dead bodies. Snow briefly describes the scene, setting up the enigma – 'Why are there dead bodies here, and what has this to do with the election?' This enigma is developed by Snow's next sentence, which answers the first question

by referring to the death squads, but, teasingly, leaves the second open. The enigmatic power of the scene is intensified by two more descriptive shots (what Christian Metz would call a 'descriptive syntagm') revealing close-ups of a vulture and an empty pair of boots.

(Lewis, 1991, p. 137)

Clearly, Lewis is well able to draw on screen theory to examine his text. But the difference from screen theory is in Lewis's use of audience readings to help think through his theory in resolving his own enigma: what, textually, is the difference between the West Bank and the El Salvador news items that leads to such differences in audience understanding?

From here Lewis moves on to consider, not screen theory, but David Morley's other *bête noire*, Fiske's 'semiotic democracy'. If, says Lewis,

TV news has, through its structure, relinquished the use of narrative to manipulate the viewer's understanding, does it have less power? Does it, in fact, open up space to viewers to construct their own readings? Does the gap between encoding and decoding pass power from the hands of producers to consumers in a kind of semiotic democracy?

(1991, p. 139)

The answer, says Lewis, is 'no'. The absence of a narrative logic in the news does not leave its viewers free to construct any meaning they like. Sometimes images are powerful, at other times words are powerful.

What made images or statements powerful was . . . their position in the news item and the ideas that viewers were ideologically attuned to receive. . . . [M]eaning is contingent upon the semiological or ideological resources available to the viewer. . . . The structure of news forces viewers to draw more actively upon their own ideological resources to make sense of what is going on . . . The fragmented narrative structure of news means that the 'preferred meaning' of a news item is usually limited to these moments of discursive or ideological resonance.

(1991, pp. 141–3)

The power of television news works, Lewis argues, via associative logics, not via narrative logic. This associative logic is often created by television itself: 'foreigners are violent to each other'; 'British Leyland equals strikes equals militant workers'. As Lewis says, even though the workers in the news item 'directly contradicted this logic, their significance in the discourse relied upon it' (1991, p. 146).

We need, says Lewis, 'to know all kinds of different things to be able to construct an effective critique of TV news. We need, for example, to have an understanding (of events) that goes beyond the range of discourses that the news delivers.' (1991, p. 152) How can this be achieved? The next study, using a very different methodology, looks at ways in which the discourse

'British Leyland equals strikes equals militant workers' discourse was challenged, and with what results.

Strikes and militant workers

In his 1990 study, Greg Philo of the Glasgow University Media Group, gave groups of people from different parts of Britain news photographs from the 1984/85 miners' strike, and asked them to imagine they were journalists writing their own news stories. They were also questioned about their memories of the strike, and what they had believed about specific issues: was picketing, for example, mainly peaceful or violent?

A significant and (to Philo) surprising result was the closeness of the 'news programmes' produced by these groups to original stories as they had appeared on the BBC and ITN news broadcasts at the time of the strike. Philo reports a group from Essex who wrote: 'As the drift back to work in the mines began to gather momentum, violence erupted' (1995, p. 37). Similarly, a Glasgow group wrote: 'On a day that saw an increased drift back to work . . . further violence was taking place.' Philo compares this to the original ITN news item on 12 November 1984: 'Worst picket violence yet but miners continue their drift back' (1995, p. 37).

Philo notes how the phrase 'drift back' had stuck in people's minds; and quotes journalists at the time of the strike commenting on the 'skilful propaganda' by the National Coal Board, whose term 'the drift back' signified an inevitable process of defeat for the strike. Virtually everybody in Philo's study also thought that most picketing shown on television news was violent, though whether they *believed* this was another matter. 'The extent to which they believed in the television version of the world depended on several factors, particularly on whether they had access to alternative accounts. No one who had actually been to a picket line thought that picketing was mostly violent' (Philo, 1995, p. 38). In contrast, for those without direct experience of the strike, television's version was likely to be important.

Philo's research is particularly interesting, however, where it goes beyond these predictable generalities to showing how his specific methodology could tease out the complications of situated readings. One woman working in a solicitor's office in Croydon, south London, for example used a photograph of a shotgun lying on a table to construct an unexpected account, understandable only via the details of her personal history. She wrote: 'Serious disruption and fear was caused by the police today at the coal mines, as a result of them using arms and threatening behaviour towards the pickets and the coal miners (Philo, 1995, p. 38).

Nothing in the socio-economic position of this woman predicted this account; and nor did her personal affiliations (her father was a police constable and her boyfriend was a CID officer). However, a complex mix of discursive resources and personal experience did explain her news story. From her professional experience in seeing court cases reported, she thought that the media concentrated on the sensational. Consequently, she focused her story on violence, even though she herself did not believe most picketing had been like this. While she also believed that the gun probably belonged to a miner, her personal experience told her that police do not always do things 'by the book': 'It wouldn't surprise me if an officer had picked up the gun and used it. Things which I have been told by police officers which they have done to people taken in for questioning might surprise some people, but in certain circumstances it would be understandable' (Philo, 1995, p. 39).

This respondent felt that the police should not have been put in this situation in the first place during the miners' strike, since the 'miners and pickets may have sorted it out between themselves. When I see the police I associate them with criminals and the miners are not criminals' (Philo, 1995, p. 39). So, she tended 'to see things from both sides', sympathising with the miners to some extent, but also being very sympathetic to the police. As Philo says,

> Because she was so close to the police, she could both sympathize with them and know they might sometimes break the rules. At the same time, she had a clear and professionally defined view of what police responsibilities are. Through this extraordinary set of filters she was able to envisage a situation in which the police might fire unlawfully at pickets, while retaining sympathy both for them and the miners. At the same time she used her professional background both to assess how the police should act and to reject the media account of what occurred.
>
> (1995, p. 39)

In his study Philo emphasises the importance to audience interpretations of having available 'alternative' sources of information. These might come from other media forms: 16 per cent of his sample of people compared accounts from the 'quality' or local press with the television news accounts of the strike. Or they could come from personal biography and memory: women from working-class areas in Glasgow and London remembered queues for food and the loss of jobs in the dispute; and one middle-class woman from Essex also remembered the hopelessness of families and 'shortage of money', drawing on her own personal history as a child in the steel works of Wales and the harsh consequences of unemployment for her own family. Still, Philo says:

> we should not underestimate [the] power . . . of television to influence public belief. Most of the people in the study did not have direct experience of the strike and did not use alternative sources of information to negotiate the dominant messages on issues such as the nature of picketing. . . . It is . . . clear that it can be very difficult to criticize a

dominant media account if there is little access to alternative sources of information. In these circumstances we should not underestimate the power of the media.

(1995, p. 41)

Media power and the skilfulness of audiences

Much of the emphasis in the 'resistive reading' tradition of media analysis has derived from the appropriation of Bourdieu's notion of 'cultural capital'. Thus, for instance, Hodge and Tripp (1986, p. 187) argued that children acquired cultural knowledge about the 'complex operations of power' in the school, and by analogy society, by way of watching the Australian soap opera, *Prisoner*, since they recognised and enjoyed the parallels between the 'total institutions' of school and prison. Curthoys and Docker also argued that *Prisoner* was popular with children because of 'its portrayal of a situation not so very different from that of school' (Curthoys and Docker, 1989, p. 67). Yet the Tullochs' research indicated that even where clearly 'alternative' and 'resistive' accounts of social processes are presented textually, students (particularly the working-class students who are the main focus of the *Prisoner* analyses) often do not understand these explanations of social and institutional causality. It is one thing to argue that some children see parallels between their school and the prison: via perceived similarities between their teachers and the prison screws. It is quite another to suggest that they will therefore extrapolate from the fact that the prison governor 'is subject to control from above' to a wider societal recognition of the potential 'limits of the powers of the powerful' (Hodge and Tripp, 1986, p. 187).

It is true that *Prisoner*, as a soap opera is far more accessible (and continuous) than Ken Loach's *Which Side Are You On?* But the contrasting audience responses to *Which Side Are You On?* and the soap opera *A Country Practice* were more to do, the Tullochs argued, with *ACP*'s embedding of its 'progressive' message within conventional scripts, schemata and community repertoires than with a simple generic difference. There is a tendency, they suggest, within much of the work on cultural competence and 'resistive readings' to emphasise the skilfulness of audiences rather than the power of conventional socio-cognitive frameworks in the media (as Murdock rightly complains). Both Justin Lewis's and Greg Philo's work on television news confirms the importance of audience analysis re-engaging with these frameworks, and the relationship between these and different audience members' symbolic resources.

Each of the methodologies used here was very different. But as David Morley has said (citing Graham Murdock), questions of methodology are ultimately pragmatic ones, 'to be determined according to the resources available and the particular kind of data needed to answer specific questions' (Morley, 1992, p. 13). Each of the 'methodological choices (ethnography included) incur what an economist would call "opportunity cost" – in terms of the possibilities excluded by *any* particular choice of method' (1992, p. 13). Morley thus agrees with Murdock that, for some purposes, properly constructed quantitative survey is the most appropriate method of research.

> Critical work is not defined by the techniques of inquiry it employs, though a number of commentators have proceeded as though the 'soft' data produced by observation, depth interviewing and personal testimony offer the only permissible evidence, and all forms of 'number crunching' are to be rejected on principle . . . [as] . . . a compromise with empiricism.
> (Murdock, 1989, p. 226, cited in Morley, 1992, p. 13)

It is undoubtedly on the basis of these theoretical and methodological views, which I share with Murdock and Morley, that I have chosen the particular studies of this chapter. They all engaged at some level with the television 'text' as a feature of embedded institutional practices. And they vary substantially in methodology, according to the kind of research need they specify. Lewis, for example, is led to his particular open-ended/probing qualitative methodology via his respondents' 'surprising' lack of recall about key 'preferring' devices in television news; and he then moves on from there to a theory about television news as hermeneutically a very different TV genre than dramas, quiz shows, sport, and so on. He relates this back to work values of practice in print journalism. Philo adopts an 'active' methodology, asking respondents to construct their own news stories with existing news photographs of the miners' strike, but in their own words and order. This is, indeed, a 'test' of the 'active audience', embedded in the context of 'dominant' (National Coal Board), 'alternative' (e.g. the *Guardian*) and 'oppositional' (miners' union) discourses. Philo thus puts to work some of the key theoretical concepts developed by Morley and others for audience study, but extending this via an 'active' methodology that looks at various audience groups' daily, practical resources for telling industrial stories.

Morley's, Lewis's and Philo's work is all within a reflexive materialist tradition; and all indicate that even when the prevailing symbolic imbalance of television is challenged, 'resistance' is severely impaired by the symbolic resources available among both young and older audiences – especially in relation to 'political' matters like industrial relations, and especially within the working class.

|11|

Conclusion:

Cult, talk and their audiences

A major theme of this book has been audience pleasures and audience anxieties and fears. A theoretical theme has been reflexivity, and the role of the researcher in situated 'tales from the field'. It seemed appropriate, therefore, to conclude with the pleasures (and anxieties) of the audience researchers themselves.

Fandom has been a preoccupation of audience theorists within cultural studies for some years now; and some of those audience theorists have been fans themselves. As we saw in chapter 2, many theorists explain this preoccupation as an outcome of postmodernism. 'Postmodern media culture creates the condition of fandom, of affective investment in appropriated objects wherein the investment further empties them of meaning' (Munson, 1993, p. 14). Fandom is the site and stake of a society without 'impassioned commitment' to rational discourse and narratives of knowledge or liberation. Fandom marks the affective society, but also, I have argued, the society of risk – the society where experts are dethroned.

This concluding chapter looks at three recent studies of fandom which I have enjoyed. Only two of these academics have *been* fans of the subject matter they have analysed. The other researched and wrote a study of fandom because of her anxiety, as a feminist, about the TV programme, *Beverly Hills 90210*, that she was studying.

So only two of the three researchers would self-describe as a fan of cult television. The third saw the cult of *90210* as something that *others* (mainly the young women she taught as an academic and musician) were into. What difference did this make, theoretically and methodologically, to these research projects and their 'audience' findings? What can we learn about cultural and media studies from a study of academic fans (and non-fans) writing about other fans?

Television, gender and identity: fans of *90210*

E. Graham McKinley, a heterosexual female academic, is immediately reflexive about herself as researcher and how this initially related to the series, *90210*, that she explored.

> All analyses are positioned, and the reader should understand that I have spent much of my life struggling with the identity issues raised here. An academic achiever who grew up in the progressive 1970s, I always expected I would find satisfaction in work as well as in personal relationships. Indeed, in my several careers as musician, journalist, and college professor, I have found arenas in which I can nurture and serve others while retaining an individual identity apart from those professional roles. In my jobs I encountered communities of both care and respect – something I did not encounter as a married woman, and therefore I have chosen not to remarry, though I enjoy close friendships and a long-term, committed relationship. In thus rejecting the culturally accepted roles of wife and mother because of their identity implications, I continue to grapple with issues of dating, appearance, and so forth raised by both the show and the interviewees, and I have struggled against the double-edged sword of interrogating gender norms while taking advantage of the ways in which they sometimes privilege me.
>
> (McKinley, 1997, pp. 11–2)

McKinley, an infrequent television watcher, became both fascinated and enlivened by the 'intense conferences, even arguments, about *90210* among a number of junior-high-school girls' (1997, p. 1) with whom she worked as a choir and drama director. 'I wondered what this talk accomplished. . . . This study is the outgrowth of my desire to understand whether and how such talk accomplished identity work' (1997, p. 2).

Still actively concerned with her own sexual and gender identity work, McKinley was distinctly *not* a fan at the start. 'To me – an infrequent television watcher – the show seemed a largely empty portrayal of an ensemble of wealthy, unsupervised young characters with improbable cheekbones. Though its dramas highlighted salient social issues, to my eye it represented a typical Hollywood effort: superficially liberal in its treatment of individual rights, but ultimately perpetuating conservative values' (McKinley, 1997, pp. 1–2). McKinley is decidedly not a 'generation-x' academic of the kind that Henry Jenkins once described himself to me as: brought up on, and working one's identities through, the considerable 'postmodern' pleasures of popular television.

And even though the undertaking of 'this analysis was a journey of discovery' for McKinley, still, at the end of her several months of closeness to the fans, she had not become a lover of *90210*.

I must admit, I do appreciate the show's many strengths, including its
focused acting and seamless production quality. . . . But my own experiences as a single woman challenging traditional female roles in both
domestic and professional spheres lead me to object strongly to a text
that both naturalizes dominant notions of female identity and conceals
how difficult it is to break out of those moulds.

(McKinley, 1997, pp. 28–9)

Thus it is that 'My urgent, concerned, and even angry voice will be heard
throughout this book' (1997, p. 28).

Symptomatic of McKinley's position as researcher, academic, professional and single woman is her analysis of *90210*'s portrayal of the character Lucinda, originally the wife of a college professor who, though a married
woman, flirts with one of the male leads, Brandon (brother of 'the bitch'
Brenda). Later, when Lucinda is divorced, she teaches a feminist course that
Brenda, Kelly ('strong, independent'), Donna (the 'airhead' virgin) and
Andrea (the 'intellectual') take. Brandon at this point contacts Lucinda
again and they have a torrid affair.

McKinley emphasises that the girls' talk about Lucinda 'was particularly
distressing to me' (1997, p. 208). For McKinley, 'the most painful aspect of
this construction' (1997, p. 207) was her audiences' condoning of textual
conflict between women when a man is involved. The girls McKinley interviewed were very negative about Lucinda.

Despite the fact that Brandon is at least as active as Lucinda in initiat-
ing the liaison, only Lucinda's behavior was censured, and that relatively consistently. . . . Lucinda [the girls said] is 'on the loose.' What
was fascinating to me was that no one seemed to remember Brandon's
persistence in pursuing Lucinda, against her better judgment, after her
divorce. . . . [B]oth reads are available in the text – Lucinda as seducer,
and as seduced. Viewers, however, uniformly constructed her as
predatory, perhaps because of her power position as teacher and as
older than the students.

(McKinley, 1997, p. 205)

In addition, the girls were very hostile to Lucinda's sexual forwardness in
putting the moves on Dylan; whereas they would have found it perfectly
acceptable if the reverse had happened. One group dismissed Lucinda as 'a
nympho', arguing that if she wanted his money, teasing him with kisses was
all right, 'but she *wanted* to sleep with him' (McKinley, 1997, p. 206).

It was completely natural for a kiss to come with a price tag. It was
Lucinda's sexuality that was threatening, that branded her as 'on the
loose.' On the one hand, women were praised when they say what
they think and go after what they want. But when what they want is a
particular male, then this behaviour is condemned. Lucinda was
judged with reference to the yardstick that men should pursue, women

attract; men are active, women passive or possessing only negative agency. The talk actively reified and perpetuated this dominant female identity.

(McKinley, 1997, p. 206)

McKinley was especially disturbed over a scene where Kelly (who had fended off Brandon because she was currently with Dylan) was jealously aggressive to Lucinda in class because she has learned that Lucinda has attempted to seduce Dylan, and is full of righteous anger.

> This confrontation episode between the two ... ends with Kelly breaking completely from Lucinda [from whom she was gaining feminist ideas]. As she snuggles up to Dylan, Kelly promises she will abandon her feminist opinions; an approving Dylan characterizes himself as 'old-fashioned' (an odd statement for a 'rebel' James Dean-type male to make, underlining perhaps that even rebels are sexist). The text firmly closes down Lucinda as a viable identity possibility once one of our community, Kelly, rejects her. I am not suggesting, incidentally, that it is wrong to feel pain in betrayal or to fight to preserve a relationship. I am simply pointing out that, in this talk, the forum for such a struggle was between women. Within the couple, the woman is silenced. And the text closes down the possibilities that in some contexts, a woman could be in control of her sexuality and be defined without reference to a male. Instead, the way the choice is presented discredits that voice, 'clawing back' the female identity into the patriarchal status quo.
>
> (McKinley, 1997, pp. 208–9)

The series *and* her interviewees' 'story-telling' about Lucinda, the feminist college teacher, deeply disturbs McKinley, the feminist college teacher, and she is both open and reflexive about it. Some feminist theorists of soap opera, of course, would argue that a soap opera is multi-stranded, and so that – were she looking – McKinley could equally find examples where the text does the opposite, or at least opens alternative gender positions. But it is the closure of alternative possibilities which is the focus of McKinley's analysis of *90210*; and this particular debate leads us directly into questions of methodology and theory.

Methodology

McKinley's discussion of the scene where Kelly confronts Lucinda over Dylan in class well illustrates her methodological approach. She describes the way in which her 'viewers applauded Kelly and criticized Lucinda *as they watched* an in-class confrontation between the pair' (my italics; McKinley, 1997, p. 207). McKinley emphasises that a 'top priority was given to preserving to the greatest extent possible the naturalness of the viewing and discussion settings. . . . With one unhappy exception of an interview that took place in my office . . . interviews took place in the homes and dormitories of participants' (1997, p. 243).

So keen was the researcher to achieve this natural setting, that she describes how, in a particularly bitter New Jersey February and March, she trudged 'uncertainly through the drifts of the Princeton University campus' (1997, p. 3) on the Wednesday evenings when *90210* went to air. Again, because of her concern to achieve the naturalness of the viewing situation, she chose friendship groups who normally watched together anyway, via her various work situations (as a Rider University lecturer, at a Protestant Church where she worked as music director, and in a newsroom where she was part-time copy editor). She then expanded her number of groups via the 'snowball' method whereby respondents found more respondents, until 36 girls and young women, ranging from sixth grade (age 11) through college (age 22), were interviewed. These all described themselves as fans of *Beverly Hills, 90210*, and were chosen from a range of socio-economic classes. Though there were three American-born Asian girls included in the study, McKinley deliberately avoided the complicating factor of race/ethnicity in her study, feeling that age, gender and class difference made the study complex enough already.

Influenced by the recent British tradition of audience analysis, she used qualitative methods, visiting dormitories and homes, tape-recording the viewers' talk, loosely following a set of questions (which McKinley prints in her book: p.245). Her innovation, as she says, was in recording 'their spontaneous talk during viewing, a procedure I have not seen elsewhere but one that proved exceptionally generative' (1997, p. 3). In particular, as in the Kelly vs. Lucinda scene, it enabled her to trace the way a *community* of viewers related to the community of main characters to construct outsiders (like Lucinda) as 'other'.

Like other researchers of young audiences (e.g. Hodge and Tripp, Tulloch and Tulloch), she also used excerpts from the series to cue discussion; and conducted a few long (one-to-one) interviews. Despite the innovatory value of her methodology, there were times in reading the book when one wishes that she had used the one-to-one interview more often; in particular to counteract her own very strongly positioned discourse. I will illustrate one example of this in her discussion following the Kelly/Lucinda debate.

She notes that only one group of viewers, women at Princeton University, 'deliberately constructed themselves as "above" this preoccupation with relationships; as superior to, and looking down on, the traditional female dependence on relationships and the "whole scene" of clothing, hairstyles, relationships, etc – the terms that permeate talk about *90210*. . . . [T]hey celebrate their strength and rejected those who conform with the traditional female identity or, as Ruth put it, of "selling herself" to the husband and 2.5 children' (1997, p. 211).

After quoting excerpts from the Princeton discussions where they criticise the *90210* characters for conforming to dominant notions of female identity, however, McKinley argues that these otherwise strong comments have a certain 'wistful' character. She quotes the following:

Courtney: I wish I were called to do like executive business-type work. I really wish I could just have a normal life. . . . Get up in the mornings, go work out, you know, live the life of the professional and get – go to work in spiffy outfits and hang out with your friends after work for drinks.

Ruth: (Inaudible) I feel like I'm doing something worthwhile.

Courtney: That's so true. And I was like, I really wish I were called to do that. I'm just not called to do that. You know, I have to do what I feel like I'm called to do.

Int: Which is med school?

Courtney: Which is med school, yeah.

(1997, p. 213)

McKinley here makes much of Courtney's words 'called to do'.

Courtney . . . spoke of this key life decision not in terms of the people she could heal as a doctor, or the service she could provide, or even the financial independence it could provide. Rather, she spoke of her rejection of a 'normal life', with its attendant emphasis on appearance and relationships. . . . The Princeton women were voicing their resistance to dominant notions of female identity. What is distressing is the disempowerment with which this position was voiced. Courtney was 'called' over and above her desire for what is 'normal'. Resistance to norms is hard to do; swimming against the tide has brought the undercurrent of fatigue into even these young voices.

(1997, pp. 213–14)

Against McKinley's analysis of the Princeton women I would argue that the 'normal life' that Courtney was interested in was *not* Ruth's 'husband and 2.5 children' but living 'the life of a professional'. And what is wrong with her wanting hours where she could meet and drink with friends more often, and wear 'spiffy outfits'? Clothes – even 'spiffy outfits' – mean different things, with different degrees of female agency in different situations: especially as between Ruth's woman 'selling herself' to a husband, children and domesticity, and Courtney's executive business woman.

But the fact that I read the Princeton discussion differently from McKinley is not the point. In one sense it demonstrates the value of qualitative analysis which liberally cites respondents' actual talk, so that the reader can come to a different opinion. But my point here is that, given McKinley's honestly acknowledged position *as* a professional 'achiever', some long, one-to-one interviews here with Ruth and Courtney might have alerted her to them having rather different views from her (or indeed my) own.

Political economy

One of the valuable features of McKinley's book is that it re-stitches the global with the local by examining the textually constituted and self-constituting audiences together. *Beverly Hills, 90210* was one of a package of new programmes (including *The Simpsons* and *Melrose Place*) which Rupert Murdoch's Fox Network designed to bring a youth-audience strategy into play in its attempts to infiltrate the oligopoly of network television. McKinley notes that Murdoch's News Corporation was attempting what many thought was impossible: to make Fox an equal player in a US television scene which had been wrapped up, locally as well as nationally, by the big three networks – ABC, CBS and NBC. Fox's entry occurred during a period of overall broadcast decline, where new media technologies – and particularly the proliferation of cable which tended to equalise the reach of VHF and UHF stations – gave Fox infrastructure advantages. Moreover, audiences were beginning to channel-surf as a result of the multiplication of options. New loyalties were being formed, and Fox, as *TV Guide* reported in 1992, struck boldly and cleverly with its line of taking young people seriously. 'An entire network, Fox, was created with the idea of targeting its programming (*Melrose Place, Beverly Hills, 90210*) to those under the age of 35' (cited in McKinley, 1997, p. 15). Fox thus benefited shrewdly from (and contributed to) the decline of a once 'monolithic' television audience as it was segmented into the 'speciality' audiences that advertisers were able to target more efficiently. Aimed at the high spending 'Generation X' audience, even quite lowly ranked series that pulled in this young audience could outsell in ratings revenue from advertisers much higher ranked shows with an older audience. *The Simpsons*, for example, drew the same $160,000 per 30 second advertisement rate when it was still only 49th in the Nielson ratings as the second-ranked *60 Minutes*. And, as a cleverly written prime-time soap, *90210* very quickly did much better than that.

Fox's senior vice-president of research and marketing saw college students as 'the opinion leader audience', arguing that they are the first to switch channels if not satisfied. *Beverly Hills, 90210* was consequently thrown in initially against the market leader with the college audience, *Cheers*, in its Thursday night time slot – and did very well. Almost immediately, *90210* became the fourth most popular show with college students, after *Cheers*, *The Simpsons* and *The Cosby Show* – and, McKinley notes, it was the only one of these that was not a comedy. Its soap opera format enabled Fox producers and writers to consciously self-promote its 'responsible' youth policy, by regularly including 'issues' like drug addiction, date rape, teenage pregnancy, abortion, AIDS, breast cancer, racism and smoking. But the youth focus was also evident in the 'James Dean' iconic play via the character Dylan; and, as McKinley says, the young audience, especially the female audience, was also courted by way of commercials which regularly promoted feminine health and beauty products (shampoos, perfume, tampons, pregnancy tests), clothing (jeans, lingerie, shoes, pantyhose which 'trims your tummy, slims your hips, shapes your thighs' (1997, p. 18)), fast food, and low-priced cars.

In her analysis of audience talk around *90210*, McKinley thus drew attention to her respondents' major emphasis on personal appearance, and buying clothes and other products.

> With often raucous, self-confident, authoritative voices, these girls and young women explored – indeed, stretched, amplified, and very occasionally challenged – the notions of appearance available in the television text. But this talk served mostly to perpetuate the idea – so condemned by feminists – that appearance is inextricably intertwined with identity. It is encumbent on us to be concerned with female appearance; our appearance is separate from our core selves; nevertheless, Kelly is pretty and nice, and I like her – and I want to look like her and in doing so, on a certain level, *be* her. The girls' and young women's talk hegemonically concealed the ways in which they were hailed by an ideological subject – the pretty, nice, passive female.
> (McKinley, 1997, p. 82)

The voices of these girls and young women, says McKinley, 'resonated with disempowerment' (1997, p. 81). Her talk about hegemony and the women being 'hailed by an ideological subject' takes us to a different area of her theoretical project.

Cultural studies

McKinley says that, as a postgraduate student, 'sifting through realms of material' written by academics about television, she decided to base her 'analysis on the cultural studies research tradition because it has focused on the interaction of both females and young people with the media' (1997, p. 31). She rightly draws attention to the central debate dividing cultural studies researchers 'over whether and how media empower or oppress' (1997, p. 31).

Focusing on 'agency – with whether we can initiate changes in our lives, and in the meanings we make of events and power relations' (1997, p. 31), McKinley outlines the work on agency, resistance and Gramscian hegemony theory coming out of Britain in the 1970s, particularly the work on 'resistant' subcultures (Willis, McRobbie). But she also points to the ways in which subcultural resistance – in the case of Willis's working-class 'lads' resisting school and McRobbie's working-class girls' use of teen magazines – actively worked to reinforce their subordinate status to capitalism and patriarchy. She emphasises the continuing relevance of Gramsci's notion of hegemony ('how the consent of the dominated to their lot is won rather than coerced' (1997, p. 34)) in important American work, such as Radway's on women reading the romance, Jhally and Lewis's on the fans of *The Cosby Show*, and Press's on working- and middle-class women watching television. Thus cultural studies also became a major underpinning of her own research assumptions about how a woman's activity in watching television 'serves to rewin her consent to the dominant ideology, especially the patriarchal and capitalist status quo (1997, pp. 34–5).

McKinley speaks of the early influence on her as a student of Fiske's more optimistic notions of the polysemic text and of viewers 'pleasurably playing with the boundaries between reality and fantasy' (1997, p. 128). Mary Ellen Brown was even more important to McKinley than Fiske, in so far as Brown had moved the debate from researcher-talk about the polysemic text, to the area of *audience talk and language* – which, as we will see in the next section, is the most innovative aspect of McKinley's theory. Brown, for instance, while accepting to some extent Althusser's notion of a viewing subject being 'hailed' ('interpellated') by a dominant ideology, also argued that women could gain pleasure in resisting that hailing. For Brown, talk by women around soap opera was importantly political in creating the 'oral networks' of 'fanships'. This was, centrally, McKinley's subject matter, and she was very interested in Brown's notion of the political effectivity of women finding emancipation in groups as 'spectators' became 'agents' through participating in talk. Talk was something that McKinley's girls and young women who watched *90210* did lengthily and passionately. Could this theoretical approach counter the researcher's own first impression of the series? Could 'Talking about soap operas . . . help groups of women become politically active on other fronts'? (1997, p. 45).

At the end of the day, it could not. After her research and analysis was over, McKinley revisited her cultural studies mentors.

> [T]he endlessly fascinated discussions of female appearance seemed empirically to confirm Fiske's (1987) theory of a polysemic text with which empowered viewers make multiple meanings. This talk also generated the pleasurable community seen by, for example, Ang (1985) and Brown (1994), support groups that these researchers said empowered the viewers. However, I suggest that resonating under this lively variety of communal responses ran a single meaning – the ominous pedal point of a narrow and restrictive female identity. Moreover, the way this talk reified and perpetuated that identity was concealed by the ubiquitous authorial voice, the 'expert' viewer who positioned herself as the source of her meanings. This voice delightedly concealed the role of the television text in offering the identities that viewers eagerly and actively appropriated for themselves.
>
> (McKinley, 1997, p. 236)

In fact, one suspects that it was Gramscian notions of hegemony which strongly influenced this non-fan academic from early on. Certainly, it is not a coincidence that McKinley's first two *90210* chapters are about:

- 'appearance' (where, 'positioning themselves as agents in their ability to judge beauty and purchase beauty products, viewers concealed ways in which the experience of community [with *90210*] and pleasure perpetuated the patriarchal and capitalist system' (1997, p. 77)); and
- 'characterizations' (where viewers 'used that community as a way of exploring the identity of the strong, cocky, aggressive woman . . . but this exploration was conducted along hegemonic lines delineated by patriarchy that . . . women's voices must be modulated if they are to relate to men romantically' (1997, p. 114)).

McKinley's description of female audience discussion of the 'strong, aggressive' women of *90210* is typical of her resort to hegemony theory, as well as of her reflexivity within the debates of cultural studies.

> Female characters who said what they thought, did what they wanted, and didn't care – in short who were aggressive – painted a picture of female agency, even if against a background of defensiveness. Women are not supposed to be cocky and aggressive, viewers said, but, at the same time, 'it's nice to see that'. I became excited as I wondered if these viewers were exercising discursive agency, exploring a subject position that flouts convention and breaks the 'pretty and nice' rules for female conduct by saying what they meant, and doing what they wanted.
>
> (McKinley, 1997, p. 109)

McKinley does not hide her disappointment in both the community of women she studied, and the feminist researchers she had drawn on to study them. 'Watching soap operas put women in a position of agency, researchers said. These researchers saw women watching soap operas as in control of their viewing experiences, and as actively empowered by them' (1997, p. 42). That phrase 'researchers said' (about women's agency) resonates throughout McKinley's text, alongside her own, highly visible and 'disturbed' voice.

The discursive self

From cultural studies (and particularly Mary Ellen Brown's cultural studies) McKinley moved on to social constructionist theory. This was for two reasons: because social constructionist theorists grounded their work in major figures of European thought like Wittgenstein, Adorno, Horkheimer, Saussure, Habermas and Derrida, who also underpinned much of the thinking in postmodern, poststructuralist and cultural studies theory; and because they were especially interested in the issue of identity.

> Social construction begins by questioning western culture's notion that we each have a unique inner self that is the author of our private

thoughts and feelings. While our ideas and emotions may be private in the sense of not necessarily communicated to others, social construction points to ways that our culture and language 'author' them, not solely we ourselves. Our inner life is not wholly the product of the autonomous self, but rather is shaped by the ways we have to express it, and by the communities that give it meaning. The pleasure or pain we feel around an event or object stems in large measure from the way it is valued in our community. . . . [S]ymbolic representations including language work to construct our notion of what is real. Talk is action. . . . A key theme in this discussion, and one that will be central to my study, is the nature and importance of narrative in identity construction and community formation.

(McKinley, 1997, pp. 48–9)

Several key ideas come together here to genuinely advance audience theory. First, McKinley's emphasis on the fact that 'talk is action' lifts the debate about agency – as Brown and other poststructuralists would insist – to the discursive level. Her focus on the cultural frames within which people talk (more than on the content of what they say) begins to answer those many critics of 'active audience' theory who argue that it takes for granted that meaning resides in the conscious interpretation of viewers (or, worse, in what they consciously decide to tell researchers!). Frequently, McKinley reiterates, that what she is most interested in is not so much what a viewer said, or 'what caused viewer "read" ', but rather 'what their reads accomplished' (1997, p. 85) in terms of the construction and reconstruction of female identity. Hegemony thus operates via talk as it works to reproduce (as though 'natural' *and* individually 'authored') dominant values and ideologies.

Second, this social constructionist approach (often from within psychology itself, as in the case of Shotter, Potter, Walkerdine and others) challenges the pyschological model of identity. 'The psychological "subject" of the European post-Enlightenment tradition is a discursive construct. . . . [I]dentity talk is the re-expression of self in terms that already have social currency' (McKinley, 1997, pp. 50–1). McKinley, who already intuited that the girls she originally chatted with about *90210* were using the series as part of their identity exploration, found that the social constructionist approach spoke to her own experience.

This way of thinking about identity is full of possibilities for analysis of girls' and young women's talk about *90210*. It suggests that this talk can be analyzed, not for the psychological processes that underlie what the viewers say, but rather for the cultural taken-for-granteds that underpin the way viewers' talk orders and makes sense both of the show and of their own world. Talk about fictional characters and situations both produces and makes possible certain ways of being in the world and relating to others, certain identities, and the same talk conceals and closes off other possibilities. This understanding of the way in which interaction works to construct identity provides a lens through which to scrutinize active viewers working on texts to open up identity possibilities, and hegemonic texts winning consent of viewers to dominant notions of female identity.

(McKinley, 1997, p. 52)

Third, social construction theory 'offers another take on community' (1997, p. 52). Rather than the 'resistant reading' approach of subcultural emphases, the notion of community is raised to the discursive level.

Using Shotter's (1993) suggestion that community has to do with a discursive construction of who 'we' are, as opposed to who 'they' are, I looked at the way in which viewer talk created community, not only with each other but also with the characters. This theory helped me foreground ways viewers discursively grouped themselves, not just with their friends, but with Kelly, Brenda, Donna, Andrea. The talk created and sustained new relationships between viewer and character that in turn cycled back into meanings viewers made of their own lives. And in discursively grouping herself with a character, a speaker joins a community whose values are set by the text, even as the viewer takes authorship of the discursive link – it is *I* who have recognised myself in the character, not the producers and advertisers who have seduced me into normalizing this beautiful, youthful blond, this upper-class lifestyle, and their preoccupation with gossiping, shopping and dating.

(1997, p. 52)

As McKinley recognises, she takes significantly further here Jhally and Lewis's work on the hegemonic naturalisation of class, and Press's analysis of working-class women's naturalising of middle-class values. She draws also on Giddens's 'risk' notion of self-narrative as it works to bind and make coherent identity; in the case of *90210* by an interweaving of characters' narratives and one's own. It is 'not done' to date a friend's boyfriend or the college professor (and his wife); so the *90210* characters that do this (including the professor's wife) are assessed, and made 'other' to the community of the series (as in Lucinda's case) where they were found wanting. This establishment of a 'community' of values around the series' own representation of deeply conservative societal values is then accepted as individually 'authored' by each respondent, as an essential outcome of her unified 'being'.

Fourth, then, McKinley engages centrally with poststructuralism's rejection of the autonomous, individualised identity. But she does not use this to celebrate the endless 'democracy' of polysemic texts and alternative readings. Rather, multiple subjectivity is seen by McKinley as the radical, feminist *target* to be achieved. Multiple subjectivity is also the major victim of audience readings which claim cultural readings as, in fact, created by the autonomous reader – the reader who, as 'fan', additionally takes pleasure in the following ways:

- in commenting as 'expert' on characters' clothing style;
- in pontificating on gender ethics, finding self-satisfaction in being 'independent' and 'tough' in talk (though only, McKinley discovers, in talk with parents and girlfriends, not with men);
- in 'calling' what is going to happen in the next scene on the basis of cultural and generic stereotypes; and
- in 'pleasurable guessing' about what will happen in the next show (so that watching the promos becomes essential viewing) and what will be said as friends talk.

In a very different feminist take on fantasy from Ang's (and stressing, like Jhally and Lewis, the American ideology of individualism), McKinley therefore says that 'In this study, I argue that the language of individualism and the desire for community play an important role in concealing the ways talk about a television show can colonize our dreams and desires, thoughts and actions' (1997, pp. 55–6). Perhaps her most interesting innovation in the agency/hegemony debate is to show the ways in which a society's macronarratives are appropriated as 'expert' audience discourse. Following Bellah *et al.* (1985) she discusses American biblical, republican, utilitarian and expressive individualist narratives; following Gergen (1991) she traces romantic and modernist narratives; and following Gilligan *et al.* (1990) she explores 'good' (nice, passive, pretty) adolescent female narratives and 'bad' (selfish, bitchy, tough) adolescent female narratives. Thus:

> Though I was delighted to hear the rejection of 'pretty and nice', the more I thought about these voices, the more I became convinced that I would be mistaken to applaud this elevation of 'cocky and aggressive'. The alternate subjectivity that many feminists would have women explore is the recognition that meaning is multiple, and that patriarchy's construction of femininity must be denaturalized. Radway (1994) called for a female identity that values intimacy and relationality alongside autonomy and success; Gilligan (1982) suggested that women have a dual responsibility to act responsively toward self and others. Once again, I was forced to conclude that this talk was working hegemonically to preserve patriarchal categories – that contrast the 'good girl' and the 'bitch'; that suggests that ownership of one's sexuality is irreconcilable with caring for others; that insists on speaking in one's own voice is incompatible with preserving connection.
>
> (McKinley, 1997, pp. 113–4)

Fifth, by way of her reflexive encounter, not only with the voices of the *90210* fans, but also with those of a history of cultural studies and social construction theory, McKinley discovers her poststructuralist voice on agency. From Press she adopts the view that 'agency must be linked to interrogation of, if not changes in, culturally based power structures' (1997, p. 38). And since this is 'a tall order for researchers who must seek to prove that link' (1997, p. 38), via the social constructions' emphasis that 'talk is action', she arrives at Chris Weedon's poststructuralist concept that 'subjectivity is neither unified nor fixed. Unlike humanism, which implies a conscious, knowing, unified, rational subject, poststructuralism theorizes subjectivity as a site of disunity and conflict, central to the process of political change and to preserving the status quo' (Weedon, 1987, p. 21). Crucially, this leads McKinley to a view of poststructuralist subjectivity which, far from being a delirious and democratic *play* of meanings, is one of access to symbolic resources. 'The decentred, destabilized subject opens the possibility of changing the status quo, of gaining access to new subject positions, and of suggesting alternative subjectivities that might advantage women more than those currently available in patriarchy' (McKinley, 1997, p. 260).

The final political word for McKinley is 'interrogating' not 'play'.

> I am personally convinced that interrogating the authorial voice [of the *audience*] can tear down roadblocks that have brought to a halt conversations about, for example, bigotry of all kinds. . . . [O]n one level I am deeply sympathetic to the young woman who celebrated the cocky, aggressive female. Certainly, shouting is better than being silenced. What I object to is women's definition of the problem in patriarchal terms, greedily appropriating what the culture used to reserve for men, without examining underlying values. . . . This study does not make a case for 'ugly' and 'mean'. Being pretty and nice can often be useful and appropriate for both genders.
>
> (McKinley, 1997, p. 241)

CASE STUDY

What makes McKinley's *Beverly Hills, 90210* such a readable (and, I believe, valuable) audience case study is the way in which all of these voices (of fans and of academic theory) are worked through a series of case studies. For example, her chapter 'Dating: the passive female' resonates both with 'the passionate and enthusiastic voices that had attracted my attention to *90210* in the first place' (1997, p. 189). It is also overtly underpinned by the researcher's honest reflexivity about her 'stubbornly and futilely' persistent attempts 'to channel the talk into issues against a flood of talk about dating' (1997, p. 194).

I conclude my discussion of McKinley's book with a case study taken from her penultimate chapter on 'the microprocesses of hegemony'. I choose this because it illustrates well how the various aspects of her analysis – her reflexivity as a professional, as researcher and as a woman; her methodology of watching the series with her respondents; and her complex weaving of cultural and social construction theory – come together in micro/macro analysis.

In her case study of the *90210* story, 'Blind Spot', McKinley describes the introduction to the storyline of a young women who is a blind piano teacher, with whom the regular character David (earlier discussed because of his 'drugs' problem) quickly becomes infatuated. This woman, Holly, forms one of a number of narrative strands which together provide what the fans rather dismissively call the 'politically correct' profile of the series.

In this episode there are 'dating' parallels: one is a gay story (which McKinley also analyses); one is an exploration of cross-racial dating; and finally there is the blind girl story. As such, this 'balancing' or 'paralleling' of 'issues' is a familiar feature of any soap opera which seeks a 'quality' profile (we saw a similar generic ploy in my earlier analysis of the Australian soap opera, *A Country Practice*). This relates to the 'political economy' slant on this episode: the market-driven thrust of Fox for a college-rich audience.

McKinley, however, prefers to emphasise the methodological advantage of watching the episode with her viewers, observing and recording their second-by-second construction of identity by way of establishing, disestablishing, re-establishing their identification with the 'community' of characters. In the parallel plot-line of Steve and 'the gay guy', for instance, McKinley shows how audience talk was 'more equivocal and layered than the talk about David's drug use' (1997, p. 179), where identification was entirely with the 'community' character. Here, in contrast, moment by moment they

- identify with Steve's discomfort as he discovers he is in a gay coffee house (thus immediately positioning the gay man as 'other': 'They're in a gay bar, oh God!' – 'Could this happen to me? Might I inadvertently find myself in a gay coffee house?' (1997, p. 180);
- enjoy the fact that the 'macho frat rat' is exposed to this particular embarrassment;
- adopt a liberal identity of tolerance to the gay man, Mike Ryan, while at the same time doubting the likelihood of him being in a college fraternity (Maybe he 'is "trying to deny his sexuality". The girls pleasurably consented to the status quo [of male-dominated college fraternities], and used the expert voice to naturalize it' (1997, p. 182));
- vehemently censure Steve's response to Mike with 'Ahhh, you jerk!', 'You're an asshole!';
- and finally, restoring the 'community' with: 'You see, I don't understand if he's gay why he wants to be in a house full of bigots'.

McKinley analyses this sequence thus:

> This excerpt provides a microcosm of a process I found particularly distressing. For a moment, these girls truly explored an alternate subjectivity; they connected on a deep level with Mike Ryan's marginalized position. They strongly critiqued Steve and worked to interrogate the notion of bigotry. Their backgrounds gave them ways of attending

to the show, and the show's meaning cycled into, and expanded, the meanings they made of their lives. But during the break their usual way of thinking about Steve, and about gays, reasserted itself. From then on, the girls' 'activity' was harnessed in an effort to patch the community back together, to re-establish equilibrium – to perpetuate the status quo.

In the case of the scenes with the blind woman, Holly, McKinley again analyses the audience responses second-by-second alongside the unfolding text. Her analysis includes:

- the girls' opening gambit of 'Oh no. The beautiful woman piano teacher', combining, McKinley argues, both generic recognitions of stereotype and the tantalizing possibilities of how this would impinge on the males in the *90210* community (the profession – piano teacher – came last in their talk, says McKinley, almost as an aside);
- the girls' (and David's) response to the point-of-view shot (from the back, from David's perspective) giving way to a close-up of her face as lack of animation and exaggerated mouth gestures signify she is blind: the girls negotiate this, finding her first 'weird', then 'paralysed', then 'blind' – this last an instant 'expert' reading of cues by one girl that was recognised and applauded by the others' expert-recognising response of 'Good call';
- this pleasurable closing down of her identity ('a blind girl'), McKinley argues, leads to an equally pleasurable 'expert' guessing: 'I predict in future episodes, she like asks him out, he kisses her, and then he decides he never could go out with a blind woman' – the blind woman is thus essentialised and her agency (as a blind woman piano teacher) 'boiled down to her potential for a relationship with a male' (1997, p. 227);
- her sexuality is also closed down (unlike Lucinda's) because of her handicap. 'The bottom line is, Holly is blind, "other".' (1997, p. 228). The text is complicit in this reading, giving Holly silly lines like 'Let the music play you' and 'feel the spray in your face, the wind in your hair';
- consequently the girls declare her 'a cheeseball', 'kind of scary' and 'don't like her';
- finally the girls distance themselves from her 'otherness' and, ironically, from their favourite show's 'PC theme for the night'.

Says McKinley,

In a few moments, the discussion had moved from 'She's blind' to 'I don't like her'. Further, the girls constructed Holly as *essentially* unlikable; it was this move that closed down the possibility of exploring, her subject position was closed off. The viewers segued from Holly as other, to Holly as unworthy of our community. In so doing, they cemented closed the door they might have given entree to an exploration of her point of view. . . . The possibility of an intimate relationship with someone 'other' was one that had resonance for these girls.

It is a way of being in the world that they could potentially experience. However, both threat and potential were defused, and the possible exploration routed onto familiar ground. . . . Despite her talents and abilities, and her plucky acceptance of her blindness, Holly ultimately is defined by her relationship – or lack thereof – with men. In the end, the viewers' consent to this disadvantaging status quo was won without resistance. For all their educational training and privileged backgrounds, these girls were not using the text as a resource to explore alternate subjectivities.

(1997, p. 234)

McKinley's whole set of concepts, methods and theories is evident in this case study: her methodology of observing the girls talk throughout the episode; her caution not to forget the 'complicity' of the text; her cultural studies debate between resistance and hegemony; her social constructionist focus on talk as action; her poststructuralist emphasis on agency and multiple subjectivity; and finally the reflexivity with which she began the book.

As it happens, I am a musician, and my first thoughts about Holly related to the difficulty of learning music when you are blind. Everything must be learned by ear (by listening to recordings), by rote (having someone else teach you the notes), or from Braille music (which cannot be felt and played simultaneously), and of course you always have to play from memory. To me, she represented an admirable subject position, a triumph over a handicap. However, this position was not explored by either the text or the girls. Instead, they focused on her potential to relate to a male.

(1997, p. 227)

What prevents Holly's female audience from taking pleasure in alternative subjectivities, is lack of symbolic resources: different discourses, differently circulated cultural experiences. But these missing symbolic resources are not seen by McKinley as a 'lack' in a series of psychological stages (as, say, in Hodge and Tripp). Rather, here, they are thoroughly in the hands of hegemonic ideologies of patriarchy and capitalism.

Textual poachers of *Star Trek*

I said earlier that my reflexive marker for this chapter would be: what difference does it make – theoretically and methodologically – whether the television audience *researcher* is a fan? Henry Jenkins, author of *Textual Poachers: Television Fans and Participatory Culture* and (with myself) *Science Fiction Audiences: Watching Doctor Who and Star Trek* is a long-term fan of *Star Trek*. His own account (in the latter book) of how this built into his biographical experience indicates a considerable difference from E. Graham McKinley's relationship with *Beverly Hills, 90210* and its fans.

What is noteworthy is the way in which *Star Trek* both helped generate a politics for Jenkins, and then – as his own identities developed – was found wanting. Important here was Jenkins own growing awareness of his sexual preferences. To begin with, *Star Trek* offered – as popular science fiction does for many of its fans – an alternative space where the narrow, hetero-sexual ideology of one's home town could be escaped. Later, with the devel-opment of the gay and feminist movements, the series, as Jenkins says, disappointed him and many other fans with its ideological compromises. Yet, as with a close friend or relative who disappoints you, Jenkins and the fans continued to work *with* the series, rather than rejecting it. Two of his most important and revealing chapters in *Science Fiction Audiences* are about fans working within the series to try and convince its producers to include regular gay characters without making a big deal of it, and about female fans working within the series in a different way, by adding in their own writing the places and spaces of romance to the rationalistic and gen-dered world of TV science fiction.

The book, *Science Fiction Audiences* makes the distinction between sci-ence fiction 'fans' and 'followers', and that marks, reflexively, the differ-ences of involvement of the two authors. Though I had watched virtually every episode of *Doctor Who* since its first episode in November 1963, I was not a member of fandom in the grassroots way which Jenkins describes. I was a 'follower' not a fan (and perhaps a modernist rather than postmod-ernist). But Henry Jenkins was, passionately, a fan: reserving the authorial 'we' in the book not for his writing partnership with me but with his mem-bership with fandom. This relates to his central polemic of *Textual Poachers* also: against the 'expertise of the academy [which] allows its members to determine which interpretive claims are consistent with authorial meaning' (Jenkins, 1992, p. 25).

This fandom, he writes in *Textual Poachers* is 'a social group struggling to define its own culture and to construct its own community within the context of what many observers have described as a postmodern era . . . a group insistent on making meaning from materials others have character-ized as trivial and worthless' (1992, p. 3). It was that 'trivial and worthless' opinion, often attached to the fans themselves, that Jenkins was especially keen to reject publicly and for all time: which is why he was so angry (and threatened to remove his authorial name) when the cover of the paperback version of *Science Fiction Audiences* infantilised the fans. How different, he argued, were the covers of his two books: *Science Fiction Audiences* with its 'infantilising' *Doctor Who* and *Star Trek* 'dolls'; and *Textual Poachers*, with its pre-Raphaelite style painting by a fan-artist, featuring the two 'gay' characters: Tasha Yar and Data!

Our differences as 'follower' and 'fan' also strongly influenced our dif-ferent methodological and theoretical choices in *Science Fiction Audiences*.

Mine, more distanced and sociological, tended to rely on focus group interviews *with* fans (and followers) – some forty groups of them which I trailed
through the developing theories of audience (Morley), reading formation
(Bennett), orders of discourse (Fairclough), and agency/structure (Giddens).
But Jenkins *was* a fan, and his methodology was more thoroughgoingly
ethnographic. His account was as a member of that grassroots media activist
community of fans, which he inflected with his own political and sexual
biography while developing, with many others, *Star Trek* fandom's conjoint
mix of political utopianism and active disillusionment over compromise. He
says fans of *Star Trek* are often asked why, given their political disappointment with the series, they don't simply walk away from it. The question, he
says (speaking for himself as well as the fans)

> fails to grasp the particular character of their relationship to the pro-
> gramme. *Star Trek* has been a consistent presence in their lives for
> more than twenty-five years, a text which has offered them endless
> amounts of pleasure and fascination, even if it has not always deliv-
> ered all they want from it. *Star Trek* continues to be important as a
> utopian space for their fantasies, still offering them a taste of 'what
> utopia feels like' even if it refuses to show them what (*their*) utopia
> might look like.
>
> (Tulloch and Jenkins, 1995, p. 263)

Like McKinley, Jenkins is a university teacher. But whereas McKinley ago-
nises through her 'disturbing' worries about *90210*'s representation of the
feminist college teacher Lucinda, Jenkins recognises even in the midst of his
own MIT students' modernist *Star Trek* pleasures (with their realistic
dreams of working next at NASA) the compromises the series has made,
and the readings it has allowed.

> We have seen that this group's reading of *Star Trek* is preoccupied
> with issues of technology and science as they interpret the series
> through a discursive competency in both real-world science and hard
> science fiction. Their reading pulls to the surface the series' roots in
> technological utopianism. Their reading places primary importance on
> scientific accuracy and technical precision, issues which surface both
> in their attention to narrative developments and their particular fasci-
> nation with special effects. Such an approach allows them to exercise
> their growing mastery over the rules and contents of scientific knowl-
> edge and reconfirms their professional ideology at a time when they
> are developing their identity as members of the scientific community.
>
> (Tulloch and Jenkins, 1995, p. 236)

Jenkins recognises that, just as in his own case but in different ways, *Star
Trek* works deeply in relationship to both symbolic resources and emotional

needs among his MIT students. They respect the 'command authority' figures, and deplore the 'lack of emotional control' of characters like Troi and Wesley Crusher.

> Through this process, *Star Trek* is made to speak to MIT students about the pressures they experience and the problems they face. What allows them to resolve their personal anxieties and to confront their professional doubts is the optimistic vision *Star Trek* offers them of a future perfected through advanced technology.
>
> (Tulloch and Jenkins, 1995, p. 236)

How different are the utopian strategies that Jenkins recognises among his fellow fans! In his chapter 'Gender and *Star Trek* fan fiction', he describes the emphasis on social change and political transformation in the fan novels of Leslie Fish, the mixture of romance and science fiction in Jean Lorrah, and the Le Guin-style feminism of Jane Land.

> *Star Trek* invited female fans to think of themselves as active contributors to its utopian future, yet offered them little substantive representation within the programme episodes. As these fans began to write and publish their own *Star Trek* stories, they were logically drawn towards the task of reconceptualising the series' sexual politics.
>
> (Tulloch and Jenkins, 1995, p. 199)

Thus Leslie Fish presents a more militant Uhura, frustrated with the social structures which block women from achieving their full potential within Starfleet. In novels that express 'female fans' frustrations over the programme's unwillingness to realize the social vision its publicity proclaims' (Jenkins, 1995, p. 200), Fish tends towards open rebellion against the Federation. In contrast, Jean Lorah's

> potent mixture of romance and science fiction allows fans to envision a world where men and women can work together and love together as equals: a world of affect. Such narratives often begin with a recognition that perceived gender differences block full intimacy within contemporary society. Cold Vulcan logic, the desire to suppress all signs of emotion, make Spock and his father Sarek rich figures for examining the emotional repressiveness of traditional masculinity.
>
> (1995, p. 201)

Thus rather than overturning the Federation, Lorrah expands the spaces in the interstices of the series, developing a woman's world where it seems most repressed, on Vulcan. Jane Land rescues *Star Trek*'s most unfeminist character, Chapel from her unrequited mooning over Spock in the series' subtexts, and makes of her 'a consummate professional who nevertheless possesses unfulfilled emotional, romantic and erotic desires for Spock' (Jenkins, 1995, p. 204).

As Henry Jenkins says, given 'the complexity of this fan culture, no single fan narrative can adequately summarize the forms of ideological critique and rewriting represented' (1995, p. 203). But all the feminist fan writing does what McKinley's *90210* fans do not do: they take seriously the programme's publicity about its 'issues' and 'ideas', find disappointment in *Star Trek*'s failure to deliver, and rewrite the series in terms of a new utopia. Moreover, similar to Mary Ellen Brown's analysis of soap opera fandom (except that science fiction fans write as well as talk), Jenkins argues that

> Writing the romance is only the first step, however, since circulating these romances brings these female fans in contact with other women, allows them to share and talk about those concerns within a broader social context. Writing and sharing these fan romances represents a move from domestic isolation towards community participation, often allowing for alternative sources of status as these women gain recognition for their creative output. The political importance of fan fiction cannot therefore be reduced to the content of the stories alone, but must be understood in terms of the dramatic step towards self-determination that comes when someone decides to share their story with the wider women's community of fandom.
>
> (Tulloch and Jenkins, 1995, p. 203)

Jenkins's theoretical approach derives centrally from his position as a fan. He has respect but no sympathy, for example, for Camille Bacon-Smith who from her more 'distanced anthropological perspective' (1995, p. 19) converts science fiction fans into pained victims rather than women with some discursive power. 'Fandom constitutes a site of feminine strength, rather than weakness as women confront and master cultural materials and learn to tell their own stories, both privately and collectively, through their poached materials' (1995, p. 203).

It is that term 'poached materials' which lies at the centre of Jenkins' theoretical choice *as* a fan. Invading, as fan, the sites of academia and cultural studies, Jenkins could himself act as 'bricoleur', as he found the 'strategies' and 'tactics' of Michel de Certeau.

> [D]e Certeau seeks to document not the strategies employed by this hegemonic power to restrict the circulation of popular meaning or to marginalize oppositional voices but rather to theorize the various tactics of popular resistance. . . . De Certeau perceives popular reading as a series of 'advances and retreats, tactics and games played with the text', as a type of cultural bricolage through which readers fragment texts and reassemble the broken shards according to their own blueprints, salvaging bits and pieces of the found material in making sense of their own social experience. Like the poachers of old, fans operate from a position of cultural marginality and weakness. Like other popular readers, fans lack direct access to the means of commercial

production. ... Fans must beg with the networks to keep their
favourite shows on the air, must lobby producers to provide desired
plot developments or to protect the integrity of favorite characters.

(Jenkins, 1992, pp. 26–7)

Jenkins' chapter 'Queers and *Star Trek*' in *Science Fiction Audiences* is all
about that begging and lobbying the producers, Paramount, 'to acknowledge a queer presence in the twenty-fourth-century future represented on
Star Trek: The Next Generation' (1995, p. 238). But it is *also* about the con-
notative tactics of the gay fans in reading queer characters into the texts.

And that is precisely the problem which *Star Trek*'s producers hadn't
foreseen. In refusing to demarcate a certain denotative space for
homosexuality within the text, they left *Star Trek* open to wholesale
reclamation. ... Soon all of the characters are potentially queer – at
least on the level of connotation.

(Tulloch and Jenkins, 1995, p. 262)

Using a range of tactics – a character's over-investment in heterosexuality
said to signify repressed homosexuality, use of iconography and stereotypes
of queer identity, the analogy with the gay civilisations of the cowboy and
frontiersman – the fans may conclude that 'it is "not theoretically impossible" that any or all of these characters could be bisexual' (1995, p. 262). But
says Jenkins, 'the double negative here is suggestive of the fans' insecurity
about their own interpretive moves. The speculations can crumple almost as
fast as they appear' (1995, p. 262). That is the problem with (as well as the
strength of) de Certeau's 'tactics'. 'Tactics can never fully overcome strategy; yet, the strategist cannot prevent the tactician from striking again'
(1992, pp. 44–5). Nor, indeed, from striking from many directions.
Because, as well as the gay viewers' connotational readings, there are the
feminist romance writers, the filksingers (Jenkins, 1992, pp. 250–76), the
slash eroticists – and also the MIT students (since Jenkins insists, against
Stuart Hall's more classifiable 'negotiated' and 'oppositional' codes, that
tactics and resistant readings are not always progressive). Many of these tac-
tical moves produce material objects. 'Fan texts, be they fan writing, art,
song, or video, are shaped through the social norms, aesthetic conventions,
interpretive protocols, technological resources, and technical competence of
the larger fan community. Fans posses not simply borrowed remnants
snatched from mass culture, but their own culture built from the semiotic
raw materials the media provides' (1992, pp. 49). It is not surprising, given
Fiske's own emphasis on de Certeau and semiotic resistance, that Jenkins
describes himself as 'one of a generation of young American cultural studies
scholars strongly influenced by the powerful mentorship of John Fiske'
(1995, p. 21). But, as a *fan*-scholar, it is not surprising either that Jenkins

experience of growing dissatisfaction with *Star Trek* and frustration
with its inability to keep pace with the political growth of its audiences

pushed him against the easy optimism that sometimes characterizes Fiske's work. Semiotic resistance was not always enough to offset the producer's refusal to represent certain groups and concepts within the primary text; the primary text retained an authority, an aura which could not be successfully met by the home-made secondary texts which circulated around it.

(1995, p. 21)

Thus it is that Jenkins calls for a political economy of fandom and the media which is too often missing from Fiske's optimism. But, on the other hand, Jenkins resisted also de Certeau's pessimism about the power of the media, and his inability to extend his concept of poaching to the television audience. 'Fan critics pull characters and narrative issues from the margins; they focus on details that are excessive or peripheral to the primary plots but gain significance within the fans' own conceptions of the series' (1992, p. 155).

It is that position as academic-researcher-fan that constitutes so clearly Jenkins's particular 'cultural studies' play between hegemony and agency, strategy and tactics. It determines his methodology, and his theoretical 'bricolage'. Via Jenkins, fans' 'lay knowledge' enters the academic discussion of *Star Trek*. But, as we have seen from McKinley's account of *90210*, fan knowledge is also 'expert' knowledge. What is so different between the accounts of Jenkins and McKinley is how they see that fan expertise working. For McKinley, it continues to centre the most conservative ideological values of patriarchy, capitalism and modernism (via the authoring 'I') against the more progressive challenge of poststructuralist emphases on multiple subjectivity. For Jenkins, fan expertise grabs tactically (and always temporarily) the power of symbolic interpretation away from modernity, and on behalf of the 'multiple sets of discursive competencies' (1992, p. 34) of postmodernity. Both McKinley's and Jenkins's fans find power in talk: but for McKinley this talk re-instantiates the 'strategies' of dominant structures and ideologies; for Jenkins, it poaches these values and tactically reworks them, at least for a time and until the next tactic is employed.

McKinley and Jenkins differ profoundly as fan and non fan; they differ consequently in their choice of theoretical engagement with the agency/hegemony debate within cultural studies; and – crucially – they differ in their genre of attention, which opened up or closed off pleasures to their personal biographies in the first place. 'Issues' in science fiction can become a formative part of the fans' political, social and sexual development, their disappointment with their show, their determination to rewrite it. 'Issues' in soap opera, in McKinley's analysis at least, are mere 'PC' formality, whereas the real passions lie much closer to hand, in the reproduction – by text as well as by audience – of the cultural rules of dating.

Towards cult(ural) studies

My third case study in this chapter consists of a brief discussion of current cult audience research by Matthew Hills. This will not do justice to a complexly argued Ph.D. thesis which I had the pleasure to assess recently; but space is short, and in any case Hills will soon tell his own tale in his forthcoming book.

Hills challenges the very heart of the ethnographic project as it developed in media and cultural studies during the 1980s and 1990s. Drawing attention to the boom in fan and 'cult' studies, he argues that 'the fan' has been produced within a highly specific cultural studies narrative, particularly that of the move towards valorising active audiences. In line with a lot of important feminist work, Hills argues (in a familiar postmodernist mode) that this hegemonic narrative of fan 'resistance' has privileged *rationalist* discourses, emphasising the cognitive, rational subject intent on displaying textual knowledge and mastery at the expense of 'dimensions of affect, attachment, and even passion'.

For Hills, this 'cognitivist' prejudice in audience studies leads to an untheorised, face-value acceptance of fans' own accounts of *their* 'mastery' of the text. Media academics, Hills argues, are good at embedding these self-celebrating fan accounts within their own (academic) political narratives and strategies; but much less good at situating them within the contradictory identities and changing (biographical and historical) time frames of the fans themselves.

Hills immediately notes key methodological implications that attend his project. His emphasis on fans' *affective* relationship to cult television 'renders ethnographic methodology problematic: it cannot be assumed (as is so often the case in Cultural Studies) that cult fandom acts as a guarantee of self-presence and transparent understanding' (Hills, 1999, p. 9). Hills points acutely to the imbrication of Jenkins *et al.*,'s political polemic (against the objectivist infantilising of fans) with a claim for fans' 'expert knowledge'. This positioning of fans slips easily into cognitivism.

> This emphasis on the fan's knowledge, and on the display of knowledge, acts, in part, as an alibi for the ethnographic process: given the fan's articulate nature, and immersion in the text concerned, the move to ethnography seems strangely unquestionable, as if it is somehow grounded in the fan's (supposedly) pre-existent form of audience knowledge and interpretive skill. And yet this grounding figure of 'the fan' is itself a reduction of subjectivity; a reduction which operates as a foundational legitimation of, and for, ethnographic methodology. Fandom is largely reduced to mental and discursive activity occurring without passion, without feeling, without an experience of (perhaps involuntary) self-transformation . . . without an inkling that the discursive justifications of fandom might be a fragile construction, albeit

socially-licensed and communal constructions. This is **not** to argue
that fans *cannot* discuss their feelings, passions and personal histories
of fandom in any meaningful manner; it is instead meant to push
towards the realisation that *such fan-talk cannot be accepted merely
as positivistic evidence of fan knowledge but must instead be interpreted and analysed in order to focus upon its gaps and dislocations,
its moments of failure within narratives of self-consciousness and self-
reflexivity, and its repetitions or privileged narrative constructions
concerned with communal (or subcultural) vindication in the face of
'external' hostility.*

(Hills 1999, pp. 9–10)

It is arguable that McKinley has, in fact, focused upon the gaps and dislocations in fans' overt language claims. But in the analysis of science fiction
fandom, there has been a tendency to take these claims at face value.

In practical terms it comes down to this:

- when the president of the *Doctor Who* fan club in Australia spoke to me
  of his distress at the way in which a peak-viewing current affairs show
  had infantilised the fans in its '25th anniversary' item on the series by
  persuading a young fan to be filmed going to bed in his Tom Baker (4th
  Doctor) scarf and hat; and
- when the *Doctor Who*, *Star Trek* and various other cult fandoms (with
  the *exception* of the *Rocky Horror* fandom) refused the request of the
  Australian Broadcasting Company to 'dress up' for their appearance on
  the televised talk show *Couchman*,

they were responding (as Jenkins was over the *Science Fiction Audiences*
book cover) in terms of 'communal vindication'. The dismissive (and later
retracted) put down of *Star Trek* fans by William Shatner (the first
Enterprise captain) to 'get a life' has long resonated in cult fandom circles;
and Tony Howe, the Australasian *Doctor Who* president, worked consistently to resist the media's regular representation of cult fans as 'weirdo',
'infantile' and 'other'. In all my meetings with him, this was – in Hills's
phrase – a privileged narrative construction, and it certainly had material
effect *on-screen* as Howe (and his fan club executive colleagues) appeared in
a variety of television programmes around the 25th anniversary of the
series.

But, Hills would argue, what about the gaps and dislocations in this
reflexive self-account? Why would a fandom which clearly gets considerable
pleasure from dressing up as various Doctors, and in inventing life-size moving Daleks and K-9's which circulate among the fans at conventions, feel so
repressed when on television – particularly in contrast to the *Rocky Horror
Picture Show* fans? Even when Howe sits dignified in his deep armchair in
one of his television current affairs interviews, quite deliberately projecting
the 'serious' side (as a postgraduate student of history at Sydney University)

of his passions, there is a full-size Dalek in shot with him in his study. For Hills this kind of fan performance on television (as well as *Star Trek* fans' continual emphasis on the early progressive politics of multiculturalism which drew them to the original crew) should not be simply accepted at face value. Rather these are discursive structures and repetitions 'designed to render the fan's affective relationship meaningful in a pseudo-objective (and therefore supposedly rational) sense, i.e. to ground this relationship solely in the objective attributes of the source text and therefore to legitimate the fans' love of "their" programme' (Hills, 1999, p. 12).

Hills is not in any sense criticising this necessary political tactic by fans. Neither is he suggesting that this is not a key part of the meanings and pleasures of the series for them, nor is he criticising academics like Jenkins for joining in this tactic as researcher-fan. What Hills *is* criticising is a much larger postmodernist project within the trajectory of cultural studies itself: of ignoring the individualistic, embodied and non-discursive meanings and pleasures of popular culture. 'The fallacy of internality neglects the extent to which internal community understandings are collectively negotiated precisely in order to ward off the taint of irrationality. . . . The fallacy of internality reifies the "in-group" as a source of pristine knowledge by neglecting the sociological dynamics whereby the ideologically devalued "in-group" of media fandom is compelled to account for its passions' (Hills, 1999, p. 13). These are *performative* discourses, not the 'truth' of meaning and pleasure in cult television.

A feature of Hills's 'vertiginous' narrative is the way in which he returns at suitable points in his text to key examples of his broader methodological and theoretical critique. Thus he is particularly pointed in a late chapter where he examines cult fans' use of the internet, and discusses media academics' tendency to forget their own debates about discursive construction and reflexivity in accepting these interactive texts as 'merely offer[ing] a "window" on the programme's offline, socially atomised fandom'. We need to recognise, Hills tells us, that an internet audience 'must . . . perform its audiencehood, knowing that other fans will act as a readership for speculations, observations and commentaries' (1999, p. 139). Here (as elsewhere in the thesis), Hills goes beyond his critique of current theory and methodology to offer an impressive analysis of audience 'activity' in relation to global rhythms and temporalities of commodification.

Hills's case study here of *X-Files* Usenet newsgroups is an extension of his critique of Jenkins-style ethnography. It is also a particularly good example of what Alasuutari calls 'audiencing', as the Web cult audience *performs as audience*. Hills takes this further, however, via his ongoing emphasis on the play between the global (capitalist) form of commodification and audience pleasure and play.

[T]he online *X-Files* audience . . . must . . . perform its audiencehood, knowing that other fans will act as a readership for speculations, observations and commentaries. This self-representation and self-performance of the audience-as-text therefore creates a second-order or implied commodification insofar as the online fan audience consumes a textual reification of itself alongside the originating commodity-text, with the valued novelties of the latter crossing over into the equally novel and similarly valued speculations, rewritings and framings of the former. The online audience is hence serialised insofar as the 'secondary text' of fans' detective work uncannily parallels the hyper-diegetic narrative space of the primary text.

(Hills, 1999, p. 139)

An example Hills gives here is the case of the British website member who complains 'I live in England and if I was to wait until the end of the 4th season and then write about it on the NG I would look stupid as by the time it gets to the cliffhanger, the 5th season probably would've started in the US.' Unable to fall in step with the spatio-temporal rhythms of the US group (which, Hills observes, are also 'the rhythms of the *X-Files* as an established media commodity' (1999, p. 138)), this user's poster is consigned to being 'flamed or ignored' by the US website users, as 'off-line temporal structures . . . dictate the unfolding text of alt.tv.X-Files' (Hills, 1999, p. 138).

However, Hills insists, this is not a return to the notion of 'audience as dupe'. Certainly, the commodity form and scheduling of *X-Files* is crucial to this 'new technology' audience. But the Usenet audience is active too. Hills gives an example of the way in which the 'delusions of conspiracy' theme so embedded in the *X-Files* perpetuated hermeneutic narrative can be playfully appropriated by a newsgroup member in relation to the very production of the text itself. 'My darling husband's truly awful theory: THERE IS NO FIFTH SEASON. DD and GA are being paid a year's pay in exchange for keeping quiet about the whole hoax and the death of Mulder. . . . I love that man, but sometimes he gives me nightmares' (Hills, 1999, p. 140).

This is, says Hills,

'just in time fandom'. By this, I mean that practices of fandom have become increasingly enmeshed within the rhythms and temporalities of broadcasting, so that fans now go online to discuss new episodes immediately after the episode's transmission time – or even during ad-breaks – perhaps in order to demonstrate the 'timeliness' and responsiveness of their devotion. Rather than new media technology merely allowing fans to share their speculations, commentaries, thoughts and questions, then, cmc has seemingly placed a premium not only on the quality of fan response (i.e. there is a social pressure not to be too far 'off-thread'. . .) but also on the timing of fan response. Much like the post-Fordist production process where inventory stock is ordered as and when needed, socio-technological pressures indicate here that the fan should respond as and when it is relevant.

(Hills, 1999, p. 141)

Nevertheless, the commodity text is continually supplanted in this very particular media space: 'the serialisation of the fan audience displaces this imagined space with the density of its own constantly-available meta-text of commentary and speculation circulating around the text's *perpetuated hermeneutic*' (Hills, 1999, p. 147). Indeed, group identity is formed around precisely those imaginative uncertainties generated by the text itself: 'narratives of anticipation and speculation, narratives of information, dissemination and status, narratives of detection, and narratives of conspiracy' (Hills, 1999, p. 149). This fan 'community of imagination' not only celebrates and validates the fan's knowledge (creating, Jenkins argues, fan hierarchies of prestige, reputation and power),

> it also mirrors the fan's attachment back to him or her, validating this affective experience itself. The newsgroup presents an inverted Durkheimian scene [which] . . . stems here not from the periodic and ritualised misrecognition of social forces [as in 'religious thought'], but from the constantly-available and social recognition of subjective 'rituals' – namely those belonging to media reception and consumption.
>
> (Hills, 1999, p. 152)

The Net newsgroup audience thus '*constructs itself extensively as a mediated and textual performance of audiencehood*' (Hills, 1999, p. 153).

Hills challenges Jenkins's 'reduction of the subjectivity' of the fan by drawing on an unusually contiguous (modernist and postmodernist) array of concepts and theories:

- Durkheim on the everyday and the 'sacred';
- Berger and Luckmann on the social construction of primary/secondary biographies;
- Adorno on instrumentalist rationality and commodified spectacle;
- psychoanalytic approaches to Winnicottian object-relations as a challenge (via embedding 'affect' in both age-related personal/biographical and social histories) to the universalist tendencies of more hegemonic psychonanalytical theories (like Lacan's);
- postmodern theories of social geography, tourism, place and space;
- theories of the body, discourse and the preverbal; and
- theories of impersonation, performativity and the cult body.

As a result, there are times in reading Hills's thesis when one feels that different substantive fields within 'cult' (*The X-Files* and internet fandom; or *The X-Files* and privileged tourist/location geography) are rehearsed as suitable cases for mapping the field of current theoretical debate. But this impression is, in my view, unfair to a narrative that shows (deliberately) 'vertiginous' control of its object of study: which is 'to explain the psycho-social operation of media cults in such a way that the cult fan's experience can become meaningful beyond its own claims over textual/iconic value' (1999, pp. 27–8).

For example, Hills moves beyond the Durkheimian notion of the arbitrary 'sacred' in media cults by analysing the 'family resemblances' across cult texts/icons. This is to 'trace out limits to the media cult's arbitrariness' (1999, p. 41). For heuristic reasons, Hills focuses separately on two major characteristics of these resemblances: the perpetuated narrative (and hyperdiegesis); and the cult icon. It is these resemblances that are then traced through later chapters (for example on internet fandom and on impersonating the cult body), which, in addition point to both:

- biographical histories (from the near-withdrawal state of a young child playing to the fixated concentration of adults' intersubjective passion at the fan club); and
- social histories (of increasing capitalist individualisation, as well as the residual romanticism of 'cult' fantasy as the 'other' of the Enlightenment project).

Thus, cult 'family resemblances' appear over time, historically re-activating the individualistic traditions of romanticism within different cultural and generic contexts. Similarly, by 'returning to the body', Hills argues, we can see how the cult body's very particular, historically located 'pleasures are dependent on the culture industry but they also surpass the provisions of those industries, the subject then confronting the system which is hostile to it, and being reincorporated (but, again, never entirely) within the system' (Hills, 1999, p. 189).

Hills draws on Virginia Nightingale's valuable work on fan impersonators, to indicate how these 'practices can *simultaneously* intensify the commodity's contradictions between use and exchange-value, *and* allow the reinscription and extension of commodified exchange value' (1999, p. 186). Thus Nightingale takes Baudrillard's bleak world of simulacra head on.

> 'The fear of the replacement of the real world by the world of the image, by simulacra, is repeated as cautionary tale in acts of Elvis and Marilyn impersonation. The impersonation exceeds repetition or commemoration and points to the deeper psychic dangers of a world in which the image has assumed disproportionate power. The psychic power of the impersonator is linked to the courage with which they address such dangers' (Nightingale 1994, p. 13). By treading that knife-edge between the complete loss of self and the 'wholesale' writing of the body, the impersonator's life-as-the-star threatens to reproduce those very contradictions inherent in the original star's existence within capitalism's fantasy of pure exchange-value. The repetition of a 'cautionary tale' can therefore, at worst, attain precisely the original tragedy of the cult icon.
>
> (Hills, 1999, p. 188)

It is this historically located micro/macro engagement with individual and social histories that is particularly innovative in Hills's analysis.

Importantly, those personal and social histories include Hills's own reflexivity as fan and researcher. Like me, Matthew Hills approached academic audience analysis via his deep and long-term enjoyment of *Doctor Who* (so we return here, but in a much more sophisticated way, to my argument of chapter 1). Hills emphasises in his own introductory section that he wants to draw 'attention to the place of the intimately personal within my theoretical undertaking. I am both an academic and a committed fan of media cults' (Hills, 1999, p. 24).

Theoretical work should, Hills argues, just 'like the "sociological imagination" [that] Mills (1970) advocates, be capable of shuttling back and forward between the minutiae of biographical data and the larger issues of social structures and systems. In my own case, this movement between autobiography and theorisation is clearly pronounced insofar as I have been a fan (and latterly a "cult fan") of *Doctor Who* for almost as long as I can remember' (1999, p. 24).

Hills, of course, entered the field of cultural studies at a very different time from my own; at a time (to use Nightingale's perceptive coinage (1996, p. 124)) of 'fan-omenology'. As Hills says,

> the task which confronts Cultural Studies at this moment in time (and it is a task which is relevant given the historical state of the field, and not as a matter of *a priori* or essentialist dogma) is to theorise the media cult and its fandoms through a primary allegiance to the role of 'fan' and a secondary allegiance to 'academia'. These priorities have been tactically reversed in Henry Jenkins' work.
>
> (Hills, 1999, p. 24)

Jenkins's position as fan-academic (or, Hills would say, academic-fan) was 'a rhetorical tailoring of fandom in order to act upon particular academic institutional spaces and agendas' (1999, p. 26). Thus, for example, Jenkins challenged those 'psychologising' disciplines which pathologised fans' pleasures. But in doing so,

> he explicitly re-inscribes the non-fan in psychological terms. . . . Preserving the social and historical difference of the fan by the counter-transference of psychologism (projecting this back on to the non-fan) leaves Jenkins' argument dangerously exposed to accusations of idealisation. Fandom deserves to be represented more on its own terms.
>
> (Hills, 1999, p. 25)

Jenkins's fan-narrative places himself (as fan-academic)

> squarely within a 'progressive' framework, assuming that Jenkins' hybridised identity constitutes a more adequate 'recognition' of an ontological similarity between 'fans' and 'academics', rather than considering this as a constructed pseudo-similarity with its own discursive capacity for academic self-legitimation via a *rationalisation* of the cult fan.
>
> (Hills, 1999, p. 26)

The privileging of the learned *fan club* in the work of academic 'fan-ome-
nologists' privileges at one and the same time the 'expert knowledge' of cultural studies academics. It is an important symptom of a hegemonic
'populism' within cultural studies which many (e.g. Ang, Morris, Corner,
McGuigan, etc.) have criticised. It is for this reason of questioning the very
methodological/theoretical procedures of some of the very best of these
'populist' cultural studies fan/academics (e.g. Jenkins) that Hills thrusts his
argument into the very centre of 'cult(ural) studies'.

Hills's 'auto-ethnographic' project seeks to avoid this populist 'pitfall' via
the postmodernism of a 'more vertiginous form of critical cultural engagement' (1999, p. 27). So, 'although I attempt to side primarily with affective
fan experiences which have been neglected within academic representations
of fandom, I continue to use academic discourses (of cultural studies, psychoanalysis and sociology) to register this absence' (1999, p. 27). The main
task for Hills is 'to explain the psycho-social operation of media cults in
such a way that the cult fan's experience can become meaningful beyond its
own claims over textual/iconic value' (1999, pp. 27–8), as well as beyond its
appropriation within academic (cultural studies) politics.

Alongside, and interweaving with, Baudrillard's postmodern world of
simulation (commodification) and Beck/Wynne's 'risk society' (of tragic
individualised reflexivity and lay knowledge), Hills discovers the global
world of performance (Austin, Butler); and argues for a renewed historical
understanding of the entire project of the 'rejection of mimesis' (1999, p.
198) from Plato to Screen Theory. Mimesis has been 'philosophy's founding
scapegoat', says Hills (1999, p. 198). But neither 'performance' nor 'mimesis' should be seen as transhistorical and homogenous universals. Rather,

> the concrete practices which surround and embody the media cult in
> its specificity must be addressed as thoroughly historical instances,
> belonging to a precise and dialectical constellation of technology, cul-
> ture and psyche. . . . The primary historical difference of the media
> cult is, then one of intense self-reflexivity regarding the constant man-
> agement of fluid boundaries between self (cult impersonator) and
> Other (icon).
>
> (Hills, 1999, p. 200–1)

Beck's reflexively individualising society as 'risk society' becomes here the
more agentive and performative society – with cult impersonators as the
avant-garde of the new transformation. Remember, says Hills, those *Rocky
Horror* fans (who so worried *Doctor Who* fan Tony Howe).

> Addressing cult movies *en passant*, Dayan and Katz note that: 'With
> their midnight processions of costumed spectators, of look-alikes
> duplicating the main character in the film: with the collective singing,
> dancing, miming by which their audience greets the sequences displayed
> on screen, cult movies [and *The Rocky Horror Picture Show* in particular

here – MH] start as fiction texts but move from mere spectacle toward the realm of performance. They are turned into ceremony' (Dayan and Katz 1992, p. 118). This description – of texts rendered as ceremonial *and* necessarily embodied performances, of characters remade as 'looka-likes' – partially demonstrates how the 'aura of publicity' inherent in 'the look of some admired . . . figure' has been remade by the media cult through a confluence of Romantic ideologies which in turn are framed by 'postmodern' social conditions: 'midnight processions of costumed spectators' replace the more general social ideals of emula-tion, and a 'large audience' has been consciously and romantically rejected in favour of a smaller audience which is minutely self-defined and self-reflexive as a participatory group.

(Hills, 1999, p. 202)

As an exemplary instance, the cult text/fan relationship can, in Hills's view, introduce a new 'Cultural Studies . . . adequately reconfigured as a form of Cult(ural) Studies, becoming more closely attentive to the kinds of lived value and religious sentiment which are both ontologically embedded within, and historically realised through, cultural practices' (Hills 1999, p. 226).

This will be a Cultural Studies which returns to the question of textual value in terms of the affectivities and passions of audiences. I would suggest that further research could seek to *codify these forms of audi-ence response more precisely within a non-reading-based metaphor*, moving from preferred/negotiated/oppositional readings or *decodings* (Hall 1980) to a less one-dimensionally cognitivist concern with *affec-tive engagements of attachments*. Cult fandom could, therefore repre-sent only one subsection within a wider field of affective engagements which are adopted by different media audiences within different socio-historical contexts and at different times.

(Hills, 1999, pp. 215, 223)

It is, ultimately, the modernist 'secularisation thesis' within cultural studies itself which is Hills's target. It is this modernist fixation within cultural stud-ies (that explains its anti-affective and 'non-devotional' prejudices) which the 'rationalist academic self-identity' (Hills, 1999, p. 224) underpinning the 'ethnographic turn' is all about. Thus it is not ethnographic methodol-ogy itself which Hills critiques. Indeed, he concludes that 'research remains to be carried out which combines aspects of ethnographic practice (claiming encounters with "the real") with elements of psychoanalytical theory (i.e. examining the absences, lapses, breaks and affective investments within dis-cursive resources)' (1999, p. 221). Rather his target is the 'division within Media Studies between "audience studies" and "textual analysis" [which] has tended to be reproduced as a split between ethnographic (sociological) and psychoanalytical methodologies' (Hills, 1999, p. 221).

Hills's call is for a 'psychoanalytical ethnography' which *'means that the cultural critic must strategically adopt modes of clinical practice'* (1999, p. 223). His own work, drawing on clinicians like Christopher Bollas's 'virtually heretical call for a "person anthropology" ', is an attempt to avoid what he calls cultural studies' de-historicising meta-narratives (e.g. Freud and the Oedipus Complex, Lacan and the Mirror Phase), and tries to preserve instead the 'idiosyncrasies and infinite variability of psychological formations with which clinical practice confronts the analyst, and which are lost in the move to theoretical meta-narratives detached from clinical puzzles, irresolutions, contestations and even historicities' (Hills, 1999, p. 223).

This is complex language, and large claims: with which more psychoanalytically oriented theorists than myself may wish to engage. But Hills's work does exemplify what Lincoln and Denzin call the 'current moment' of qualitative research – as 'tales of the field' where the 'concept of the aloof researcher has been abandoned' and the 'search for grand narratives will be replaced by more local, small-scale theories fitted to specific problems and specific situations' (Denzin and Lincoln, 1998, p. 22). Hills's 'clinical puzzles' model is one where 'tales from the field' are jointly negotiated and narrated by 'experts' and 'fans', as they reflexively monitor their different child/adult, rationality/affectivity and self/other relationships.

It is thus that Matthew Hills seeks to avoid the fate of his favourite cult show's intellectuals, *Doctor Who*'s timelords, whose pleasure resides in contemplating, without *either* action *or* affect, the infinite plurality and difference of the universe. At the same time, Hills's thesis engages in a very sophisticated way with 'third generation' (Alasuutari, 1999) audience theory which seeks to revisit text/audience relations via notions of embodied 'audiencehood'.

Conclusion: fans and enemies of talk shows

The discussion in the academic literature about fans as audiences of popular television has gone well beyond soap opera, science fiction and cult shows. The nature of television talk shows – where the technology of television has introduced audience's everyday experiences into the studio itself, and where camera, microphone and studio seating have focused attention on these audience (rather than expert) voices – has encouraged a new focus on Habermas's concept of the public sphere. In this debate, we can see McKinley's anxieties and Jenkins's pleasures exemplified in a way that represents the modernist/postmodernist history and field of cultural studies itself.

As we saw earlier, for Habermas the early modern public sphere was a forum that encouraged the *reasoned* formation of public opinion. Many media academics – particularly those who see their task as 'deconstructing' media representations of power and its different publics – would see themselves as contributing to this reasoned formation of public knowledge. Others, though, now find themselves contemplating with pleasure that task being taken out of their hands, and residing instead in the new fora of the media.

Thus, while Habermas became very pessimistic about the survival of the classical public sphere in the face of its commodification by commercial forces (including, especially, the media), various recent writers have argued for the existence of a new electronically defined 'common place' within the television talk show (Carpignano *et al.*, 1990). Here, in a new 'audience'-centred studio layout, with greater mobility of the microphone, and transparency of production, a number of theorists find a public place for the circulation of discourse, often the alternative discourse of marginalised and subordinated populations. For Carpignano *et al.*, talk shows

> Call into question the very structure of the separation between production and consumption of cultural products, they problematize the distinction between expert and audience, professional authority and layperson. . . . The process of formation of common sense is illustrated by the dynamics that the talk show institutes between the experts and the public. The confrontation is not between scientific knowledge expressed by the panel of experts and the 'natural' immediacy of ordinary people. In fact, the sort of experts appearing on these shows espouse theories that are based on practical knowledge.
>
> (1990, pp. 35, 52)

The practical knowledge of social workers and therapists underlines that 'the purpose of the talk show is not cognitive but therapeutic. The structure of the talk show is not a balance of viewpoints but a serial association of testimonials' (Carpignano *et al.*, 1990, p. 51). Thus, they argue, the 'talk show can be seen as a terrain of struggle of discursive practices' (1990, p. 52), a new public form of politics. If, Carpignano *et al.*, argue, we think of politics as representational democracy, the traditional institutionalisation of the public sphere in terms of parties, unions, and so on, then we face a crisis of politics. But if on the other hand we consider politics in terms of new interactive technologies and the 'available data base of acquired discursive practices' (1990, p. 54) of the television talk show, then 'new light' is cast on the problematic of the public sphere.

> [I]f we conceive of politics today emanating from social, personal and environmental concerns, consolidated in the circulation of discursive practices rather than in formal organizations, then a common place that formulates and propogates common senses and metaphors that govern our lives might be at the crossroad of a reconceptualization of collective practices.
>
> (Carpignano *et al.*, 1990, p. 54)

Feminists, in particular, have developed this theme, arguing (in extending the re-valorisation of 'talk' discussed earlier this chapter in relation to soap opera) that talk shows constitute an 'oppositional' public sphere. Masciorotte (1991) argues that the sheer variety of subject positions in talk shows entails the 'irritated architecture of subject to subject', and undermines singular, authoritative voices. The talk show operates according to the 'privileging of the storied life over the expert guest', and the 'plurality of positions on the panels privileges the performative gesture or the spectacle of speaking, thereby confusing the most visible sociological categories' (Masciariotte, 1991, pp. 86–7). As Masciarotte sees it,

> Restoring the issue is not the function of the talk show, displaying the space for stories is . . . Here . . . the spectacle of uncontrolled or out-of-control emotions . . . highlights the pain of the social body through the fiction of the private body. . . . Thus the citizenry postulated by talk is one of resistance to the community at large stemming from interventionist identity politics. Talk shows afford women the political gesture of overcoming their alienation through talking about their particular experience as women in society.
>
> (1991, pp. 88, 90)

In a detailed discussion which compares the generic positioning of knowledge in various TV genres, Livingstone and Lunt (1994) suggest that in talk shows the variety of 'common sense' voices achieves greater credibility than expert voices which speak on behalf of some institution or authority. In an interesting, focus-group-based extension of risk theorists' emphasis on lay discourse as a context-embedded challenge to expertise, Livingstone posits women's pleasures (and competences) in talk shows in terms of interpersonal affect. Like Brian Wynne's Cumbrian farmers, Livingstone argues that women's judgements are more contextual than abstract.

The talk show fan's situation is close to the 'affective reflexivity' in Matthew Hills' account, where the performance and spectacle of 'heartfelt conversations of situated individuals' (Livingstone, 1994, p. 438) represents a different moral reasoning compared with the voices of the inappropriately intellectualising men. In so doing, the female fans of talk shows establish a community based on the circulation of discursive practices, a 'forum for the expression of multiple voices or subject positions' (Livingstone, 1994, p. 433).

> [A]udience discussion fans construe the genre more in terms of the oppositional or plural public sphere, valuing the conjuncture of contributions from diverse, lay publics, seeing these debates as of social value, and relishing the confrontation of elite experts and ordinary people. They are less concerned than non-fans about whether the debates are emotional, ill-expressed, include non-normative views or 'fail' to reach a consensual conclusion. Consequently, they are more

participatory: these viewers engage with the openness in the genre more than do non-fans both in terms of responding to perceived invitations to offer thoughtful, valued and personally relevant contributions of their own and in terms of finding interest in the conjunction of alternative positions.

(Livingstone, 1994, p. 444)

Women enjoy talk shows as a communicative, interactive form of sharing the emotions and experiences of ordinary people, while men are more concerned with the communicative purpose *behind* the genre. Women audiences of talk shows *enjoy* their connectedness to each other. For Livingstone, the 'different' and marginalised (but also pluralised) talk exposed in talk shows 'resists these disconnections and disassociations, and speaks relationally, staying connected with concrete others, with lived responsibilities, with the self' (Livingstone, 1994, p. 439). This is, Livingstone argues, a plural public sphere, which values the contributions from diverse lay publics. The talk show, one might say, in Beck's 'risk' formulation is the emerging genre of a new sub-politics.

Thus, as Tolson notes, though much analysis of talk shows moves directly between the technology of the genre to postmodernist accounts of Baudrillard's schizophrenic or multiple subject (the subject of 'affect' not knowledge; see, for example, Munson, 1993), in recent feminist (audience-focused) analysis we see more precisely situated accounts of the spectacle and performance of everyday life. These talk show fans may be much more diverse than Hills's midnight procession of costumed cult spectators, but the sense of local connectedness, pleasure and affect is still strong.

Not everyone, however, agrees with this optimism about a new, television public sphere; and what is clear from scrutiny of the talk show debate is that precisely the same frames that we have seen operating in the McKinley, Jenkins, Hills positions are working here too. Empirical audience research has not been as evident in talk show analysis (with important exceptions in the case of Livingstone and Lunt), and theoretical frameworks have been very varied (from the ethno-linguistic approach of Carbaugh on *Donahue* to the Lacanian postmodernism of Masciarotte on *Oprah Winfrey*). Despite this, it is very easy to trace the debate across the same conceptual frames we have explored in this chapter. As with McKinley, the analytical frames of the debate are are those of political economy, cultural studies and social constructivist discourse analysis.

Political economy

Like McKinley, a number of talk show theorists attempt to examine textually constituted and self-constituted audiences together. Thus Jane Shattuc (1997) reminds feminists of the importance of continuing to account for the corporate context of talk shows: for example, the relationship between

Oprah Winfrey's company and the syndication company, King World Productions, for which it has been a major advertising revenue earner. The analytical focus here is on the demographic targeting of 18–49-year-old women, because this age/gender category contains the largest percentage of habitual viewers *and* the group who are still the main buyers of household items. In this context, Shattuc speculates on a familiar 'contradiction' within capitalist popular television. On the one hand, the focus of talk shows on rationalist psychotherapeutic 'self-help' advice (via a cadre of 'bourgeois feminist' experts), encourages an individualised, consumer orientation.

> Although the program/expert/product is necessary to confront the problem, the viewer/guest is called upon to be active and use the method/therapy to his or her own advantage. The commercials handily extend this sensibility; advertisements for weight-loss clinics, cleaning products, and personal-injury lawyers emphasize the logic of immediacy, choice, and fulfillment. Perhaps herein lies the Foucauldian nightmare: the daytime talk show manufactures consumer desires as it produces a notion of the emptiness of the self.
>
> (1997, p. 121).

Shattuc is following the same 'political economy' path here as McKinley, who similarly notes the relationship between feminine health and beauty products and *90210*'s construction of the self. But Shattuc is also more ambivalent than McKinley, noting that talk shows appeal to

> women who have historically been taught to efface their needs and themselves in the name of family. . . . The affirmation of the power and rights of the individual might be a rare moment of illumination for the lower-class housewives who dominate the shows' audiences. . . . In the end daytime talk shows are not caught up purely in pragmatic individualism: they also solicit a collective consciousness – the female audience.
>
> (1997, p. 121)

Cultural studies

The emphasis on the empowerment of a female collective audience through talk was one, as we saw, that McKinley negotiated (via Mary Ellen Brown's work on soap operas) in her study of the *90210* audience. A number of feminist theorists of talk shows (e.g. Masciarotte on the heightened emotionalism of the *Oprah Winfrey Show*, Livingstone on women fans' pleasure in a communicative form of sharing emotions) have followed the 'empowerment' path. Others, like Lisa McLaughlin have (like McKinley) finally disagreed.

As McLaughlin argues, the distinction that Livingstone and others make between expert (male) and common sense (female) voices in relation to talk shows is compromised by the historical construction of lay discourse. Following Foucault's analysis of the apparatus of sexuality (ensembles of discourses, institutions, regulations, moral propositions, scientific and other 'official' disciplinary knowledges) in manipulating relations of power, McLaughlin insists that the 'social formation of common sense . . . can be seen as arising out of official – scientific, medical, legal, political – discourses. . . . Here, it becomes nearly impossible to locate common sense discourses left untouched by official or expert discourse' (1993, p. 47). McLaughlin returns to an earlier (1970s/1980s) preoccupation (as, for example, in Terry Lovell's 1981 analysis of *Coronation Street*) with Gramscian notions. The focus here is on the colonisation of common sense by powerfully organised ideologies in any particular historical moment. Like McKinley, who also reverts to Gramsci, McLaughlin's emphasis is on oppression rather than empowerment. She thus discusses the appearance of a prostitute on *Donahue*.

> [H]er authority is undermined, not through a confrontation between common sense and expertise, but through a confrontation managed by both of these – the confrontation between deviant and 'normal' sexuality. The rejection of the prostitute-expert's authority does not represent a moment of working-class triumph amidst clashing discourses in the way that Carpignano *et al.*, describe . . . [T]he prostitute's discourse of expertise is sabotaged by her status as a symbol of female folly, dating from the American Revolution, when women were viewed as foolish and easily corrupted and, therefore, dependent on men for moral direction and authority. Under male authority, chastity was established as the cardinal virtue of womanhood and passion its chief vice.
>
> (McLaughlin, 1993, p. 163)

Andrew Tolson adds to this, that we should 'consider where this view of prostitution is coming from: that men should be giving to their wives and children the money they take to prostitutes. It reminds me of popular nineteenth-century morality tales – where the demon drink, also, could lead weak men astray' (1999, p. 112). Tolson (following Shattuc) elaborates this theory of the connection between talk shows and melodrama, thus adding a specific history of form to McLaughlin's history of common sense. Thus traditional melodrama and talk shows are similar in their individualisation of problems; their class perspective (where individuals like prostitutes are the victims of powerful agents); their emphasis on the sanctity of the family, marriage and the private sphere; and their performance of the spectacle of emotion. Tolson sees this aspect of 'affect' very differently, however, from Hills or Livingstone. Speaking of the appearance of women who are 'addicted to sex' on American talk shows (including

McLaughlin's prostitute), and the fact that both studio audiences and those phoning in from home often give these women such a hard time that they cry, Tolson says:

> For Foucault such gestures of authenticity are, in fact, the products of discursive techniques such as confession, or its allied bodily instrument, torture. In the Inquisition, the heretic cries out with pain as a result of the techniques which are applied to his body; in the confession, the speaking subject bursts into tears as previously repressed secrets are revealed.
>
> (Tolson, 1999, p. 110)

On the one hand, some of Livingstone's 'ordinary' women cry as they self-reveal; on the other hand McLaughlin's prostitute is denied her expertise.

> She and Rivers engaged in a lengthy dialogue in which French attempted to establish prostitution as a work option and Rivers attempted to re-focus attention to the deviant activities and bodily secretions involved in prostitution. . . . Attention to sexual techniques and techniques of the body is prevalent in talk shows featuring sex work; in the talk show, topics and issues are subsumed under spectacle, as the reasons for a woman's entering prostitution and its status as labor become buried under the talk about techniques of oral sex and fingernail polish color. . . . It is much more common for audience members or 'callers' (those who telephone the *Donahue* show while it is taping) to express their disapproval of prostitutes, unloading a barrage of epithets on prostitutes, questioning their maternal abilities . . . than to speak out on the decriminalization or even the regulation of prostitution.
>
> (McLaughlin, 1993, p. 50)

McLaughlin (and Tolson) are, at one level, arguing for a return to 'textual' analysis; or, more precisely to the new 'third generation' synthesis of production, text and audience analysis in terms of 'moral frames' that Alasuutari calls for. In criticising theorists like Carpignano *et al.*, McLaughlin argues that 'Many of their assertions are based on a discursive approach that isolates and privileges the audience/public and ignores the location of the subject by the text' (1993, p. 53). The relationship between 'representational apparatuses' at all levels of power (including talk shows) is, in her view, what is missing from 'populist' audience analysis.

> Since common sense discourses are contaminated by, indeed depend on, 'official discourses', and since representational apparatuses promote 'normal' categories and discourage other ways of seeing, is it at all possible to locate alternative discourses in the talk shows or any other genre? The problem, it seems, is not in locating feminine voices or feminist-inspired arguments but rather, in the degree to which they

challenge the traditional representational apparatus, that which produces and inscribes ideologies of gender, race, and class and positions
some groups as subordinate to others . . . The representational apparatus is comprised of 'expert' knowledges (including those of journalists) and 'public' knowledges, neither ideologically innocent nor
uninformed by history. The current trend, in popular cultural studies,
to focus on the active role of audiences in constructing the text runs
'the danger of romanticizing and sentimentalizing audiences as they
exist in certain inhumane social conditions' (Schudson 1987, p. 64).
Romanticizing the audience as working class limits analysis to
unearthing resistances, the alternative practices of 'pop readers', with
resistance replacing revolution in the description of working class
action.

(McLaughlin, 1993, pp. 50, 53)

McLaughlin's is an older (modernist) call of 'impassioned commitment':
that to achieve a democratic public sphere 'requires structural transformation, a new media apparatus with a new set of politics directed toward new
forms of public life, not the reconstitution of an exclusionary public sphere
amidst existing structures masquerading as "democratic" ' (p. 53–4). Like
McKinley, she is, at the end of the day, unimpressed with the emancipatory
power of fan 'affect'. Her analysis is closer to the ideology-critique tradition
we examined at the beginning of our survey of the police series (and later in
McKinley) than to the more postmodern position of Carpignano *et al.*,
Livingstone and Lunt, and Masciarotte.

Social constructionism and the discursive self

As we saw earlier in this chapter, McKinley emphasises social constructionist theory for: lifting talk about human empowerment and agency to the discursive level; challenging classical psychological models of the self;
understanding the notion of 'community' as a matter of discursive performance; and viewing multiple subjectivity as a target to be achieved via
increasing women's symbolic resources (rather than celebrating it as simpler
postmodern theories tend to do). All of these features of 'the discursive self'
debate have also been central to discussion of the talk show.

For example, Andrew Tolson draws on Krause and Goering's comparison
of German and American talk shows to discuss the cultural and historical
positioning of psychological theories of the self. He notes that

to the extent that national differences exist, any judgments about the
talk show's potential as a 'public sphere' might also need to be differentiated. . . . There is a distinction here between two types of narrative
discourse: between the 'self-oriented' narrative of personal transformation (America) and the national narrative of a common culture

(Germany). In this way the dramatis personnae, in their different settings, are performing different kinds of cultural script.

(Tolson, 1999, pp. 103–4)

But what does this self-oriented American psyche represent? Tolson draws here on Donal Carbaugh's (1988) ethno-linguistic account of *Donahue*, where he analyses ideological categories at work in American talk.

Carbaugh traces the meanings of the American concept of 'self' (as independent, aware, communicative) and points to its interesting metaphorical realization as a personal space, an inner essence of 'personhood'. It is then said, repeatedly on programmes such as *Donahue*, that personhood can be transformed through the recovery of 'self' (such as by becoming 'self aware') in therapy. The truth of this claim is publicly demonstrated in the stories an individual tells about their self-transformation: the personal story . . . is the key performative act, and this performance of being 'true' to oneself recalls an American myth which is itself reproduced through an oral narrative tradition. . . . Thus the talk show would seem to provide a cultural 'scene' . . . for the dramatic retelling of personal stories which collectively reproduce an American consciousness.

(Tolson, 1999, pp. 105–6)

As in McKinley's analysis of the way in which a very traditional American (individualised) 'community' is manufactured in fans' talk about *90210*, so Carbaugh understands talk shows like *Donahue*.

The general point is: persons jointly produce through their talk a cultural sense of self. This plurivocal sense is then interpretable along the semantic dimensions of unique independence, awareness, and communicativeness. While each dimension is not always relevant, all are salient in hearing the communal dialogue – a dialogue that is used prominently to construct and evaluate a common sense of self. This performance of self highlights the meanings of unique independence as *the American community* converses through their separate, but common, identity.

(Carbaugh, 1988, p. 72)

Just as McKinley discusses the *90210* fans talk as 'microprocesses of hegemony' – an active construction of American, individualised communities as audiences and textual characters interact – so too Carbaugh discusses the way in which talk show texts (via the therapeutic help of talk show host and experts) establishes a community, even as the audience-participant claims authorship of the discursive link. As in McLaughlin's analysis also, the 'pluralism' of voices leads back to a very established and traditionalist populist discourse.

In contrast, Livingstone and Lunt, as we will see next, have a very different view, drawing centrally (like Henry Jenkins) on De Certeau's 'tactics'.

Poaching and tactics

Livingstone and Lunt note that various authors have pointed to the popular transformation of scientific and expert explanatory systems as a matter of:

- using only selected subsets of the concepts present in expert theory;
- keeping these concepts isolated from an overarching theoretical system; and
- incorporating these concepts within other frames of experience in popular thought.

Thus, as Jenkins notes of de Certeau's concepts of poaching and bricolage, the public 'fragment [expert] texts and reassemble the broken shards according to their own blueprints' (Jenkins, 1992, p. 26).

Similarly drawing on de Certeau, Livingstone and Lunt examine the talk show as a prime site where experts lose their authority.

> For de Certeau (1984), the increasingly common expectation that experts should speak in the public, nonspecialist domain – to popularize, to be accessible, to disseminate, to be accountable – inevitably results in a loss of expertise. As specialist knowledge cannot be communicated in a public, nonspecialist domain without significant transformation and impoverishment, their only qualification to speak is based on the authority granted them because of their specialist knowledge, rather than on that specialist knowledge itself. There is a danger that the media might, unintentionally or otherwise, deconstruct the expert as a repository of knowledge.
>
> (Livingstone and Lunt, 1994, p. 96)

Livingstone and Lunt clearly take considerable pleasure in that 'danger', plausibly examining a range of specific devices in the talk show which 'deconstruct the expert'. Thus:

- As talk shows extend television's increasingly conversational style, experts are often pushed into oversimplified arguments, and so are driven to rely on status alone. 'Undoubtedly, experts are regularly frustrated in their desire to draw comparisons, pursue analogies, identity complexities and moral difficulties, locate arguments in their historical or cultural contexts, and so forth' (Livingstone and Lunt, 1994, p. 95).
- Experts on talk shows often undermine each other's status.
- Talk shows establish an 'epistemology' in which lay narratives are preferred over expert abstractions, and where authenticity is conferred on information that is 'hot' (as against cold and impersonal), relevant, grounded in experience ('in depth'), practical and 'real'. 'Audience discussion programmes adopt an anti-elitist position which implicitly draws on these alternative epistemological traditions, offering a revaluation of the life-world, repudiating criticisms of the ordinary person as

incompetent or ignorant, questioning the deference traditionally due to experts through their separation from the life world . . . and asserting instead the worth of the "common man" ' (1994, p. 102).

- The formal set up of the studio often places the experts among the audience, where they often have to fight to have their say, and frequently face more demanding questions from their hosts than other audience members. Hosts, moreover, generally prioritise anecdotal responses out of everyday life over more abstract or scientific accounts; and thus the more successful experts are the ones who themselves draw on personal, everyday experiences and practical knowledge.

Livingstone and Lunt thus argue that:

> The subject position of 'ordinary person' is created when the studio audience 'tell their own story'. They construct the folk category of speaker in which animator, author and principal are the same, and so gain communicative power through the construction of authenticity. . . . The discussion programme . . . strengths lie in the revelatory retelling of personal experiences, using the credibility of the source to validate the message. The display of spontaneity, self-disclosure and direct experience are vital for grounding the argument. . . . Evidence counts only if it can be produced in the studio.
>
> (1994, pp. 129–0)

Through these various formal features of the talk show, then, audiences (both in the studio and at home) 'fragment [expert] texts and reassemble the broken shards according to their own blueprints' (Jenkins, 1992, p. 26). Like Jenkins, Livingstone and Lunt reject, here, modernist for postmodernist notions of power, knowledge and authority in the public sphere of television.

> In the work of Foucault (1970), which anticipates much of postmodernism, the various ways in which power is dispersed among social institutions can be contrasted to both positive and Marxist conceptions of power as residing in rational and economic processes respectively. This dispersal of power is reflected in expressions of diverse interests through discourse, so that, in contrast to the attempts to construct a consensus with which to challenge established power, discussion should give free rein to difference. In this sense, proponents of the oppositional public sphere are postmodern: proposing that an institution could provide a context for diverse voices, representing different subject positions with different power bases, to generate a discourse as part of the social dispersal of power.
>
> (1994, pp. 94–5)

Livingstone and Lunt are not so universally 'postmodernist' as this, however; arguing that different television genres produce different epistemologies.

Following the modernist separation of expertise and common sense, with the former becoming increasingly specialized and privileged while the latter is degraded and personalized, television genres which involve both expertise and ordinary experience (for example, documentaries, current affairs) have traditionally valorized the expert by opposing experts to the laity. . . . Yet in the audience discussion programmes, experts and lay people are put together, setting an agenda of social issues and offering both established elites and ordinary people the opportunity at least to discuss the lived experience of current-affairs issues in relation to expert solutions. In this context, it is interesting to observe the spread of the audience discussion format into other genres, such as news, documentary and current affairs.

(1994, pp. 101, 132)

Thus, for Livingstone and Lunt's analysis of talk shows, just as for Jenkins's analysis of science fiction, de Certeau's pessimistic inability to extend his concept of poaching to the television audience is rejected. The fan and participant audience member is seen to pull the power of symbolic interpretation away from modernity, on behalf of the 'multiple sets of discursive competencies' (Jenkins, 1992, p. 34) of postmodernity. However, while Jenkins also pulls away from Fiske's more optimistic account in arguing for a political economy of *Star Trek*, Livingstone and Lunt do not answer the 'modernist' argument posed by McLaughlin, Carbaugh and Shattuc. This is that expert and lay knowledge – the abstract and the everyday, the 'hot' and the 'cold' – are differentially (but also inextricably) intertwined within the political economy and ideological hegemony of television in different cultural places at different historical times. As with the risk society thesis which also tends to construct a romantic opposition between expert and lay knowledge, we need (following Matthew Hills's account) a more historicised analysis of 'technology, culture and psyche' than most postmodernist analyses provide.

In this final section I wanted to show how discussion of fandom – whether of soap opera, science fiction, cult television or talk shows – highlights the central pleasure/risk problematic of this book. Thus I have not concluded with a summary of the book, because each chapter has been a reflexive summary of the field – pointing, I hope, to the continuing strengths of 'older' (modernist) theories and methods within current debate. And each chapter has developed some of the central issues of the book – of expert and lay knowledge, reflexivity in theory and methodology, pleasure, anxiety and risk – in particular ways associated with academic audience work in its particular generic field. I wanted to keep that degree of a plurality of voices open.

So, rather than a closing summary of what has gone before, we might take the last case study of the book, Matthew Hills's analysis of cult audiences, as a useful launching pad to that further programme of 'live' performance/audience research I referred to in the Introduction. With his focus on internet fans on the one hand, and his emphasis on the 'midnight procession of costumed spectators' on the other, Hills's insistence that we still need a theory (and a method of accessing) affective experiences among smaller, minutely self-defined, reflexive audiences is a pathway to both new technology audiences and those 'live' audiences of theatre, painting and street carnival that I mentioned earlier.

Like Hills, other theorists seek a 'new way' beyond the now stale binary of, on the one hand, social conservatism (see Tolson, 1999, pp. 92–6), with its intense anxiety about the breakdown of (both right and left) utopias of consensus, and, on the other, 'resistance' discourses (whether modernist or postmodernist). Like Pertti Alasuutari, Andrew Tolson seeks a 'new way' for cultural studies which focuses on discourses as regulators and performers of moral judgements.

> Perhaps 'new way' might be putting it too strongly, for this has been prefigured in previous work, but it does at least offer an alternative to the cycle of attacks on, and defences of, popular cultural genres with which we are all too familiar. The field which opens up, it seems to me, in Shattuc's account of the talk show, is . . . in connection with 'moral regulation'. That is to say, the debate about talk shows now becomes, not an assessment of their problematic or progressive tendencies, but rather a study of their place in the discursive formation of morality, characterized by preferred or dispreferred ways of making moral judgments. Popular culture, especially in its melodramatic forms, can be understood as a site for the reproduction of moral discourses.
>
> (Tolson, 1999, p. 117)

'What is it', Andrew Tolson asks, 'about academic commentators on popular culture that they frequently seem unable to resist making . . . apocalyptical remarks' (1999, p. 99) about social 'disintegration' – whether this is the pessimistic conclusion of rationalistic 'public sphere' thinkers or the positive evaluation of postmodernists? This book has heard much from both pessimistic 'ideology critique' modernists and risk modernists and from the postmodernists' 'promiscuous promotion of "affect" ' (Tolson, 1999, p. 99). Matthew Hills's 'affective reflexivity' seems to me to be a useful coinage for the kind of conjuncture that Tolson, Alasuutari and others are looking for towards a 'new way'. In my reading at least, it offers the potential to conjoin both emotional experience and critical cognition. It concerns itself with both the fans' pleasure and the critics' engagement with moral discourse as everyday performance. At the same time, by concentrating (as Hills does) on:

- the affective engagements which are adopted by different audiences within different socio-historical contexts and at different times; and

- the 'smaller audience which is minutely self-defined and self-reflexive as a participatory group' (Hills, 1999, p. 202).

we can widen our analysis far beyond the field of cult television.

We can even go beyond what Lisa McLaughlin quite rightly calls 'popular cultural studies' to *unpopular* (or 'high') cultural studies, for example to audiences of theatre and painting, where we can see different affective engagements of different 'smaller audiences' in different 'participatory groups'. As any theatre marketing manager will tell us, their economy can actually involve itself with both the *Rocky Horror Picture Show* 'costumed spectators' and Shakespeare fans, depending on the particular local context, space and site of any one theatre. In one current case I am looking at, a theatre inscribes both sets of fans within one season of plays; and additionally, by performing Janet Suzman's *The Free State*, confronts audiences with the pluralistic black (male and female) voices of post-Mandela South Africa in confrontation and unison with the post-serf voices of Chekhov's *Cherry Orchard*. Here, to borrow McLaughlin's terms, the focus is on the colonisation of common sense by powerfully organised ideologies in a particular historical moment (South Africa, 1994); and the bodies, songs, uncontrolled emotions and voices of (old and new) losers of different races, colours, tribes, genders and histories are performed on behalf of what a new public, post-Mandela sphere might look like.

In some other spaces than television talk shows, then, the relationship between expert and common sense discourses – as intertwined hegemony and liberation – is engaged with reflexively by both performers and audiences. Fans can be found here too; and clearly both reflexive cognition and affect are profoundly important for them. We live in a performative society (Kershaw, 1994; Abercrombie and Longhurst, 1998; Tulloch, 1999); one where 'life is a constant performance; we are audience and performer at the same time; everybody is an audience all the time. Performance is not a discrete event' (Abercrombie and Longhurst, 1998, p. 73). This 'audience all the time' is, as Abercrombie and Longhurst say, a 'diffused audience' in so far as being an audience member in the performative society is 'constitutive of everyday life' (1998, p. 68). But, as Abercrombie and Longhurst are also careful to emphasise, the 'simple audience' (those who attend a range of public events from plays to carnivals and football matches) also exists in the performative society; and it may well be here – in the interfacing of performance as 'theoretical event' and performance as 'everyday' activity, that reflexive cognition and affect are especially important.

To return to my discussion of chapter 1 – and Denzin and Lincoln's fifth moment of qualitative research – we are (as work on the talk show so clearly indicates) in a phase of theory read in narrative terms, as 'tales of the field' where the expert researcher gives way to the plurality of local tales. But this 'risk' scenario (of contestation among and downgrading of experts' rational discourse) is by no means the only one in the field; as actors and producers (like Janet Suzman), as well as academics, continue to display and perform the voices of their own ethnographies. The first question of this book, 'why does methodology matter?' will get a different answer according to whether the respondent adheres to a modernist or postmodernist position on expertise, cognition and affect. But it will be obvious from the academic tales about audiences that I have told in this book, that my own commitment is to both cognition and affect – and to an 'affect' that is not always singly related to the media circulation of narratives (as my discussion of Sparks, Kellner and the paleosymbolic in chapter 3 indicates).

Affective reflexivity – in neither part of which *Doctor Who*'s timelords were notably strong – is then needed to take us beyond the status of those cult intellectuals whose pleasure resides in contemplating, without action, the infinite plurality and difference of the universe. In that quest, neither pleasurable, pluralistic play nor the universalist cognition of cataclysmic risks can be our single goal.

References

Abercrombie, N. and Longhurst, B. 1998: *Audiences: a sociological theory of performance and imagination*. London: Sage.

Adam, B. and Allan, S. 1995: *Theorizing culture: an interdisciplinary critique after postmodernism*. London: UCL Press.

Alasuutari, P. (ed.) 1999: *Rethinking the media audience*. London: Sage.

Allen, R. 1985: *Speaking of soap operas*. Chapel Hill: University of North Carolina.

Allor, M. 1988: *Relocating the site of the audience. Critical studies in mass communication*. 5, 217–33.

Alvarado, M. and Buscombe, E. 1978: *Hazell: the making of a TV series*. London: Latimer/British Film Institute.

Ang, I. 1996: *Living room wars: rethinking media audiences for a postmodern world*. London: Routledge.

Ang, I. (with Hermes, J.) 1996: Gender and/in media consumption. In Ang, I., *Living room wars: rethinking media audiences for a postmodern world*. London: Routledge.

Barker, M. 1984: *The video nasties: freedom and censorship in the media*. London: Pluto Press.

Barker, M. 1989: *Comics: ideology, power and the critics*. Manchester: Manchester University Press.

Barker, M. 1993: Seeing how far you can see: on being a 'fan' of 2000 AD. In Buckingham, D. (ed.), *Reading audiences: young people and the media*. Manchester: Manchester University Press, 12–31.

Barker, M. 1997: The Newsom Report. In Barker, M. and Petley, J. (eds), *Ill effects: the media/violence debate*. London: Routledge.

Baudrillard, J. 1984: *The evil demon of images*. Sydney: Power Institute Publication.

Baudrillard, J. 1988a: *The ecstasy of communication*. Trans. B and C. Schutze, ed. Lotringer, S. New York: Semiotext(e).

Baudrillard, J. 1988b: *Selected writings*. Cambridge: Polity Press.

Beck, U. 1992: *Risk society: towards a new modernity*. London: Sage.

Beck, U. 1995: *Ecological politics in an age of risk*. Cambridge: Polity Press.

Beck, U. 1996: Risk society and the provident state. In Lash, S., Szerszynski, B. and Wynne, B. (eds), *Risk, environment and modernity: towards a new ecology*. London: Sage.

Beck, U. 1997: *The reinvention of politics: rethinking modernity in the global social order*. Cambridge: Polity Press.

Beharrell, P. and Philo, G. 1977: *Trade unions and the media*. London: Macmillan.

Bellah, R., Madsen, R., Sullivan, W., Swindler, A. and Tipton, S. 1985: *Habits of the heart: individualism and commitment in American Life*. New York: Harper and Row.

Bennett, T. and Woollacott, J. 1987: *Bond and beyond: the political career of a popular hero*. Basingstoke: Macmillan.

Bennett, T., Martin, G., Mercer, C. and Woollacott, J. (eds) 1981: *Culture, ideology and social process*. London: Batsford.

Berry, C. and Clifford, B. 1985: *Learning from television news: effects of presentation factors and knowledge on comprehension and memory*. Unpublished manuscript. North-East London Polytechnic.

Brunsdon, C. and Morley, D. 1978: *Everyday television: 'Nationwide'* London: British Film Institute.

Buckingham, D. 1987: *Public secrets: 'EastEnders' and its audience*. London: British Film Institute.

Buckingham, D. (ed.) 1993: *Reading audiences: young people and the media*. Manchester: Manchester University Press.

Carbaugh, D. 1988: *Talking American: cultural discourses on Donahue*. Norwood. NJ: Ablex.

Carpignano, P., Anderson, R., Aronowitz, S. and Difazio, W. 1990: Chatter in the age of electronic reproduction: talk television and the 'public mind'. *Social Text 25/6*, 35–55.

Clarke, A. 1986: 'This is not the boy scouts': television police series and definitions of law and order. In Bennett, T. *et al.* (eds), *Popular culture and social relations*. Milton Keynes: Open University.

Cohen, S. and Young, J. (eds) 1973: *The manufacture of news: social problems, deviance and the mass media*. London: Constable.

Collins, W. 1983: Social antecedents: cognitive processing and comprehension of social portrayals on television. In Higgins, E., Ruble, D. and Hartrup, W. (eds), *Social cognition and social development: a sociocultural perspective*. Cambridge: Cambridge University Press.

Connell, R. 1983: *Which way is up? Essays on sex, class and culture*. Sydney: Allen & Unwin.

Corner, J. 1991: Meaning, genre and context: the problematics of 'public knowledge' in the new audience studies. In Curran, J. and Gurevitch, M. (eds), *Mass media and society*. London: Arnold.

Cottle, S. 1998: Ulrich Beck, 'risk society' and the media. *European Journal of Communication*, 13(1), 5–32.

Curran, J. 1996: The new revisionism in mass communication research: a reappraisal. In Curran, J., Morley, D. and Walkerdine, V. (eds), *Cultural studies and communications*. London: Arnold.

Curran, J. 1990: The 'new revisionism' in mass communication research. *European Journal of Communications*, 5(213), 135–64.

Curran, J., Morley, D. and Walkerdine, V. (eds) 1996: *Cultural studies and communications*. London: Arnold.

Curthoys, A. and Docker, J. 1989: In praise of 'Prisoner'. In Tulloch, J. and Turner, G. (eds), *Australian television: programs, pleasures and politics*. Sydney: Allen & Unwin.

Dennington, J. and Tulloch, J. 1976: Cops, consensus and ideology. *Screen Education*, 20 (Autumn): 37–46.

Denzin, N. and Lincoln, Y. (eds) 1998: *Collecting and interpreting qualitative materials*. London: Sage.

Donald, J. 1985: Anxious moments: 'The Sweeney' in 1975. In Alvarado, M. and Stewart, J. (eds), *Made for television: Euston Films Limited*. London: British Film Institute.

Drummond, P. 1976: Structural and narrative constraints in 'The Sweeney'. *Screen Education* 20: 15–35.

Fiske, J. 1987: *Television culture: popular pleasures and politics*. London: Methuen.

Gergen, K. 1991: *The saturated self: dilemmas of identity in contemporary life*. New York: HarperCollins.

Giddens, A. 1991: *Modernity and self-identity*. Cambridge: Polity.

Gillespie, M. 1993: The Mahabharata: from Sanskrit to sacred soap. A case study of the reception of two contemporary televisual versions. In Buckingham, D. (ed.), *Reading audiences: young people and the media*. Manchester: Manchester University Press.

Gilligan, C., Lyons, N. and Hanmer, T. 1990: *Making connections*. Cambridge, MA: Harvard University Press.

Gray, A. 1987: Behind closed doors: video recorders in the home. In Baehr, H. and Dyer, G. (eds), *Boxed in: women and television*. New York: Pandora Press.

Gray, A. 1992: *Video playtime: the gendering of a leisure technology*. London: Routledge.

Grossberg, L. 1987: The in-difference of television. *Journal of Communication Inquiry*, 10(2), 28–46.

Grossberg, L. 1988: Wandering audiences, nomadic critics, *Cultural Studies*, 2(3): 377–92.

Gunter, B. 1985: *Dimensions of television violence*. Aldershot: Gower.

Gunter, B. 1987: *Television and the fear of crime*. London: John Libbey.

Hall, S., Clarke, J., Jefferson, T., Critcher, C. and Roberts, B. 1978: *Policing the crisis: mugging, law and order and the state*. London: Macmillan.

Hartley, J. 1982: *Understanding news*. London: Methuen.

Heath, S. and Skirrow, G. 1977: Televison: a world in action. *Screen*, 18(2): 7–59.

Henriques, J., Hollway, W., Unwin, C., Venn, C. and Walkerdine, V. 1984: *Changing the subject*. London: Methuen.

Hetherington, A. 1985: *News, newspapers and television*. London: Macmillan.

Hill, A. 1999: A social drama: media violence controversies and anti-violence campaign groups. In Berry, D. (ed.), *Ethics and media culture: practices and representations*. Oxford: Butterworth-Heinemann, 248–61.

Hills, M. 1999: *The dialectic of value: the sociology and psychoanalysis of cult media*. Ph.D. thesis, University of Sussex.

Hills, M. forthcoming: *Cult media and fan cultures: consuming texts and icons*. London: Routledge.

Hodge, R. and Tripp, D. 1986: *Children and television: a semiotic approach*. Cambridge: Polity Press.

Hopkins, G. 1985: The Monster of Peladon. In Bentham, J. (ed.), *Doctor Who: an adventure in space and time*. London: Cybermark.

Hurd, G. 1976: 'The Sweeney' – contradiction and coherence. *Screen Education*, 20 (Autumn): 47–53.

Jameson, F. 1984: Postmodernism and the cultural logic of late capitalism. *New Left Review*, 146: 53–93.

Jenkins, H. 1992: *Textual poachers: television fans and participatory culture*. New York: Routledge, Chapman and Hall.

Jhally, S. and Lewis, J. 1991: *Enlightened racism: the Cosby Show, audiences, and the myth of the American dream*. Boulder, CO: Westview Press.

Jordan, G. and Weedon, C. 1995: The celebration of difference and the cultural politics of racism. In Adam, B. and Allan, S. (eds), *Theorizing culture*. London: UCL Press.

Kellner, D. 1989: *Jean Baudrillard – from Marxism to postmodernism and beyond*. Cambridge: Polity Press.

Kellner, D. 1995: *Cultural studies, identity and politics between the modern and the postmodern*. London and New York: Routledge.

Kershaw, B. 1994: Framing the audience for theatre. In Keat, R., Whitely, N. and Abercrombie, N. (eds), *The Authority the Consumer*. London: Routledge.

Krause, A. and Goering, M. 1995: Local talk in the global village: an intercultural comparison of American and German talk shows. *Journal of Popular Culture* 29(2), 189–207.

Lewis, J. 1991: *The ideological octopus: an exploration of television and its audiences*. New York: Routledge.

Livingstone, S. 1994: Watching talk: gender and engagement in the viewing of audience discussion programmes. *Media, Culture and Society* 16 (3), 431–47.

Livingstone, S. and Lunt, O. 1994: *Talk on television: audience participation and public debate*. London: Routledge.

Lovell, T. 1981a: *Pictures of reality: aesthetics, politics and pleasure.* London: British Film Institute.

Lovell, T. 1981b: Ideology and Coronation Street. In Dyer, R., Geraghty. C., Jordan, M., Lovell, T., Paterson, R. and Stewart, J. (eds), *Coronation Street.* London: British Film Institute.

Lupton, D. 1999: *Risk.* London: Routledge.

Lupton, D. and Tulloch, J. 1998: The adolescent 'unfinished body': reflexivity and HIV/AIDS risk. *Body and Society* 4(2): 19–34.

Lyotard, J-F. 1984: *The postmodern condition.* Manchester: Manchester University Press.

McGuigan, J. 1992: *Cultural populism.* London: Routledge.

McKinley, E.G. 1997: *Beverly Hills, 90210: television, gender and identity.* Philadelphia: University of Pennsylvania.

McLaughlin, L. 1993: Chastity criminals in the age of electronic reproduction: reviewing talk television and the public sphere. *Journal of Communication Inquiry* 17(1), 41–55.

Mandler, J. and Johnson, N. 1977: Remembrance of things parsed: story structure and recall. *Cognitive Psychology* 9, 111–51.

Masciarotte, G. 1991: C'mon, girl: Oprah Winfrey and the discourse of feminine talk. *Genders* 11, 84–108.

Messenger Davies, M. 1997: *Fake, fact and fantasy. Children's interpretation of television reality.* Mahwah, NJ: Lawrence Erlbaum Associates.

Modleski, T. 1982: *Loving with a vengeance: mass produced fantasies for women.* New York: Methuen.

Modleski, T. 1986: Introduction. In Modleski, T. (ed.), *Studies in entertainment: critical approaches to mass culture.* Bloomington/Indianapolis: Indiana University Press.

Moores, S. 1993: *Interpreting audiences: the ethnography of media consumption.* London: Sage.

Moran, A. 1982: *Making a TV series: the Bellamy project.* Sydney: Currency.

Morley, D. 1980: *The Nationwide audience.* London: British Film Institute.

Morley, D. 1981: The Nationwide audience: a critical postscript. *Screen Education,* 39: 3–14.

Morley, D. 1986: *Family television: cultural power and domestic leisure.* London: Commedia.

Morley, D. 1992: *Television, audiences and cultural studies.* London: Routledge.

Morley, D. 1996: Populism, revisionism and the 'new' audience research. In Curran, J., Morley, D. and Walkerdine, V. (eds), *Cultural studies and communication.* London: Arnold, 279–83.

Moss, G. 1993: Girls tell the teen romance: four reading histories. In Buckingham, D. (ed.), *Reading audiences: young people and the media.* Manchester: Manchester University Press.

Munson, W. 1993: *All talk: the talk show in media culture.* Philadelphia: Temple University Press.

Murdock, G. 1989: Critical inquiry and audience activity. In Dervin, B., Grossberg, L., O'Keefe, B. and Wartella, E. (eds), *Rethinking communication: volume 2, paradigm exemplars*. London: Sage, 226–48.

Nightingale, V. 1989: What's 'ethnographic' about ethnographic audience research? *Australian Journal of Communication*, 16: 50–63.

Philo, G. 1990: *Seeing and believing. The influence of television*. London: Routledge.

Philo, G. 1995: Audience beliefs and the 1984/5 miners' strike. In Philo, G. (ed.), *Glasgow media group reader, volume 2: industry, economy, war and politics*. London: Routledge.

Philo, G., Beharrell, P. and Hewitt, J. (Glasgow University Media Group) 1977: One-dimensional news – television and the control of explanation. In Beharrell, P. and Philo, G. (eds), *Trade unions and the media*. London: Macmillan, 1–22.

Potter, J. and Reicher, S. 1987: Discourses of community and conflict: the organization of social categories in accounts of a riot. *British Journal of Social Psychology* 26, 25–40.

Press, A. 1991 *Women watching television: gender, class and generation in the American television experience*. Philadelphia: University of Pennsylvania Press.

Radway, J. 1988: Reception study: ethnography and the problems of dispersed audiences and nomadic subjects. *Cultural Studies* 2(3): 359–76.

Radway, J. 1991: *Reading the romance: women, patriarchy and popular literature*. Chapel Hill: University of North Carolina.

Richards, C. 1993: Taking sides? What young girls do with television. In Buckingham, D. (ed.), *Reading audiences: young people and the media*. Manchester: Manchester University Press.

Schlesinger, P., Dobash, R. E., Dobash, R. and Weaver, K. 1992: *Women viewing violence*. London: British Film Institute.

Sefton-Green, J. 1993: Untidy, depressing and violent: a boy's own story. In Buckingham, D. (ed.), *Reading audiences: young people and the media*. Manchester: Manchester University Press.

Sharpe, S. 1976: *'Just like a girl': how girls learn to be women*. Harmondsworth: Penguin.

Shattuc, J. 1997: *The talking cure: TV talk shows and women*. London: Routledge.

Silverman, D. 1993: *Interpreting qualitative data: methods of analysing talk, text and interaction*. London: Sage.

Skirrow, G. 1985: Widows. In Alvarado, M. and Stewart, J. (eds), *Made for television: Euston Films Limited*. London: British Film Institute, 174–84.

Sparks, R. 1992: *Television and the drama of crime: moral tales and the place of crime in public life*. Buckingham: Open University Press.

Tolson, A. 1999: Talk shows. In *Popular genres, popular pleasures and cultural values*. Open University Cultural and Media Studies Masters Programme. Milton Keynes: Open University.

Tulloch, J. 1981: *Legends on the screen: the narrative film in Australia, 1919–1929*. Sydney: Currency, ch. 10/11.

Tulloch, J. 1989: Approaching the audience: the elderly. In Seiter, E., Warth, E., Kreutzner, G. and Borchers, H. (eds), *Remote control*. London: Routledge, 178–203.

Tulloch, J. 1990: *Television drama: agency, audience and myth*. London: Routledge.

Tulloch, J. 1999: In Alasuutari, P. (ed.) *Rethinking the media audience*. London: Sage, 151–78.

Tulloch, J. and Alvarado, M. 1983: *Doctor Who: the unfolding text*. Basingstoke: Macmillan.

Tulloch, J. and Moran, A. 1986: *A Country Practice: 'quality' soap*. Sydney: Allen & Unwin.

Tulloch, J. and Tulloch, M. 1992a: Discourses about violence: critical theory and the 'TV violence' debate. *Text* 12, 183–231.

Tulloch, M. and Tulloch, J. 1992b: Attitudes to domestic violence: school students' responses to a television drama. *Australian Journal of Marriage and Family*, 13, 62–9.

Tulloch, J. and Jenkins, H. 1995: *Science fiction audiences: watching Doctor Who and Star Trek*. London: Routledge.

Tulloch, J. and Lupton, D. 1997: *Television, AIDS and risk: a cultural studies approach to health communication*. Sydney: Allen & Unwin.

Tulloch, J., Lupton, D., Blood, W., Tulloch, M., Enders, M. and Jennett, C. 1998: *Fear of crime*, volumes 1 and 2. Canberra: National Campaign Against Violence.

Tulloch, J. and Tulloch, M. 1993: Understanding TV violence: a multifaceted cultural analysis. In Turner, G. (ed.), *Nation, culture and text: Australian cultural and media studies*. London: Routledge.

van Dijk, T. 1984: *Prejudice in discourse: an analysis of ethnic prejudice in cognition and conversation*. Amsterdam: John Benjamins.

van Zoonen, L. 1991: Feminist perspectives on the media. In Curran, J. and Gurevitch, M. (eds), *Mass media and society*. London: Arnold.

Walkerdine, V. 1985: Video replay: families, films and fantasy. In Burgin, V., Donald, J. and Kaplan, C. (eds), *Formations of fantasy*. London: Routledge.

Walkerdine, V. (with the assistance of Melody, J.) 1993: 'Daddy's gonna buy you a dream to cling to (and mummy's gonna love you just as much as she can)': young girls and popular television. In Buckingham, D. (ed.), *Reading audiences: young people and the media*. Manchester: Manchester University Press.

Weedon, C. 1987: *Feminist practice and poststructuralist theory*. Cambridge: Blackwell.

Wellman, H. 1990: *The child's theory of mind*. Cambridge: MIT Press

Willis, P. 1978: *Learning to labour*. Farnborough: Saxon House.

Wood, J. 1993: Repeatable pleasures: notes on young people's use of video. In Buckingham, D. (ed.), *Reading audiences: young people and the media*. Manchester: Manchester University Press.

Wynne, B. 1996: May the sheep safely graze? A reflexive view of the expert-lay knowledge divide. In Lash, S., Szerszynski, B. and Wynne, B. (eds), *Risk, environment and modernity: towards a new ecology*. London: Sage.

Index

Kellner, Douglas 19, 22–24, 39–41, 46, 55, 84, 248
Kojak 42
Kuhn, Annette 62

Lacanian 6, 8, 229, 234, 237
Lay knowledge 27, 29, 30, 85, 239, 245
  reduced to 'irrationality' by expert knowledge 43
'left realist criminology' 43
  and emphasis on over-rationalist anxiety 44
  and fandom 224
Levi-Strauss, Claude 126, 127
Lewis, Justin 157–178, 193–197, 200, 201
'Linguistic turn' 120, 125, 126
Lisa (CCRR 'Fear of Crime' interviewee) 56–60, 73, 128
live cultural performances 14, 245, 246
lived experience 8, 45, 88, 93, 97, 100, 101, 150, 199, 229, 245
Livingstone, Sonia 85, 236, 237, 239
Livingstone, Sonia and Lunt, Peter 29, 236, 237, 241–245
Loach, Ken 99, 106, 107, 111–113, 117–119, 128, 180, 200
Local/global account 31, 208
Lovell, Terry 7, 39, 63, 80, 180, 239
Lucinda (*Beverly Hills 90210* character) 204, 220
Lupton, Deborah 24, 75, 76, 78, 79, 81
Lyotard, Jean-Francois 21

McKinley, E. Graham 203–220, 222, 224, 226, 234, 237–239, 241, 242
  methodology of McKinley's *Beverly Hills 90210* study 205–207, 216
McLaughlin, Lisa 238–242, 245, 247
McLuhan, Marshall 20
McRobbie, Angela 64, 159, 160, 209
The Manufacture of News (Cohen and Young) 41, 43
Marx, Karl 21, 68
  Marxist account of 'active audiences' 161, 172
Masciarotte, G. 236–238, 241
masculinist pleasures 89
'mean world' thesis (Gerbner) 44, 49, 54
Media ethnography as both 'expert' and 'local' knowledge 30
Media producers 30, 31, 77–79, 81, 104, 105, 108

Media sociology on under-privilege and risk, 41
  versus 'textualization' 180
Media Watch 54
Melodrama 66, 86, 189, 239
Messenger Davies, Maire 134–137
'Metaphysics of presence' 8
Miami Vice 37, 39–41, 84
  male subject positions privileged 41
Mimesis 232
Miner's strike (Britain 1984/5) 105–108, 110–113, 115, 117–119, 191, 192, 198–201
Mise-en-scene 189
  of various cop shows, 37
MIT 220, 221, 223
Modality 128, 129, 134, 136, 140
Modernism/postmodernism 24, 219, 220, 229, 234, 241, 244, 245, 248
Modernity 21, 24, 148, 245
  and single-subjectivity 40
  and the city in cop shows 47
  and coherence in moral frames 55
  and secularisation 233
Modleski, Tania 62, 63, 68, 69, 80, 104
Monster of Peladon (*Doctor Who* story) 3–6, 9
Moonlighting 65, 69
'Moral frames' 13, 30, 31, 33, 49, 50, 83, 91, 92, 240
  realist moral frame (Angela, CCRR interviewee) 52, 54, 55
'Moral panics' 43
Moran, Albert 37
Morley, David 6–8, 12, 36, 71, 85, 179–194, 197, 200, 201, 220
  on 'methodological choices' 201
Morris, Meaghan 19, 31, 157, 232
Moss, Gemma 147, 149, 151, 152, 156
MTV 39
Munson, W. 21–24, 202, 237
Multi-generic research strategy 88, 93, 96, 97, 101, 167
Multiple narratives in soap operas and cop shows 38
  soaps and risk 76–81
  soaps and audience activity 91
Mulvey, Laura 62
The Muppets 131–133
Murdoch, Rupert 17, 208
Murdock, Graham 102, 103, 108, 111, 156, 200, 201
Myth (Barthesian) 35, 142